PROGRAMMING
S E R I E S

Introduction to Programming

Que Development Group

Introduction to Programming

© **1992 by Que® Corporation**

Library of Congress Catalog No.: 92-61694

ISBN: 1-56529-097-6

95 94 93   8 7 6 5 4 3 2

Interpretation of the printing code: the rightmost double-digit number is the year of the book's printing; the rightmost single-digit number, the number of the book's printing. For example, a printing code of 92-1 shows that the first printing of the book occurred in 1992.

Trademarks

Credits

Publisher
Lloyd J. Short

Associate Publisher
Rick Ranucci

Publishing Manager
Joseph Wikert

Acquisitions Editor
Sarah Browning

Product Development Specialist
Jay Munro

Production Editor
Jodi Jensen

Editors
Bryan Gambrel
Kezia Endsley
Charles A. Hutchinson

Technical Editor
Greg Guntle

Production Manager
Corinne Walls

Proofreading/Indexing Coordinator
Joelynn Gifford

Production Analyst
Mary Beth Wakefield

Book Designer
Scott Cook

Cover Designer
Dan Armstrong

Graphic Image Specialists
Dennis Sheehan
Jerry Ellis
Susan VandeWalle

Production
Jeff Baker
Claudia Bell
Julie Brown
Jodie Cantwell
Paula Carroll
Laurie Casey
Michelle Cleary
Brook Farling
Bob LaRoche
Jay Lesandrini
Cindy L. Phipps
Linda Seifert

Indexers
Joy Dean Lee
Loren Malloy
Suzanne Snyder
Tina Trettin
Johnna Van Hoose

Composed in Utopia and MCPdigital by Prentice Hall Computer Publishing

Screen reproductions in this book were created by means of the program Collage Plus from Inner Media, Inc., Hollis, NH.

About the Authors

Dave Linthicum has over ten years experience in the computer industry. He currently works with Mobil Oil in Fairfax, Virginia as a Senior Software Engineer. In addition to his work in the software field, Mr. Linthicum is an associate professor of computer science at Northern Virginia Community College in Sterling, Virginia, and is currently teaching courses on system analysis and design and database design. He has written for a variety of popular technical publications and technical book publishers and has spoken at technical conferences throughout the country. You can contact him on CompuServe at 72740,2016.

Marcus Johnson has been working with computers since the mid-1970s and with microprocessors since the early 1980s. He currently is a member of the technical staff at Precision Systems in Clearwater, Florida.

Lisa Ann Monitto is the president of Broadway Bound, a New York City computer and software consulting firm that caters to the needs of entertainment professionals and businesses. Ms. Monitto is also a screenwriter, photographer, and former stage actress. Her contribution to this book marks her debut as a print writer.

Jay Munro has been working with computers since the early 1980s. In 1980, he received a Bachelors Degree in Cinema from the University of Bridgeport and has worked in many areas of photography, video, and computers. He has been an assembly and BASIC programmer for the past four years, is a frequent contributor to *PC Magazine*, and moonlights as a Sysop on ZiffNet. Recently, he joined Prentice Hall Computer Publishing as a Product Development Specialist for Que programming books. You can reach Mr. Munro on CompuServe at 75230,1556 or ZiffNet at 72241,554.

Greg Perry has been a programmer and trainer for the past 14 years. He received his first degree in Computer Science and then completed a Masters Degree in Corporate Finance. He is currently a professor of computer science at Tulsa Junior College, as well as a computer consultant and lecturer. Mr. Perry is the author of more than 10 computer books and has written articles for several publications, including *PC World, Data Training,* and *Inside First Publisher*. He has traveled in several countries, attending computer conferences and trade shows, and is fluent in nine computer languages.

David Veale is the Vice President of Information Technology for Veale & Associates, Inc., a consulting company serving the financial and investment banking industries. Mr. Veale has spent the past several years working in PC software development and support, and his company specializes in the creation of multimedia computer-based training systems for a variety of computer platforms. Mr. Veale has written dozens of articles for such publications as *PC Resource, ComputerWorld,* and *Computer Language*. You can reach Mr. Veale on CompuServe at 74006,576.

Contents at a Glance

Table of Contents

19 BASIC Products **347**

Introduction

Welcome to the world of programming. Learning to write programs is not as scary as you might think. In fact, even if you have never touched a computer, you have probably done some programming already. Your VCR, car radio, microwave—even the watch on your wrist—all require some level of programming.

Who Should Use This Book?

This book is for the entry-level programmer. If you have written macros for a spreadsheet or word processor, you already are familiar with some of the concepts covered in this book. Let this book help you decide which programming language to use. Even if you have no experience with computers, this book can help bring you up to speed in no time.

What Is Programming?

Programming is a process that involves several components: a task to accomplish, the analysis of the steps to accomplish it, and the tools required to get the job done. If you think about it, these are the steps to solving any problem in life. However, instead of making a pot of coffee or building a house, your task is to create a computer program. By picking up this book, you probably have thought about the tasks you want to accomplish, whether those tasks include writing simple batch files that run your other applications or writing the next Great American Program.

After determining the task, the hardest part of writing a program is selecting and assembling the instructions that give you the results you want—with the least amount of work.

Contrary to popular belief, computers and humans are well suited to each other. Humans get bored doing the same thing over and over again, whereas computers work best when they perform mundane, repetitive tasks—and they can't complain about it. Humans don't always do what you tell them to do, whereas computers can *only* do what you tell them to do and exactly the way you tell them to do it—a perfect match.

Some people believe that computers and humans aren't compatible because the computer can't think like a human or read minds, lips, or body language. For every task you ask the computer to perform, you must provide explicit instructions. If you tell a computer to count to infinity (the programming equivalent of telling it to get lost), it will count until it runs out of numbers to count.

About This Book

This book is aimed at helping you understand the concepts common to all programming languages. Part I, "Programming Concepts" (Chapters 1 through 11), introduces you to the building blocks of programming. Along the way, you will see how a program makes decisions, handles repetitive tasks, receives data from a user, stores the data, and outputs that data in a useful fashion. Throughout the book, simple code examples support these basic programming concepts, and you can actually try them in Microsoft QBasic.

QBasic is the modern successor to BASICA for PC DOS or GW-BASIC for MS-DOS, the programming languages that have been included with DOS since it was first introduced. QBasic, introduced with DOS 5.0, is one of the easiest programming languages to understand—it's almost in plain English. Code examples written in QBasic are essentially *pseudocode*, that is, code written for explanation rather than execution.

After becoming familiar with the basic concepts, Part II, "Programming Languages" (Chapters 12 through 17), provides you with an overview of the popular programming languages. If all tasks required the same level of control over the computer, there would be only one programming language. Part II helps you discover why there are various languages.

These language overviews show the advantages and disadvantages of a specific language. Each chapter builds on the preceding chapter and illustrates the best features of a language. The goal for Part II is to help you decide which language best suits your programming needs.

After you decide which programming language to use, you must choose the tool for your work. Part III, "Programming Products" (Chapters 18 through 21), introduces you to the real world of programming—the actual brand-name products that are available. Depending on which language you choose, your compiler choices can be very limited or very broad. Part III can help you choose wisely.

Conventions Used in This Book

The following typographic conventions are used in this book:

Code lines, variable names, and any text you see on-screen appear in a special `monospace` typeface.

Placeholders—terms used in code lines to hold the place for text you will substitute—appear in *`italic monospace`*.

User input following a prompt appears in **`bold monospace`**.

Filenames appear in regular text font, usually in uppercase letters.

New terms, which can be found in the Glossary, appear in *italics*.

Ready To Go!

OK, enough of this philosophical rhetoric. It's time to roll up your sleeves and get to work. There are two things to remember as you progress from computer novice to programming guru.

First, don't be afraid to try anything in this book. There is nothing that will break your computer or damage your data. So, don't worry.

Second, enjoy yourself. Programming becomes addictive. You control the machine in front of you. Tell the computer to do something, and it does it. Coding a program and then executing it can provide great satisfaction—no matter what level of programmer you are.

So, future programmer, go to it.

I

Programming
Concepts

What Is a Program?

by Lisa Monitto

A *program* is a set of instructions that tells a computer what to do. This set of instructions, originally written by the programmer, is called *source code*.

Computer programs have become an indispensable part of our lives. They provide airline pilots with all the information they need to keep their planes in the air and to take off and land safely, and they help meteorologists predict the weather more accurately. Computer programs also print your movie tickets, record and total your purchases at the supermarket checkout line, keep track of your insurance payments, and print your daily newspaper.

Using a computer program, investigators can compare fingerprints found at a crime scene with millions of other fingerprints. Other programs can figure your taxes, make hotel reservations, and keep inventories. Do you own a digital watch? It's run by a computer program stored on a tiny chip within the case.

Just as a novel is a series of sentences properly arranged to form a complete story, a computer program is a series of statements designed to make your computer perform specific tasks. Without programs, your computer is just a hunk of metal and plastic taking up space on your desk—a body without a brain.

Various words are used to refer to a computer program, such as software, executable file, and application. These terms are interchangeable.

Early Programs

Charles Babbage (1792-1871), an English mathematician, is considered to be the inventor of the computer. Although mechanical calculators had been introduced in the 17th century by Pascal and Leibniz, Babbage's work was far more complex. He created a machine that used punched cards to store and retrieve information. Unfortunately, no models of this machine survive today; it is known only from written descriptions. Babbage eventually abandoned this effort in order to work on a newer, much more intricate machine. Although he never completed his work, the unfinished model exists and can be seen in the British Museum in London. Babbage's work laid the foundation for the modern computer.

Punched cards similar to those invented by Babbage were used later by Jacquard to automate looms to weave patterns in cloth. The punched cards used in a Jacquard loom were the forerunners of today's computer programs.

More than 50 years after Babbage's death, Vannevar Bush of the Massachusetts Institute of Technology built a machine capable of solving difficult equations. This machine is considered to be the first real computer.

When scientists were able to replace the awkward, bulky gears and levers of the machines developed by Babbage and Bush with electric current, advancements in computer development were rapid.

Early computers such as UNIVAC and ENIAC consisted primarily of vacuum tubes and relays and had to be programmed by connecting a series of plugs and wires. A team of programmers might spend several days entering a small program into one of these room-sized machines. In addition, the vacuum tubes were temperamental and subject to frequent failure. Every time a tube burned out, work had to stop while it was located and replaced. This added greatly to the time needed to complete a program.

With the advent of punched-card readers, the process became much simpler. Program code was written on paper and then punched onto stiff oblong cards with a keypunch machine. The cards were then fed through a card reader. Both programs and data were input with this method. Once entered into the computer, the information could be stored on reels of magnetic tape.

Today's computers are no longer programmed with tubes, plugs, wires, and punched cards. With the development of advanced programming languages, a programmer doesn't have to worry about crossed wires or mutilated punched cards.

Programming Languages

Programmers would have a much easier time if programs were written in standard English sentences; unfortunately, this is not the case. Programs must be written in a programming language, and there are many such languages.

Some common programming languages are Pascal, C, C++, BASIC, COBOL, FORTRAN, and assembler code. These languages are used today in much of the current commercial software development.

The following three program listings, shown in QBasic, C, and Pascal, present a short program that prints the sum of three numbers.

Listing 1.1. A simple program written in QBasic.

```
' QBASIC program to
' Print the sum of three numbers

PRINT "The sum of 7 + 3 + 5 is ";
PRINT 7 + 3 + 5
```

Listing 1.2. A simple program written in C.

```
/* C program to print the sum of three numbers */

#include <stdio.h>

main()
  {
  printf("The sum of 7 + 3 + 5 is ");
  printf("%d", 7 + 3 + 5);
  return(0);
  }
```

Listing 1.3. A simple program written in Pascal.

```
{ Pascal program to print the sum of three numbers}

Begin
   write('The sum of 7 + 3 + 5 is ');
   writeln(7 + 3 + 5);
End.
```

The preceding three programs all display a message and the sum of three numbers.

Choosing a Language

Why are there so many programming languages? Is one language better than another? The answer is yes and no. Each language was written to perform a particular function within a discipline. One language may be best for calculating graphs of the results of particle physics experiments; another language may be best for creating business reports. The language you choose for a project depends on its suitability to the task.

High-Level Languages Versus Low-Level Languages

Programming languages are broadly divided into two categories: low level and high level. A *low-level* programming language directly represents machine code instructions and is designed to be "understood" by the computer rather than by humans. Because it does not resemble an English sentence, low-level languages (such as assembler code) are more difficult to learn. However, low-level languages enable a knowledgeable programmer to fine-tune the code so that the result is a smaller, faster-running program.

A *high-level* language, on the other hand, is designed to be more readily understood by humans. The keywords and functions of a high-level language, such as BASIC, C, or Pascal, often read much like an English sentence and are usually easier to learn, read, and understand. High-level languages, however, usually must be interpreted into low-level machine code.

Different languages are suited to different tasks. High-level languages are easier to use and take less time to learn, but they sometimes result in larger programs that operate less efficiently.

Figure 1.1 shows a short assembler code listing.

```
  File   Edit   View   Search   Spell   Window   Keys   Make                    F1=Help
       1         2         3         4         5         6         7
;NUMOFF.ASM
;Turns NumLock off when run
;Masm 6.0 Syntax
;ML /FPi /Gc /W3 /Zm /Ta NUMOFF.ASM
.Model Tiny                            ;Masm 6.0 syntax
.Code
Org 100h

Start:
        Xor   AX,AX               ;clear AX to assign to use to clear DS
        Mov   DS,AX               ;clear DS with AX
        Mov   BX,417h             ;BX contains address of keyboard status
        Mov   AL,0DFh             ;use bit mask to clear numlock status
        And   [BX],AL             ;clear numlock bit (bit
        Int   20h                 ;exit
End     Start


  1:  1
File: D:\MASM\BIN\NUMOFF.ASM | Mode: Edit                            % Full: 1
```

Figure 1.1.   Assembler code sample.

Assembler Code

Assembler is a low-level computer language. A low-level language offers a great measure of control over how a program runs because a programmer can directly access memory locations and the computer's hardware. A low-level language does not contain all the statements that high-level languages have to handle input and output and direct program flow. Consequently, the details of these processes must be painstakingly broken down to their most basic steps by the programmer.

Because higher level languages have built-in routines, you can easily perform common tasks such as screen output or keyboard input with a single line of code. However, if you are using assembler, something as simple as printing Hi there on the screen can take many statements, in contrast to the single QBasic statement:

PRINT "Hi there".

Although higher-level languages offer the programmer an easier way to develop programs, the executable files will be larger. This additional size occurs because a high-level language program is built from prepackaged code blocks. Although the blocks fit together well, these prepackaged blocks always contain extra overhead. In contrast, the executable file produced from well written assembler code can be considerably smaller and faster than a comparable program written in a higher-level language.

BASIC

BASIC stands for Beginners All-Purpose Symbolic Instruction Code. The name alone can seem intimidating, yet BASIC has been a starting point for many new programmers. It was developed at Dartmouth College in the 1960s for use on mainframes and has been subsequently rewritten for personal computers. It may lack some of the sophisticated features of high-level languages like Pascal, C, and C++, but it is much easier to learn and is excellent for writing simple programs. A new BASIC programmer can begin writing programs in a relatively short time. BASIC is discussed in Chapter 14.

Pascal

Pascal is a powerful and efficiently structured high-level language. Its easy-to-understand syntax makes it a good language to use when learning OOP, or object-oriented programming, which is discussed in Chapter 11, "Object-Oriented Programming." Chapter 15 offers more information about Pascal.

C

C is a structured language that has long been the choice of programmers doing serious commercial development. C is gradually losing its dominance in the workplace due to recent advances in the development of object-oriented languages such as C++. C is discussed in Chapter 16.

C++

C++ is an advanced, high-level, object-oriented language that has much of the power and control of assembler code and some of the ease of readability of Pascal. C++ is discussed more fully in Chapter 17.

Program Complexity

Programs can be as simple as the short examples shown in Listings 1.1 through 1.3, or as complex as those used by NASA to control a space shuttle mission. A program to control the flight of a space shuttle might contain tens of thousands of program statements. The complexity of a program depends on the job it must perform.

Common Types of Programs

Walk into any software store and check the shelves. You can find computer programs of every type, size, description, and price. The following list shows some of the most popular software packages:

Word processors—WordPerfect, Microsoft Word, Ami Pro

Desktop publishing packages—Ventura Publisher, PageMaker

Spreadsheets—Lotus 1-2-3, Excel, Quattro Pro

Databases—FoxPro, Clipper, dBASE, Paradox

Drawing and painting programs—Harvard Graphics, Adobe Illustrator, CorelDRAW!

Computer-aided design (CAD) packages

Music composition programs

Animation programs

Accounting programs

Communication programs

Games

Each of the preceding items is discussed in detail in this section.

Word Processors

A word processing program reaches far beyond simple text editing. Its primary advantage is the amount of time it can save. A word processing program enables you to easily correct errors, make additions and deletions to text, check spelling and grammar, and change the order of paragraphs—all without the need to manually retype an entire document. Many word processing programs also enable you to apply various fonts, type sizes, italics, underlines and boldface, and to include figures, tables, and graphics in a manuscript. Some word processors also have extended *macro* language capabilities, which enable you to create your own short-cuts. Macros can increase a program's functionality by allowing you, for example, to pull an address from a mailing list and add it to a pretyped letter by simply pressing a key. Figure 1.2 shows a typical word processing screen.

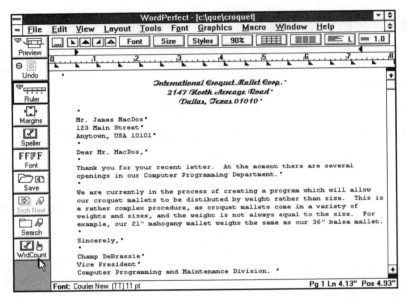

Figure 1.2. A word processing screen.

Desktop Publishing

Desktop publishing programs give documents a professional finish. Text can be made to fit into the format of a newspaper, magazine, newsletter, or any other desired layout. Illustrations can be sized to fit any space. The difference between the capabilities of desktop publishing programs and word processing programs is lessening as word processors grow more sophisticated and richer in features.

Spreadsheets

Spreadsheets are ideal for maintaining tables, calculating formulas, and producing graphs. The best-selling spreadsheets also have macro capabilities. Spreadsheets similar to the one shown in Figure 1.3 are used extensively for financial reports and calculating statistics.

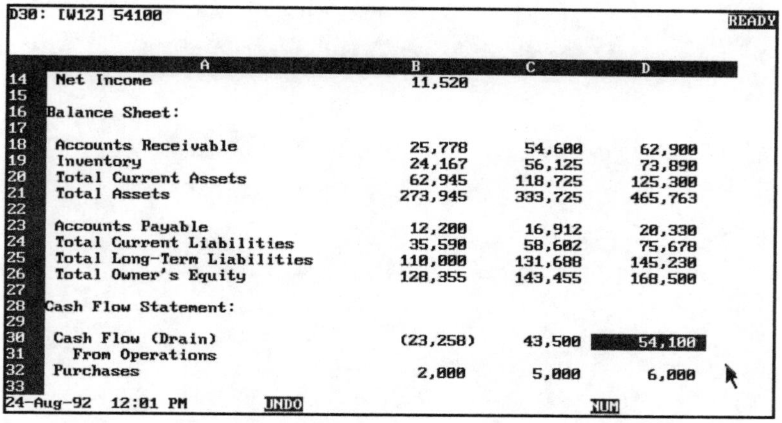

```
D30: [W12] 54100                                                    READY

            A                        B           C           D
14   Net Income                   11,520
15
16 Balance Sheet:
17
18   Accounts Receivable          25,778      54,600      62,900
19   Inventory                    24,167      56,125      73,890
20   Total Current Assets         62,945     118,725     125,300
21   Total Assets                273,945     333,725     465,763
22
23   Accounts Payable             12,200      16,912      20,330
24   Total Current Liabilities    35,590      58,602      75,678
25   Total Long-Term Liabilities 110,000     131,600     145,230
26   Total Owner's Equity        128,355     143,455     168,500
27
28 Cash Flow Statement:
29
30   Cash Flow (Drain)           (23,250)     43,500      54,100
31     From Operations
32   Purchases                     2,000       5,000       6,000
33
24-Aug-92  12:01 PM      UNDO                        NUM
```

Figure 1.3. A typical spreadsheet screen.

Databases

A database program stores large amounts of information for retrieval across a broad range of categories. A database consisting of all the names, addresses, and phone numbers in the New York City telephone directory, for example, can be searched by name, street address, or phone number. Fields or categories in a database can be linked to a field from another database containing different information. This is called a "relational database." Databases are used extensively for mailing lists, inventory records, and employee personnel information. Figure 1.4 shows a mailing list in FoxPro.

Draw and Paint Programs

Draw and paint programs range from the simple to the highly complex. The simplest ones permit basic line drawings and doodles—an electronic version of the Etch-A-Sketch. The most advanced paint programs feature thousands of colors and allow artists to render photographic-quality artwork. Figure 1.5 shows a screen from the Windows Paintbrush program.

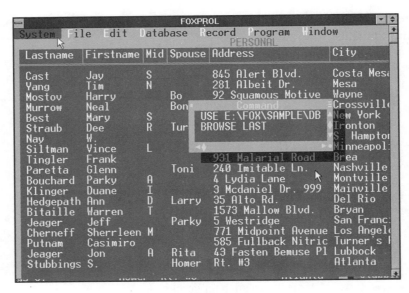

Figure 1.4. A FoxPro mailing list screen.

Figure 1.5. A Windows Paintbrush screen.

CAD

Computer-Aided Design (CAD) programs are used to create architectural blueprints, electrical wiring diagrams, and new car designs. The best CAD programs can rotate a figure on the screen so that it can be seen from all sides—in three dimensions.

Playing and Composing Music

Almost all professional composers use one or more musical composition programs. Musical notation can be entered at the computer keyboard or with a mouse; the resulting musical score can be played back instantly or saved in a file. The composer can choose the instrumentation, transpose keys, or change the rhythm. The program can also include drum parts and a bass line.

A Musical Instrument Digital Interface (MIDI) is a piece of hardware that allows music to be entered from a piano keyboard. The notes are stored in a file and displayed on-screen or printed in standard musical notation as sheet music. Figure 1.6 shows a sheet of music generated from a MIDI file.

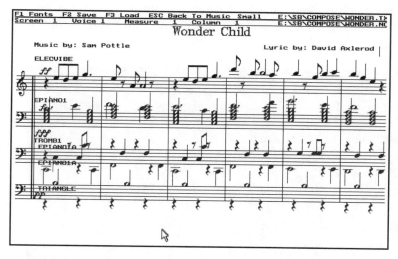

Figure 1.6. Computer-generated musical score.

Animation

A series of drawings linked together and displayed rapidly in a sequence creates the illusion of motion. Low-end animation programs can create the style of cartoons shown on Saturday morning television. High-end animation programs can be used to create startling special effects, such as those used in movies.

Accounting Programs

Accounting programs combine the information storage and retrieval capability of a database with a spreadsheet's ability to manipulate figures using formulas. Accounting programs are in widespread use for both business and personal accounting.

Communication Programs

Communication (Comm) programs use a modem to connect to the thousands of electronic bulletin boards, online information services, and communications networks available at the other end of your telephone. Local, national, and international bulletin board systems (BBS) offer research information, electronic mail, stock quotes, news services, travel and weather information, electronic shopping malls, conferencing, and a wealth of other services. You can make your computer do the job of a fax machine by using a fax card with communications software to send and receive fax transmissions. Figure 1.7 shows the dialing screen from the DOS version of the ProComm Plus communications package.

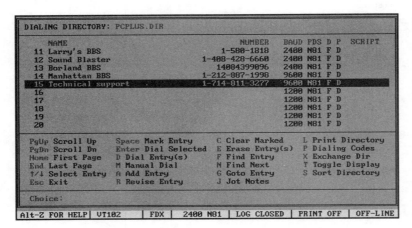

Figure 1.7. A dialing directory screen from ProComm Plus.

Games

The first game to explode on the software scene was called Pong. Primitive by today's standards, Pong was a game in which two players batted a ball back and forth across a computer screen. Today's sophisticated game programs, with their high-resolution graphics and digitized sound effects, provide game players with a far more realistic setting. The quality of the games being produced for home use rivals the games featured in video arcades.

How Do Programs Work?

The Disk Operating System (DOS) is essentially the computer's brain. The operating system is a computer program. Without it, your computer could not function. The operating system carries out instructions stored in an executable program file. The instructions in DOS provide the normal functions of displaying text on-screen, retrieving information from the keyboard, and accessing the disk. The encoded instructions in DOS don't look anything like the original program statements; they are written in machine code.

Machine Code

In order for the computer to understand a program, program statements must be translated into machine language. Machine language is a series of 0s and 1s called binary numbers. These binary numbers represent instructions in the program. Think of a computer as a United Nations diplomat who speaks only Arabic. In order to understand speeches in other languages, the diplomat must use the services of a translator. Programmers use compilers to translate their program statements into a form readable by an operating system: machine code.

Compilers and Interpreters

A programmer must use either a *compiler* or an *interpreter* to translate high-level source code to low-level machine code.

The primary difference between a compiler and an interpreter is in the way they execute a program. A compiler translates the entire program into machine language before any execution begins. An interpreter, on the other hand, reads and executes each statement, one by one. The advantage of compiler execution is that it is much

faster than interpreter execution. The disadvantage of a compiler is that the programmer must wait until the entire program has been compiled before any error (no
matter how small) is identified.

Why Write a Program?

A glance through any computer magazine, or a quick look into any store that sells
computer programs, will show you that there is a dazzling array of software on the
market. Many of these programs are excellent, some are adequate, and a few are not
worth the disks they are stored on. With such a formidable number of programs
available, you may wonder why new programs are needed. There are several good
reasons why you should write a program, four of which are discussed in this section.

Programming Small Utilities

Perhaps the most common reason to write a program is to create a small utility.
A *utility* is a program that does a specific task or tasks and usually is not terribly
elegant. Utilities simply solve a problem or fill an immediate need. Programs in this
category are often termed *quick and dirty*: they do not have polished user interfaces,
but they get the job done. Examples of small utilities are a short program that reads
a text file and formats it for a printer or a conversion program that helps reformat
data in a file.

Programming Out of Necessity

You may discover an area for which no computer programs exist or where the
existing software is inadequate. As a programmer, you must be able to analyze
these situations and determine whether a program can perform the task faster
and more efficiently. If so, it's a perfect candidate for your programming skills.

For example, consider this fictional company—International Croquet Mallet
Corporation (ICMC)—based in Dallas. You learn that ICMC distributes croquet
mallets worldwide and, therefore, receives funds not only in dollars, but in escudos,
francs, marks, rubles, and guilders. These funds are kept in the countries where
the payments are made until the dollar ratio is high enough to permit the company
maximum benefit on the exchange rate. The company's accountants check the
exchange rate daily and notify the company when they feel a transfer of funds
should occur. The company managers then execute the transfer.

You can assist this company by writing a program that automatically scans the exchange rates and identifies those countries whose currency has increased in dollar value. Your program could then direct an electronic funds transfer from the foreign bank to the company's U.S. account and calculate the amount of profit made on the exchange.

Instead of using the labor of several professionals, the program can be operated by one employee and the transfers accomplished in a matter of seconds rather than hours. There is no longer a need for lengthy and complex manual calculations and record keeping; your program stores all the information in a file that can be retrieved at any time.

Identifying a need and writing a program to fill that need are essential parts of the programmer-analyst's job.

Programming on Assignment

It would be a wonderful world if programmers could write only those programs that they found personally enjoyable and fulfilling. Unfortunately, life doesn't always work that way. The vast majority of programs are written to meet the specific requirements of the company employing the programmer. In these cases, the problem has been identified; the programmer's task is to find the solution. Your programming skills are defined by how well the program you write deals with these solutions.

Suppose you are employed as a programmer by ICMC, which produces croquet mallets of various lengths and colors. Suppose the company's senior managers want to know the particular lengths and colors that sell best in certain countries. Your task might be to write a program that scans the orders, breaks down the data into the necessary categories, and prints the information in a clear and concise manner. For this project, you may be asked to write the program on your own. For a larger, more complex project, you may be part of a team of programmers working together. As a member of a programming team, you might be responsible for one small portion of the program, which will be integrated with the work of your colleagues.

Programming for Fun

Your programming skills can be used in a variety of ways for your own enjoyment. Many programmers like to write add-ons for existing software that either correct a problem or offer easier, more elegant ways of accomplishing the program's functions. You can design your own games, instruct your computer to issue a greeting when you turn it on, catalog your collection of CDs, or keep track of your friends' and relatives' birthdays. You can even have a birthday card automatically printed and ready for mailing a few days in advance.

It is a wonderful feeling of accomplishment when you boot up your first program and see that it actually works!

Interface

Interface refers to the way a program looks and feels to its users. In most cases, a program is designed to be used by others. Interface is the general term used to designate how the program looks on the user's screen and the way in which the user communicates with it. A program has a poor interface if its screens are garishly colored, confusing or unpleasant to look at, or lack proper information to guide the user. On the other hand, a program has a good interface if its screens are distinct and logical, with functions easily accessible and clearly displayed. The choice of an interface can make all the difference between a popular, successful program and "shelfware"—a program that sits on a shelf collecting dust.

One of your main goals as a programmer is to make your program easy for the user to run.

The screen design should be readable, easy on the eyes, and unobtrusively colored. The instructions should be logical and easy to understand. Instructions which can be readily comprehended are called "intuitive." The more intuitive a program is, the easier it is to use.

Since the dawn of interactive computing, programmers have been inventing their own interfaces. This resulted in confusion when users of several popular software packages found that particular key combinations performed very different functions in different programs. Since IBM introduced a standard to eliminate the confusion, however, this obstacle is beginning to fade. The standard that IBM developed is known as the Common User Access (CUA). CUA-compliant programs offer end-users an enormous advantage. After a user learns the standard key combinations, she or he can operate other CUA-compliant programs with relative ease. Programmers can save time by writing CUA-compliant programs because they don't have to develop a unique interface for each application they write. A more complete discussion of CUA will be found in Chapter 8, "Communicating with the User."

Users become confused and frustrated when they must deal with a program that is not intuitive and lacks clear instructions. Software manuals—often written by people who are technically gifted but unable to construct a clear sentence in English—make matters worse. Nothing is less likely to inspire confidence in a user than a manual that looks like a calculus textbook.

Make sure the instructions on the help screens and in the manual are clear and logical enough to be understood by the people using your program.

Beginning a Program

Once you learn a programming language and have an idea about the kind of program you want to write, begin by writing a basic outline of what the program will do. The most important part of creating a program is being able to define each of the steps you need to achieve your goal.

Most beginning programming classes teach you how to create a flow chart. A flow chart is a blueprint of your program that details the major steps, decisions, and branches that determine how your program runs.

Many programmers combine flow charts with pseudocode. Pseudocode is another way of creating an outline of what a program should do. It is a program instruction written in plain English. The short program in Listing 1.1 might originally have been outlined as:

Print a message.
Calculate the sum of three numbers.
Print the result.

When you write the actual program, the preceding sentences are replaced with real programming statements that tell your computer to perform the tasks described. Outlining your program is an excellent way to see the task as a whole and provides you with much of the information you need to write the actual code.

Once the outline is complete, you have an overview of how your program should work.

Summary

In this chapter, you learned that a program is a set of instructions that tells a computer what to do. There are various languages you can learn in order to write programs.

The program should be selected for its ability to perform the task you want it to do. Types of programs include spreadsheets, word processors, desktop publishing programs, databases, and many others.

The four major reasons for writing a program are

- To solve a simple and immediate problem

- To fill a more complex need

- As an assignment

- Because it's fun

Computer programming offers you the opportunity to work in a creative environment and see the results of your efforts in practical applications. This book can serve as a guide to teach you the skills you need to get started.

Introduction to Programming Statements

by Lisa Monitto

Chapter 1 introduced you to programming statements. This chapter defines and describes many types of statements and shows you how they are used to create computer programs.

Learning to program is a hands-on experience. Reading theory and looking at examples can help you along, but seeing the results on your computer screen drives home the theory. This chapter begins by showing you some program examples written in pseudocode; later, you can try your luck with some QBasic examples.

Overview of Programming Statements

This section provides an overview of various programming statements. Each statement illustrates proper syntax as well as some examples of how to use the statement. These examples are designed to help you see how the statements look in a program.

In Chapter 1, you learned that programming statements are specialized sets of instructions that tell a computer how to perform a task. These statements are executed one after another until the program ends. Chapter 1 also presented three examples of a simple addition program. Listing 1.1 showed the program in QBasic, Listing 1.2 showed the same program in C, and Listing 1.3 presented the program in Pascal. To help you better understand these three programs, the following is how the AddSum program from Chapter 1 would look in pseudocode.

Print a message showing what is being added.
Calculate the sum of three numbers.
Print the result.

You can see that a program modeled from the preceding pseudocode doesn't do much. The example requires no input from a user, so there is no user interface. The output produces a message and the number 15 on a line by itself, with no explanation of what that line means. By adding some input and output statements to this program, you can make it more useful. The following pseudocode shows the AddSum program with some additional statements.

Display to the user a short description of what this program does.
Display what input it expects.
Ask for the first value.
Store the first value and call it A.
Ask for the second value.
Store the second value and call it B.
Ask for the third value.
Store the third value and call it C.
Add the three stored values together and store the result as SUM.
Display the value SUM to the user.

With just a few additions, the program this pseudocode describes has gained a measure of flexibility. A user can now sum any three numbers by running this program.

Two of the most important things programs do are receive input and produce output. As the programmer, it is up to you to decide what kind of input your program needs and what output the program produces.

By having your program ask the user for the data it requires to run, you have eliminated guesswork on the part of the user. Otherwise, the user is faced with a blinking prompt and a blank screen and no explanation of what input the program expects.

Variables

A *variable* is a fundamental element of any programming language. You may recall from basic algebra that a variable is something that changes. Computers use variables in much the same way algebra does. The data stored in a variable may change. The expanded pseudocode example in the last section asked the user for values and then stored them. These stored values are variables. Specifically, data values are stored in memory at different locations; each location may contain a value that can change. The computer must be able to manipulate data and change its values.

In algebra, a typical expression is $y = x + 2$. The value of y changes as the value of x changes; x and y are called variables because their values can change. In order to understand, visualize an empty box marked x. This box, which represents a location in memory, can accept only one item at a time. You can put any value you want in this box, and it will remain there until you change or remove it.

Now, think of each numeric address or location on your PC as represented by a box. The various types of PCs have from several thousand to millions of these locations. A programming language allows you to assign *identifiers*, or names, to these locations. Using identifiers to represent specific locations in memory is much easier than using numeric addresses.

The variables in the example are named A, B, C, and Sum. In such a short program, it is easy to remember what type of information each variable is supposed to hold and what each is used for. As a program grows, however, it becomes much more difficult to keep track of variables with such short names. A more detailed discussion of variables can be found in Chapter 3, "Simple Data Types and Elementary Operators."

You can give variables names that help you remember the purpose they serve in your program. Instead of A, B, and C, you could name your variables FirstNumber, SecondNumber, and ThirdNumber.

Longer names make your program much clearer to anyone who tries to read and follow it—and clearer to you if you have to go back and revise your code six months or a year after you wrote it.

Program Flow

The examples in this chapter have been executed in a linear fashion—the statements are read from top to bottom. The order of the statements never varies.

As programs become more complicated, however, you sometimes want to change the *flow* of the program (the order in which statements are executed) based on the value of one of the variables or the occurrence of a specific event. Changing the order in which statements are executed is called *branching*.

You can use pseudocode or flow charts to design the *flow* of the program. The program statement that causes control of the program to jump to a different point is called a *conditional* statement. You'll find out more about conditional statements in Chapter 5, "Making Decisions." Figure 2.1 shows a *flow chart* of the original AddSum addition program. Notice that it is linear and has no branches.

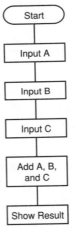

Figure 2.2.   An example of a linear flow chart for the original AddSum program.

Figure 2.2 shows a flow chart of the AddSum program that branches on a certain condition. You can see where the program branches based on the value of the variable.

Types of Statements

As you begin writing programs, you will encounter several different types of programming statements. The rest of this chapter is devoted to explaining the most common types of statements. Those included are the input, output, conditional, select case, assignment, subroutine call, function call, loop, and comment statements.

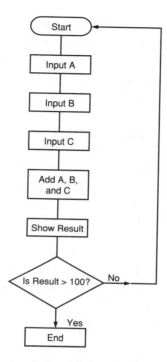

Figure 2.2. An example of a branching flow chart for the revised AddSum program.

Comments

A *comment* is an annotation or explanation of code and is an important part of a programmer's toolbox. Writing comments along with your code can help you, or anyone else who reads your program, understand what each section of your program does. Comments are implemented differently in QBasic, C, C++ and Pascal.

In QBasic, you indicate the beginning of a comment with an apostrophe ('). Everything that follows (until the end of that line) is considered to be part of the comment, and your program ignores it. *REM,* short for remark, is another way to mark a comment in QBasic. The following shows examples of the two forms comments can take in QBasic:

```
'This is a program comment
REM This is a program comment too.
```

In Pascal, everything enclosed in *curly braces* ({ and }) is considered a comment. Comments in Pascal can continue for more than one line—until the program reaches the right curly brace—as shown in the following:

```
{ This is how a comment is written in Pascal.
  Notice how the comment can continue onto multiple
  lines until the end brace is reached. }
```

In C, comments are enclosed in a slash-asterisk combination (/* and */). The beginning of a C comment is slash-asterisk and the end of the comment is asterisk-slash. Like Pascal comments, comments in C can span several lines, as

```
/* The comments in C can also continue onto multiple
   lines. The two character combination indicating the
   beginning and end of a comment serve the same purpose
   as braces in Pascal. */
```

In C++, comments are indicated with a double slash (//). Like the apostrophe (') in QBasic, everything on the line following the // is considered to be a comment and is ignored by the program. To continue a comment on a second line, you must insert another //. C++, however, recognizes the standard C comment (*/ and /*) if you prefer that style. The following example illustrates the double-slash comment:

```
// This is a comment in C++
// Notice that each line of a comment must begin
// with the double slash.
```

You should use comments liberally throughout your programs. It might seem like overkill to comment a 10-line program; but as you learn more and your programs grow longer, it becomes essential to have a record of what you were intending to do when you wrote each section of code.

Careful commenting and documentation can simplify revisions later. Comments aid both you and others who may be working on your program. To someone seeing your program for the first time, your comments are like a road map indicating what each section is supposed to do.

Commenting can also help you track program bugs. Many times a bug can be found by checking the comments to see what the program is supposed to be doing at a certain point; then, you can see if the code matches the comment.

Assignment Statements

Assignment statements assign values to a variable. An equal sign (=) is most often used to make an assignment. You can assign a value to any variable of the same type. Both

```
A = B
```

and

```
Total = Average.
```

are assignment statements.

You can *assign* any variable to a variable of the same type. You can evaluate an expression and set a variable equal to it. You also can set a variable to the result of a function. (The terms "variable" and "expression" are explained in further detail in Chapter 3, "Simple Data Types and Elementary Operators." For more information about "functions," see the section by that name later in this chapter.)

Input Statements

All programming languages have input statements. Input statements bring information into a program. A grocery list is a simple example of an input statement. You enter each item you plan to purchase at the market, and your program instructs the computer to print the list on the printer. If you design your grocery list program without the use of input statements, it will resemble the *pseudocode* shown in the following example:

Instruct the printer to print the word milk.
Instruct the printer to print the word bread.
Instruct the printer to print the word juice.
Instruct the printer to print the words frozen pizza.

This code must be rewritten every time your shopping list changes. Because this would become tedious for even the most eager programmer, programming statements exist that can make your program more flexible.

The input statement retrieves information, which the program then manipulates to produce the desired result. The following pseudocode represents a program that would input text for grocery items and display each item on the printer until you enter the word *END*.

Display the program title on-screen.
Display the program instructions to the user.

BEGIN:
　　Ask the user for an item.
　　Input the item.
　　If the item equals the word END, end the program.
　　Otherwise, print the item on the printer.
　　Go back and repeat, starting from the word BEGIN.

Whenever a program receives input interactively (from a user), you must include a user interface. The interface does not have to be fancy, but it should give the user a good idea of what he or she must do next to make the program perform correctly.

Where Does Input Come From?

Input comes from many different places. It can come from files on your hard drive or floppy disk drives, from a keyboard, mouse, graphics tablet, trackball, touch screen, modem, fax card, or numerous other sources.

The preceding pseudocode represents a program that requested user input from the keyboard. For this application, keyboard input is fine. There are many occasions, however, when you must retrieve information from a file. Getting information from a file is called *reading a file*. Storing information in a file is called *writing to a file*. Chapter 9, "Data Storage and File Handling," provides a more detailed discussion of storing and retrieving data.

Output Statements

Regardless of how good your program is, nobody will know about it if it lacks output statements. You could say that the purpose of a program *is* its output; a program must display its results.

However, *output* means more than printing to the screen. Just as input statements can receive input in different ways, output statements can send output in more than one way.

In programs that have *input* but no *output*, information can be gathered and manipulated, but the code has no effect. If you add output to a program, you can see the result of the program's actions. You can send this information to the screen, printer, file, modem, or even to a sound card so that your computer can tell you the results by voice.

All programming languages have instructions to do output in some form. For example, QBasic uses the keyword PRINT to send output to the screen. When combined with other keywords, the PRINT statement also can output to a text file on disk. QBasic has other, more specialized file output statements that can create and write to disk in structures called records. Records and other data types are discussed more fully in Chapter 3.

QBasic and other high-level languages make it easy to write to peripheral hardware connected to the computer. High-level languages standardize how you output to your hardware by referring to them as *devices*. The PRINT statement in QBasic can write to a printer device, a comm port device, or a disk file device, just by using another keyword called OPEN. Devices are called by names, such as LPT or PRN for printers, COM for communications ports, or filenames for disk files. With the OPEN statement you can tell the computer which device you want to output to.

Subroutine Calls

When a repetitive action is required and it takes two or more statements to perform the action, that group of statements is a candidate for a *subroutine*. A subroutine is actually a separate section of code, out of the main execution of the program. To tell your program to execute the subroutine, the key word CALL is used in most languages.

For example, if you are mailing a letter, the tasks you must perform are as follows:

1. Folding the letter.

2. Placing the letter in the envelope.

3. Sealing the envelope.

4. Putting a stamp on the envelope.

5. Addressing the envelope.

6. Mailing the letter.

Suppose you have a button on your desk that summons an assistant to rush in and mail your letters for you. Rather than going through these steps each time you want to mail a letter, you simply press the button. You have traded six steps for one. The assistant is called to perform the task. When the assistant is done, he returns to tell you the mail went out successfully. A program CALL works the same way. The program execution goes from the point of the call to the subroutine where the task is performed. When the subroutine is finished, execution is returned to the original calling program.

Consider a program that accepts a number from the user for its input and keeps a running total of the input. If you write such a program in a linear fashion, you must write an individual input and addition statement every time you need input from the user. Although this program will work fine if you only have to ask the user for a few values, what if the program must ask a question hundreds, or even thousands, of times? You would quickly run out of space or have very tired fingers typing input statements for each question. However, by placing the input code in a *subroutine*, and then calling that code when you need it, you can save space and typing.

Passing Parameters

A *parameter* is a variable or value that can be transferred from the main program to a subroutine the program is calling. The action is referred to as *passing* a parameter. When you pass a parameter to a subroutine, you are handing it a value. The value you pass can be literal (the number 12, or the string of text *My Dog's Name is Spot*) or contained in a variable. You learn more about variables and how to use them in Chapter 3.

You can write your subroutine to use as many parameters as you need. When you call the subroutine, you must take care to initialize each variable to a value that is both permissable and meaningful to your subroutine. You also must be careful to keep the parameter list in order.

In a restaurant, you could give the following order to your server:

1. I would like a slice of bread, please.

2. Put fried bacon on the slice of bread.

3. Put lettuce on the slice of bread.

4. Put a slice of tomato on the slice of bread.

5. Put another slice of bread on top of it all.

But more likely, you would simply say: "Please make me a sandwich with bacon, lettuce and tomato."

Your server understands the command "Make me a sandwich," and the bacon, lettuce, and tomato are good parameters to pass, because the server knows how to handle these food items.

By changing the parameters (asking for ham or turkey instead of bacon), you change the result of your order. For example, if your order to the waiter were a subroutine it would look like this:

```
CALL MakeMeASandwich( bacon, lettuce, tomato)
```

which makes a different sandwich than

```
CALL MakeMeASandwich(steak, cheese, onions)
```

Because particular subroutines expect certain values, program execution could be jeopardized if you pass the wrong type of parameters. Your waiter, or subroutine, is expecting to make a sandwich from tasty things like bacon, cheese, or tomatoes and wouldn't understand a request such as the following:

```
CALL MakeMeASandwich(bolts, tire, wheel)
```

Although the MakeMeASandwich subroutine would be terribly confused by these parameters, a ChangeAFlatTire routine would be right at home. Consequently, your program's subroutines, like these examples, can only work with the type of data or the values for which they were designed. Passing a subroutine a string of text when it is expecting a number is like passing a bolt to the MakeMeASandwich subroutine. Such a parameter, sent in error, can shut down your entire program. Chapter 7, "Structured Programming," provides more information about passing parameters.

Functions

A *function* is similar to a subroutine in that it is a group of related statements that can be executed by a single assignment statement (described earlier in this chapter). As you just learned, a subroutine returns to the main program when it is done with its task. A function does the same thing, only it brings back a value with it.

In an assignment statement, a function name can be used in place of a variable. For example, as you saw earlier with assignment statements, you can assign the value of one variable to another, such as

```
A = B
```

Now, suppose that the value you want for B actually is a complicated series of equations such as

```
(C + (D/E) - ((Z * P) / pi) + (3 * X))
```

If the program wants to assign the value of A to this equation, it begins to get a little unwieldy—especially if the assignment must occur several places in the program.

```
A = (C + (D/E) - ((Z * P) / pi) + (3 * X))
```

As with subroutines, you can put a series of program statements into a separate area and CALL it when you need it. Because a function is similar to a subroutine, you can move the complicated equation code into the function, as shown in this pseudocode:

ComplexEquation function
  (C + (D/E) - ((Z * P) / pi) + (3 * X))
   RETURN with answer   ·
End of ComplexEquation Function

To use the value, substitute the name of the function in your original assignment statement:

```
A = ComplexEquation
```

The function ComplexEquation now looks like a variable and takes the place of B. Because a function returns a value, you can use a function name within your program in exactly the same way you would use a variable name.

The following code example shows a function that returns the average of three numbers. At first glance, it appears to be very similar to a subroutine. This function takes three numerical parameters.

```
FUNCTION Average(FirstNum, SecondNum, ThirdNum)
    Average = (FirstNum + SecondNum + ThirdNum)/3
END FUNCTION
```

Now that you have written the function, the following example shows one way to call this QBasic function:

```
A = 20
B = 62
C = 88

Result = Average(A, B, C)
```

A function can also be used like a variable with other statements, such as PRINT, as shown in the following example:

```
A = 20
B = 62
C = 88
PRINT "The average is: "; Average(A, B, C)
```

PRINT is the QBasic output statement that causes information to be displayed on-screen. The function Average is called, which calculates the average value of the three parameters. The answer, or return value, of Average is then printed by the QBasic statement PRINT.

Conditional Statements

"If you can't stand the heat, stay out of the kitchen."

This is a *conditional statement*. Its name comes from the fact that it evaluates a condition and then takes an action based on that condition. For example, If (you can't stand the heat), then stay out of the kitchen.

If the words or expressions within the parentheses evaluate to True, the part of the statement following the word *then* is executed. If the expression within the parentheses evaluates to False, whatever comes after *then* is ignored. Therefore, whatever statement follows the word *then* depends on an evaluation of the condition following *if*.

If you write this example in QBasic, it looks like this:

```
IF (YouCantStandHeat) THEN StayOutOfKitchen
```

You can expand this example by adding another condition: "If you can't stand the heat, then stay out of the kitchen, or else put the roast in the oven." The ELSE statement gives you another option.

In the first case, there is only one choice. If you can't stand the heat, then you stay out of the kitchen. With the ELSE option, you are given one choice if you cannot stand the heat, and one choice if you can.

It is possible to follow an IF statement with another IF statement in QBasic.

```
IF (YouCantStandHeat) THEN
    IF (WindowWontOpen) THEN

        IF (AirConditionerBroken) THEN
            StayOutOfKitchen
        END IF

    END IF

ELSE
    WashTheDishes
END IF
```

All the stated conditions must be met before you can stay out of the kitchen, or else you must wash the dishes. IF-THEN statements are discussed further in Chapter 5, "Making Decisions."

Case Statements

Case statements are a shorthand way of writing conditional statements. If you have a long or complicated expression to evaluate and you must compare it to two or more conditional values (two or more tests on the expression), you can replace the tests with a select case statement. The following example shows a program that uses conditional statements.

```
IF FirstName$ = "Sally" THEN
    PRINT "Hi Sally!"
    END
END IF

IF FirstName$ = "David" THEN
    PRINT "Yo, Dave!"
    END
END IF

IF FirstName$ = "Cassie" THEN
    PRINT "Where's Sally?"
    END
END IF
```

The following code example uses the QBasic SELECT CASE statement to perform the same task as in the preceding example.

```
SELECT CASE FirstName$         'Variable to be evaluated
    CASE "Sally"               'Is it Sally?
        PRINT "Hi Sally!"      'Yes!
    CASE "David"               'Is it David?
        PRINT "Yo, Dave!"      'Yes, it's David
    CASE "Cassie"              'Is it Cassie?
        PRINT "Where's Sally?" 'Yes it's Cassie
END SELECT
```

The SELECT CASE statement decreased the size of the program and made the code clearer and more efficient. SELECT CASE statements are very useful when the program needs to check input against a fixed list of values.

Clarity is one good reason for using a SELECT CASE statement. Another reason is that the expression you are testing is evaluated only once, rather than once for every IF statement; this makes your program run faster. The more complicated the test expression is, the more time you save by using SELECT CASE statements. Chapter 5, "Making Decisions," explores SELECT CASE statements in more detail.

Loops

A loop repeats a statement or set of statements until a condition that you have specified has been met. There are several kinds of loop statements and you can control the flow of your program using them.

You will discover ways to construct loops within all the high-level programming languages such as C, Pascal, QBasic, and so on. The statements each language uses to create a loop vary slightly, but all loops do essentially the same thing. Loops are discussed in more detail in Chapter 6, "Performing Loops."

Summary

In this chapter, you learned how to get input to and output from your program, using several kinds of programming statements. You learned the importance of adding comments to your code so that you and others can understand what each segment of code is supposed to do and to aid in debugging and revising your code.

You also learned the importance of subroutines and functions, and how they can extend the language you are working with, and about conditional and case statements to control program flow. You've seen how assignment statements change the values of variables inside the program.

The following list summarizes the types of programming statements presented in this chapter. Accompanying each statement is an example of how to use the statement in QBasic. QBasic was chosen because it is packaged with MS-DOS 5.0.

- **Comment.** A comment is a notation, or documentation, of the intent and desired result of your program.

```
' This is a QBasic comment.
REM This is also a QBasic comment.
```

- **Assignment statement.** An assignment statement assigns a value to a variable.

```
A = B
FirstName = "Harvey"
RecordCount = 45
Total = Average(A,B,C)
```

■ **Input statement.** An input statement brings information into your program.

```
INPUT A
```

■ **Output statement.** An output statement enables the program to communicate with your computer's hardware and present the result of the program's activities in some tangible form.

```
PRINT "The total is ";Total
```

■ **Conditional statement.** A conditional statement performs a test on an expression and causes your program to branch depending on the outcome of the test.

```
IF A = B THEN C = A + B
```

■ **Case statement.** A case statement compares an expression with a series of evaluations.

```
SELECT CASE CityName
   CASE "Sacramento"
     CALL ShowMap("California")
   CASE "Albany"
     CALL ShowMap("New York")
END SELECT
```

■ **Subroutine call.** A subroutine call enables a programmer to refer to a block or series of frequently used statements with one command.

```
CALL MySubroutine(A, B, C, D)
```

■ **Function call.** A call to a function returns a value that can be assigned to a variable.

```
Score = RollDice(6,6)
PRINT "You have rolled ";RollDice(6,6)
```

Simple Data Types and Elementary Operators

by Greg Perry

People invented computers to process data. Computer programs receive raw data (usually from the keyboard or a disk file), process that data, and produce meaningful information—often seen as output. Figure 3.1 illustrates the basic model of any computer program.

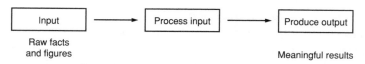

Input		Process input		Produce output

Raw facts
and figures

Meaningful results

Figure 3.1. A model that all programs follow.

A program must be able to store its input somewhere so that it can work with the data and process it into something meaningful to the user. All data processed by a program is stored in the program as either a variable or a constant.

The word *data* is actually plural for the word *datum*. This book treats the word *data* as if it were singular, such as "The data is …," because that currently is the most common usage.

The primary storage areas programs use are called *variables.* Variables are memory locations inside your computer that hold data. Variables hold different kinds of data, and the same variable might hold many different values during the execution of a program. Variable contents vary—hence the name *variable. Constants* never change. Constants are numbers, characters, or words that you put in a program. As you see later in this chapter, programmers sometimes even store constants in variables.

This chapter tries to explain the meaning behind variables and constants, the kinds of variables and constants you can use, and how variables are stored.

Storing Data

Before getting into the specifics of variables and constants, you should understand what is going on "under the hood" of your computer when you process data with a program. Inside your computer is the *CPU—*the *Central Processing Unit.* The CPU is the brain—or traffic cop—inside your system unit: it monitors, controls, and computes all the data that flows between the memory and other devices of your computer system.

Your CPU can process data only when that data is in the computer's memory. For example, you probably have used a word processor at some time. If so, you know that you cannot edit a document file until you load the file from the disk into memory. After you select the correct menu options telling the CPU what to do, the CPU sends instructions that place the contents of the file in memory.

Only when the file is in memory can you edit the file. The CPU cannot do anything with your data while it resides only on the disk. The CPU must bring the data into memory—usually called *RAM* or *random-access memory*—before it can work with the file. The CPU works closely with memory but can only direct the disk to input or output to and from that memory. The CPU cannot directly manipulate data on the disk until you bring that data into memory.

Your computer's memory is made up of thousands of characters of memory locations, which are called *bytes.* In other words, if your computer has approximately 640,000 bytes of memory, it has approximately 640,000 characters of memory, or 640,000 locations in which to store characters. Once you fill that memory, you cannot add any more data to it. If you need more memory (so that you can process larger amounts of data at a time), you must buy additional boards and memory chips.

The reason you have *approximately* 640,000 bytes and not *exactly* 640,000 is because computer manufacturers build computers based on powers of 2. Electricity must be either on or off, so there are two states of electricity. Because your computer is nothing more than millions of tiny switches going on and off, computer designers started building computers based on the two states of electricity. This *binary* state controls the amount of memory your computer can have at any one time. Therefore, if your computer has 640,000 characters of data, it really has the power of 2 closest to 640,000, which is exactly 655,360 bytes of storage. Instead of keeping track of the extra numbers, people usually say they have 640K of data; the *K* means *Kilobytes*, or approximately 1,000 bytes.

To fully understand the meaning of memory and data, you must also understand how your computer's memory is physically constructed. Each of the thousands of memory locations inside your computer contains a unique location called an *address*. Just as every house has a unique address, so does every memory location inside your computer. As Figure 3.2 shows, the addresses begin at 0 and continue from there, adding 1 each time.

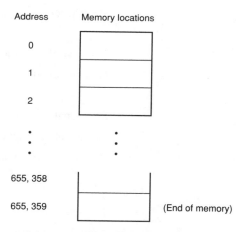

Figure 3.2. A model of a computer's 640K RAM and its addresses.

When you define a variable or constant in a program, your computer stores that data at a memory location. Depending on the magnitude of that data, it might take up one or more bytes of memory; not every data value occupies a single space of memory in the computer. You do not want to have to remember addresses. In fact, the less you have to worry about memory addresses, the better. Programming would be very difficult if you had to tell the computer to store your data at a specific memory location, and then you had to use the address of that location from then on. If you needed a payroll salary figure, you would need to tell the computer to look for it at a certain address. Addresses might help deliver the mail, but they do not help improve your programming speed if you have to keep track of them. Luckily, as you will learn a little later in this chapter, you don't have to remember the specific addresses of your data; after you assign names to your data, the program remembers the specific addresses for you.

Data Types

Data, whether held in variables or constants, takes on different types. Table 3.1 lists the standard types of data. The most common distinction among the various types is that there are both numeric and character data types.

Table 3.1. The kinds of data types.	
Numeric	
Name	*Description*
Integers	
Short integers	Small whole numbers
Long integers	Large whole numbers
Real (floating-point)	
Single-precision	Small real numbers
Double-precision	Large real numbers
Scientific notation	Extremely large or extremely small real numbers
Character	
Name	*Description*
Single characters	A single character
Character strings	One or more characters strung together

Not all programming languages support all these data types, and some programming languages break the types into even more specific categories. Most languages support these data types in some form. Some programming languages call these data types by different names. For example, in C and C++, a single-precision number is called a *float* (for *floating-point*) and a double-precision number is called a *double*. The next few sections explain each data type.

Integers

An integer is any whole number. Loosely speaking, an integer is any number that does not have a decimal point. Therefore, all the following are integers:

`23      149     0     -83      98234      -8398`

None of the following are integers, they are real numbers:

`23.0      -4390.433      0.0`

As you can see, even if the number is the same (such as 23 and 23.0), the decimal point makes the number a real number because it adds some precision (the number is known to be accurate to a specified number of decimal places). Real numbers are discussed in the next section.

Most programming languages support two kinds of integers: *short integers* and *long integers*. These integers can have different names in different languages. Short integers generally occupy only two bytes of space. Therefore, if your program used three integers, those integers would consume six bytes of memory space. Because a single memory location (byte) cannot hold large numbers (never more than 255), your program must be able to use a pair of memory locations for larger integers. A two-byte integer typically can fall within the range of –32,768 to 32,767.

Long integers might take four to eight bytes of memory. Some programming languages use no more than four bytes of memory for integers, but you usually can store very large (and very small) integers in four bytes. The range of numbers you can store in a long integer is generally –2,147,483,648 to 2,147,483,647.

Real Numbers

Real numbers, sometimes called *floating-point* numbers, are numeric values that have decimal points. The following are all real numbers:

`17.5      4.33333333      0.0      -0.0000000005      -2322.8`

Real numbers contain both a whole portion of a number and a fractional portion (the part of the number to the right of the decimal point). Precision plays an important role in real numbers. For example, if you type a number that has two decimal places (such as a number representing dollars and cents), you are implying that the number is accurate to within two decimal places. In other words, 415.68 is accurate to two decimal places. The number is not 415.67 or 415.69; it is exactly 415.68. It is implied that the number might contain additional decimal places that you don't specify; the number might be stored in the computer as 415.680001 or 415.680999, but only the first two decimal places are important.

The number of decimal places you need for precision determines whether you need to store a value in a single-precision or double-precision location. Generally, a single-precision value is accurate to six decimal places and requires four bytes of memory to store. Most programming languages enable you to store the following range of numbers in a single-precision value: 3.402823×10^{38} to -3.402823×10^{38} (which is the same as 3402823 with 32 zeros after it). Generally, a double-precision value is accurate to 14 decimal places and takes eight bytes of memory to store. Most programming languages enable you to store the following range of numbers in a double-precision value: $-1.79769313486231 \times 10^{308}$ to $1.79769313486231 \times 10^{308}$ (or, 179769313485231 with 294 zeros after it).

All that accuracy can get confusing. Often, a programming language supports *scientific notation*. Scientific notation sounds difficult, but it is not; you saw its partial use in the preceding paragraph. Many times numbers are so big (or so small) that you must resort to some other method of describing them rather than simply typing the entire number. Scientific notation is a shortcut method of representing numbers of extreme values. Many people program for years and never need scientific notation, but knowing it puts you at ease with programming manuals that use it—and you won't be surprised if your program someday prints a number on the screen in scientific notation.

It is easiest to learn scientific notation by looking at a few examples. You can represent any number in scientific notation, but the use of scientific notation usually is limited to extremely large or extremely small numbers. All scientific notation numbers are real numbers. Table 3.2 shows some numbers written in scientific notation and their decimal equivalents.

Table 3.2. Examples of numbers written in scientific notation.	
Scientific Notation	**Decimal Equivalent**
3.08e+12	3,080,000,000,000
−9.7587e+04	−97,587
+5.164e−4	0.0005164
−4.6545e−9	−0.0000000046545
1.654e+302	1.654×10^{302}

Positive numbers written in scientific notation begin with a plus sign or have no sign. Negative numbers written in scientific notation begin with a minus sign.

To evaluate the number, take the number left of the *e* (which stands for *exponent*) and multiply it by 10 raised to the number on the right. Thus, 3.08e+12 means to take 3.08 and multiply it by 1,000,000,000,000 (10 raised to the 12th power, or 10^{12}). Also, −4.6545e−9 is −4.6545 times .00000001 (10 raised to the −9 power, or 10^{-9}).

You can use either an uppercase *E* or a lowercase *e* when typing scientific numbers in a program. Some versions of BASIC use a *d* rather than an *e* when the scientific notation value is stored in a double-precision location.

The Reason for Lengths

Programming languages offer different lengths for the same type of data—long integers and short integers, for example—because you should use only the smallest possible type for your data. As you will see in a section later in this chapter, you can create variables that hold any one of these many types of data.

If you must create a variable to hold the ages of the children in a fourth grade class, you do not need to use long integers. Short integers—which can usually hold a number as large as 32,767—will suffice. If, however, you were writing a trajectory program for NASA and you needed to compute the number of miles between solar systems, you might need to use a long integer—or even scientific notation—for those larger numbers.

At first you might think you should always use the largest data type available—better safe than sorry. If a double-precision variable can hold a number as large as $1.79769313486231 \times 10^{308}$, then any value can fit in it, right? That is correct, but it is not an efficient use of space; your programs run inefficiently if you always use the largest data type available.

Figure 3.3 shows a short integer labeled `si`, a long integer labeled `li`, a single-precision real number labeled `sr`, and a double-precision real number labeled `dr`. Each of these four memory locations contains a small number—7 for the two integers and 7.0 for the two real numbers.

Which of the numbers in Figure 3.3 do you think your CPU can read from memory the fastest? Obviously, the CPU can read the short integer value faster because it only has to read a pair of memory locations to get the value stored there. You should usually only use short integers and single-precision values, although you might need to use the large memory locations for extreme values later. Your program's efficiency, and therefore speed, will be improved.

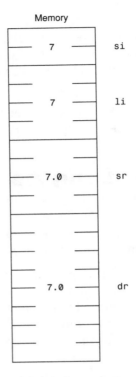

Figure 3.3. Storing several data types in memory.

Character Data

The remaining data types in programming languages are character data types. There are two character data types: characters and strings of characters. A character data type is any single character represented on your computer. A character is any letter, number, or special character (such as a question mark). Just about every key on your keyboard, including the Spacebar, represents a character. Some data is best suited for a character variable. Your initials are character data, as is each student's grade in a teacher's record-keeping program.

String data is the term applied to one or more characters strung together. Many programming languages, including C and Pascal, also support zero-length strings, meaning that a string can be zero or more characters. As you can see, a string is really just an aggregate of the character data.

Any data that is not a number is a character or a string. Some data is made up entirely of numbers; yet, your programs should store it as a string. If you are not going to perform any math with a number, you should store it as a string. For example, although phone numbers and Social Security numbers are made up of numeric digits, store them as strings of characters. You would never add two phone numbers together.

As you learn about four popular programming languages later in the book, you will see how they store numeric and character data.

Variables and Constants

Almost every programming language supports all of the data types you learned about in the previous sections. Some languages, such as C and C++, do not directly support strings as efficiently as the others, but you can easily simulate the string manipulation operations that are available in BASIC. Now that you understand the different data types, you need to see where they are used.

All the data that your program works with resides in memory. Whether it is loaded into memory from a disk file, typed at the keyboard, input from a modem or from some other external device, all your data must be in memory for the program to access it. The program's data resides in variables or constants. In most programming languages, both variables and constants can take any of the data types from Table 3.1.

Loosely speaking, a variable is nothing more than a box in memory that holds a value. A variable holds only one value at any one time. For example, a variable can hold the integer value 4. Another variable might hold the floating-point value of 45.65. (Although the number has four digits, the variable is still holding one thing—a single number.)

Even when a variable holds a string, it holds only one value—one string of characters. The important thing to remember is that if a variable holds a value and you then put another value into that variable (through programming commands that you will learn about later), the old value is wiped out when the new one goes into the variable. Variables cannot hold two values at the same time. Because you can store several values in the same variable throughout a program's execution (just never more than one value at any one time), a variable's content varies, hence its name *variable*.

A constant never varies; it always remains the same. Sometimes programmers refer to constants as *literals*. You can think of some real-life data in terms of being variable and constant. Your Social Security number acts like a constant: you have the same number your entire life. You can think of your salary as being variable. Your salary (hopefully!) increases over time.

Some data in a program is constant. For example, if you were writing a program for a driver's license bureau, and the driving age is 16 in your state, you might use a constant to represent 16. If you think the driving age might change someday, you can store it in a variable so that you can modify it at a later time.

When you need to put a constant in a program, you simply type it in the code. For example, you would probably see 16 in several places throughout the driver's license program. For numeric constants, you typically type the actual number each time it is used in the program. Character and string constants are handled a little differently in different programming languages. Most programming languages require that you put single or double quotation marks around character and string constants.

The following are character constants in many programming languages:

```
'a'      '9'      '+'      'Y'      'T'
```

Some languages require that you enclose character data in double quotation marks.

The following are string constants in many programming languages:

```
"This is a string"      "555-6543"      " "
```

The last string is an empty string, sometimes called a *null string*. Empty strings are useful if you want to blank out a string variable completely. Putting a space in a variable is not the same as blanking it out because the computer recognizes a space as a valid character. When you put a null string inside a string variable, the program acts like nothing is in the string until you put something into it.

Before you can use a variable, you must *define* it. By defining a variable, you give the variable (the box inside memory) a name and a data type. Your program has to know what kind of data you are going to put into a variable in order to assign the correct data type. Your program also requires variable names. Because you—as the programmer—are responsible for naming variables, you should understand how names work.

Naming Variables

Whether your program contains one or one thousand variables, you are responsible for creating them. More accurately, you are responsible for telling the program to create them for you. Chapters 14 through 17 explain how to define variables in four different programming languages: BASIC, Pascal, C, and C++. BASIC is less strict than most languages in that you do not have to define a variable before you use it. BASIC waits until you use a variable, looks at the context of your use, and then creates it "on the fly."

Most programming languages available today require a statement at the top of the program defining every variable used in the program. You must list all the variables and their data types in the definition/declaration statement.

All variables have names, and no two variables within the same program area can have the same name (you learn more about this later). If there were more than one variable named Salary, when you tried to print Salary, the program wouldn't know which Salary to print. Therefore, no programming language allows you to have two variables with the same name in the same program area.

There are many naming rules for variables. Because you are responsible for making up variable names, you must know how to name them. Each programming language has its own rules. You learn these variable-naming rules in the chapters that cover individual programming languages, Chapters 14 through 17. Most programming languages require that a variable name begin with a letter of the alphabet; after the first letter, the names can contain numbers and even some special characters. A space is never allowed in a variable name—if the variable had a space in it, your program would incorrectly treat it as if it were two different variables.

Whatever names you make up, be sure to use meaningful variable names. For example, if you want to store a 1992 marketing number in a variable, you could use any of these variable names:

```
xyz     w_w2     hat     MyShoes
```

Although these names are valid, the variable name is easier for you to identify and remember if you give it one of the following names:

```
Mktg92     MKT_92     MarketData92
```

Just from the variable name itself, you can determine the meaning of the variable. Your computer does not care how you name variables; when you have 50 or 60 different variables within the same program, however, you will be glad you used meaningful names.

Defining Variables

In Chapters 14 through 17, you learn the specifics of defining variables. This chapter will make much more sense to you after you see the different approaches used by the different languages. Nevertheless, the following discussion gives you a general feel for the way most languages treat the defining of variables.

Suppose you are writing a program to calculate some payroll data. You must work with several values, including hours worked, pay rate per hour, gross pay, taxes, and net pay. Your program must ask the user to type the necessary data, calculate the results, and finally display the results on-screen.

Variables are the perfect place (actually, the only place inside a program) to store the values entered from the keyboard and the values computed in the program. Table 3.3 lists some possible variable names and their data types.

Table 3.3. Some payroll variable names and data types.		
Name	**Data Type**	**Description**
HrsWrkd	Integer	Entered from the keyboard
Rate	Single-precision	Entered from the keyboard
GrossPay	Single-precision	Calculated in the program
Taxes	Single-precision	Calculated in the program
NetPay	Single-precision	Calculated in the program

Before the program can work with these variables, you almost always will see a variable definition section at the top of the program. This section defines each of the program variables by type. In C, the variable definition section looks like this:

```
int   HrsWrkd;
float Rate, GrossPay, Taxes, NetPay;
```

As you can see, defining variables is easy. All other programming languages define variables in a similar manner (although, as mentioned earlier, BASIC does not require that you define a variable before using it). When your program reads these lines, it sets aside room in memory for the variables. Although different data types take different amounts of memory, and the amount of memory for each data type varies with different computers and programming languages, an integer usually requires two bytes of storage and a single-precision, floating-point variable requires four. Therefore, the previous variable definitions set up memory similar to that shown in Figure 3.4.

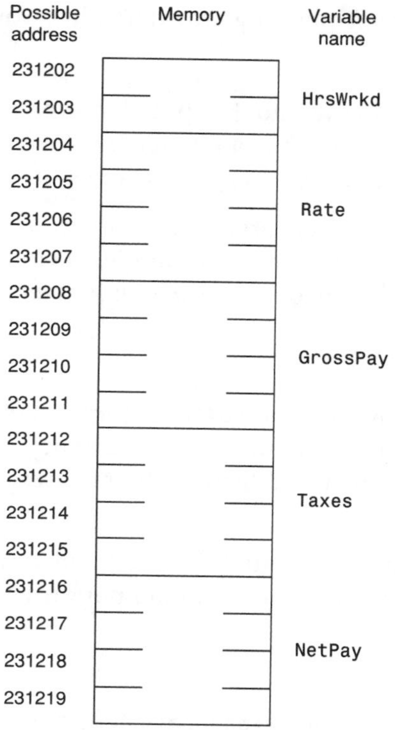

Possible address	Memory	Variable name
231202		
231203		HrsWrkd
231204		
231205		
231206		Rate
231207		
231208		
231209		
231210		GrossPay
231211		
231212		
231213		
231214		Taxes
231215		
231216		
231217		
231218		NetPay
231219		

Figure 3.4. The program reserves memory for your variables based on the variable definitions you supply.

Once you define variables, you can put values into them.

Assigning Values to Variables

Almost every programming language uses an equal sign (=) to store values in variables. (Pascal is an exception, as you will see in Chapter 15.) You can only put the same type of data into a variable as the variable definition defines. In other words, a single-precision variable stores a single-precision value; a single-precision variable cannot store a character value.

The following statement is the general format for putting values into variables:

```
variable name = a value
```

The equal sign acts like a left-pointing arrow. In other words, if you write this,

```
HrsWrkd = 40
```

the program puts the integer 40 into the space it reserved for the variable named HrsWrkd. You don't have to know the address of HrsWrkd; your program figures out exactly where in memory HrsWrkd was placed, and stores the value there.

You can assign variables to other variables; the value on the right side of the equal sign does not have to be a constant. For example, the following is permitted (assuming you have defined Sales and OldSales earlier in the program):

```
OldSales = 3454.32
Sales = OldSales
```

After the second statement, the value 3454.32 remains in the OldSales variable and is also in Sales. When you assign one variable to another, the first variable retains its original value. Assigning one variable to another causes the computer to copy the first variable's value.

Anything on the right side of the equal sign is copied into the variable name on the left. For example, you can make the computer perform math before it assigns values to variables, such as this:

```
NetPay = GrossPay - Taxes
```

This assumes that GrossPay and Taxes have values that you calculated and put in them earlier in the program. The variables NetPay, GrossPay, and Taxes must be numeric variables in order to perform arithmetic on them.

Be sure that you do not attempt to use a variable on the right side of an equal sign before you put something into it. Most languages do not automatically initialize variables before you use them. Therefore, you have no idea what value is in a variable until you—or the user—put something into the variables.

Assuming that your program contains the payroll variable definitions shown earlier, and assuming that values have been assigned to HrsWrkd and Rate, the following assignment statements compute the remaining values:

```
GrossPay = Rate * HrsWrkd
Taxes = .35 * GrossPay
NetPay = GrossPay - Taxes
```

The asterisk (*) means multiplication in almost every computer language. If you use an x instead, the program might get confused and think that x is a misplaced variable name.

There are many ways to put values into variables besides using the equal sign. As you learn a programming language, you learn how that language specifically inputs keyboard values into variables. Once you assign a value to a variable, that variable holds the value until the program ends, or until you put another value into the variable.

Operators

As you saw in the previous section, expressions often contain math operators such as addition and multiplication operators. Most programming languages support the following four operators:

- + meaning addition

- - meaning subtraction

- * meaning multiplication

- / meaning division

Some programming languages also support an exponent operator, which is represented by the caret (or "housetop") character (^). Therefore, the following expression puts the result of 2 raised to the 5th power into `Result`:

```
Result = 2 ^ 5
```

As Chapters 14 through 17 more fully explain, programming languages follow a few simple rules. All multiplication and division is performed before addition and subtraction. Therefore, the following statement:

```
Result = 2 + 3 * 2
```

stores an 8 in `Result`. Because the multiplication is done before the addition, the 3 * 2 produces a 6, which is then added to the 2 to produce 8. If multiplication and division both reside in the same expression, they are performed from left to right. Addition and subtraction also are computed from left to right. In the following statement, the subtraction occurs before the addition:

```
Result = 8 - 2 + 5
```

In the following statement, the division is done before the multiplication:

```
Result = 8 / 2 * 5
```

You can override the default order of the operators with parentheses. In the following example, the multiplication is done before the division:

```
Result = 8 / (2 * 5)
```

to produce .8 (8 divided by 10).

Updating a Variable

You often see the same variable name on *both* sides of the equal sign. For example, you might see something like this:

```
count = count + 1
```

You do not have to be a mathematician to suspect that something is wrong here. How can any variable, regardless of what value it holds, be equal to itself plus 1?

In math, nothing can be equal to itself plus one; in computers, however, the equal sign does not work exactly like it does in math. Remember that the equal sign is similar to a left-pointing arrow. The equal sign says, "Take whatever is on the right side, compute the answer if it is a formula, and store the resulting value in the variable on the left."

Therefore, the count assignment statement is adding 1 to count. The equal sign tells the program to take whatever is in the variable named count, add 1 to it, and *then* store that newly-calculated value into the count variable, replacing what was in it before. When you see a variable on both sides of an equal sign, you are *updating* the value that was in the variable.

You might need to update a variable (by adding 1 to it) when you count items, such as inventory records, people on the payroll, or customers for the week. Each time your computer processes another item, you add 1 to the count variable. When you have counted the last item, the count variable contains the total number you processed.

You can count down, if your application requires it, by subtracting 1. The following assignment statement counts down:

```
count = count - 1
```

Computers are also useful tools for keeping track of totals. You often see a variable being updated with a value other than 1. For example, suppose you see the following statement:

```
DailyTotal = DailyTotal + CashSale
```

Instead of adding 1 to DailyTotal, this statement adds the value of a variable named CashSale. This statement might be in a program that tracks cash sales as customers make purchases throughout the day. Each sale is added to the `DailyTotal` variable; at the end of the day, `DailyTotal` holds the total sales for the entire day. Of course, the following day you must make sure the program zeros-out the `DailyTotal` so that the next day's total begins at zero.

Arrays

After you have been programming for a while, you might discover a need for a special type of variable called an *array*. Different programming languages handle arrays differently. Of the four languages explained later in this book, arrays are only critical to the beginning programmer in C and C++. As you will see in Chapters 16 and 17, C and C++ use arrays to hold strings of character data. Nevertheless, you should know a little about arrays to complete this data discussion.

Suppose you must keep track of 100 scores in a cross-country tournament. You must compute the average of the scores, find the highest score, find the lowest score, and calculate some other statistics. Applying what you have learned so far in this chapter, you would need 100 variables to store the 100 scores. However, you don't want to have to make up 100 different variable names to keep all the scores in; that would be too much trouble. Also, if you wanted to add them all up, you would have to write a statement similar to this:

```
total = score1 + score2 + score3 + ... + score100
```

Once you have added all 100 scores, this statement would span several lines in a program. Programming languages offer a much better alternative: arrays. An *array* is a list of variables that all have the same name.

A few sections earlier, you learned that two variables cannot have the same name; an array, however, is a special type of variable. An array contains more than one variable, each with the same name, but there is a way for you and your program to distinguish one array variable from another. Each array variable has a unique *subscript*. A subscript is a sequential number, starting at either 0 or 1 depending on the language, that tells the computer which of the array variables you want to use.

Figure 3.5 shows a sample of what a `scores` array might look like. Each of the 100 scores is named `scores`—in other words, the array name is `scores`. The first score in the array is named `scores(1)`, the second is named `scores(2)`, and so on. (Some programming languages, such as C, use brackets ([]) to contain the subscript.)

Figure 3.5. Looking at the *scores* array.

At this point, the subscripts might seem like extra work on your part. However, instead of writing extensive statements that add 100 explicit variables, you can add 100 array variables in three short statements, such as this:

```
FOR Sub = 1 TO 100
    total = total + scores(Sub)
NEXT Sub
```

This is a loop (you learned about loops in Chapter 2) written in BASIC. Chapter 14, "Overview of BASIC," goes into more detail on how to write this loop. Even if you don't fully understand the details of a loop at this point, an array makes summing totals and performing other statistical manipulations much easier. You can step through an array's values by using a subscripting variable.

Summary

Data storage is the most critical part of writing programs. Your programs work with data in two forms: variables and constants. Variables hold data that changes throughout the program; constants are values that never change while the program executes. There are several types of data, and the data types determine the kind and amount of data the program can work with. Your program will not work at all until you define every variable your program uses.

Although you do not have to understand how data is stored internally in memory, knowing about it helps explain how the different types are stored and how their storage lengths differ. By seeing how much memory is taken up by double-precision values (as much as eight memory locations), you understand why a programmer should not define all data in a program as double-precision data unless the data justifies the extra storage. Not only is much memory wasted, but the program is less efficient than it would have been if you used single-precision data.

Lastly, you learned that arrays provide a mechanism whereby you can store many variables and give them the same name. Instead of remembering hundreds of different names and referring to each variable by its individual name, you can simply refer to each variable by the same name (the array name) and its individual subscript. You can loop through the array using commands offered in the specific programming language you are using.

Sophisticated Data Structures

by Lisa Monitto

In Chapter 3, you learned about simple data types—constants, variables, different types of numbers, and characters. These simple data types are pre-defined in most languages, using keywords specific to that language. In other words, the definitions of these data types and variables are included in the programming language. Because they are predefined, it is not necessary for the programmer to redefine a data type each time it is used.

This chapter discusses more complex data types. Most high-level programming languages allow the programmer to create user-defined data types. These complex data types are used in a program in the same way that simple data types are used—by declaring variables of that data type. Defining your own data may sound complicated and intimidating, but most languages allow you to implement your own data structures easily.

Before going into the details of these special data structures, you need to understand the difference between the concept of a data structure and its implementation. When you create your own data structure, you are creating a new data type for the purpose of your program. Before you can use the new type, though, you must create it by declaring a variable of that type. The following pseudocode creates a *record* BooklistItem.

Template called BooklistItem
  Author AS a STRING of 30 characters
  Title AS a STRING of 50 characters
  Price AS a SINGLE precision variable
  Quantity AS an INTEGER
End of Template

You have now created a template, or blueprint, for the record you want to use. The preceding pseudocode example tells the compiler what the data type is to look like. This example combines four individual variables into a structure that must always contain these variables. But this new record cannot be used yet. Your program has only defined the template, and still needs to create a variable using that template.

The following pseudocode line creates a usable variable of the type `BooklistItem`, defined in the preceding pseudocode:

CREATE *a variable using the template* `BookListItem`

You have just created (declared) a variable named `MyBooklistItem` of type `BooklistItem`. You can access this data structure from your program similar to the way that you accessed simple variables in Chapter 3, "Simple Data Types and Elementary Operators."

Just as you can have more than one variable of `INTEGER` type or `STRING` type in your program, you can also have more than one variable of the same programmer-defined type in your program. You have created a reusable type.

A variable references an actual piece of memory inside your computer. Data structures—which are composed of variables—are used to organize information within a computer's memory and make it easier to retrieve and move data. Data structures make your job as a programmer much easier.

Think of a mailing list with thousands of names. The list contains a separate first and last name, address, city, state, and ZIP code for each individual. In a large mailing list it would be difficult—if not impossible—to keep track of separate variables for each name and its related information. By using a programmer-defined record, you can create a single variable for each member of the list.

As the previous pseudocode example showed, you can combine variables of different types and sizes in a programmer-defined record. This structure in effect extends the language you are working with and gives you greater flexibility in designing your program.

Records, Structs, and Types

QBasic, Pascal, and C all allow the use of *record variables.* A record variable simplifies the use of many different types of related data by grouping them together—regardless of data types. For example, you can have someone's name (a string), yearly salary (floating-point), number of children (byte), and sex (single character) all in the same record.

In QBasic records are called *types,* in Pascal they are called *records,* and in C they are called *structs.* When you create a record variable, you are declaring a new data type. This new data type can combine any data types you want. You can include simple variables, arrays, or even arrays of record variables in a record variable field.

Listing 4.1 shows how to create a record in QBasic.

Listing 4.1. A QBasic record used to store personnel files.

```
TYPE Employee
    Name AS STRING * 20
    Salary AS SINGLE
    Kids AS INTEGER
    Sex AS STRING * 1
END TYPE
```

Listing 4.2 shows the same example written in Pascal.

Listing 4.2. The same record of personnel files written in Pascal.

```
TYPE Employee = RECORD
    Name    : STRING[20];
    Salary : REAL;
    Kids    : BYTE;
    Sex     : CHAR;
END;
```

Listing 4.3 shows the same example written in C.

Listing 4.3. The same record of personnel files written in C.

```
struct Employee
   {
      char Name[20];
      float Salary;
      int Kids;
      char Sex;
   };
```

As you saw in Listings 4.1, 4.2, and 4.3, individual variables of different types are combined into a single record, struct, or type. To use such a record variable, you must declare a variable of this type—Employee in this case. You can then refer to the fields in the record variable by name (Employee), followed by a period and the field name. Listing 4.4 shows an example written in QBasic.

Listing 4.4. A QBasic program implementing the record shown in Listing 4.1.

```
DIM Worker As Employee   'Declare a variable of
                         'Employee type
Worker.Name = "Gene Gabriel"
Worker.Salary = 1500.10
Worker.Kids = 0
Worker.Sex = "M"
```

Listing 4.5 shows the example written in Pascal.

Listing 4.5. A Pascal program implementing the record from Listing 4.2.

```
VAR
Worker : Employee; { Declare a variable of }
                   { Employee type }
Worker.Name := 'Gene Gabriel';
Worker.Salary := 1500.10;
Worker.Kids := 0;
Worker.Sex := 'M';
```

Listing 4.6 shows the example written in C.

Listing 4.6. A C program implementing the record from Listing 4.3.

```
struct employee worker;    /* Declare a variable of */
                           /* Employee type */
    Worker.Name = "Gene Gabriel";
    Worker.Salary = 1500.10;
    Worker.Kids = 0;
    Worker.Sex = "M";
```

Arrays

An *array* is a grouping of identical data types or structures. Think of an array as a row of numbered slots which store many data items of the same type. An array can hold number values, character data, pointers, or even programmer-defined data structures.

Arrays allow you to manipulate large amounts of related data easily. With only a few lines of code, you can perform the same operation on hundreds of data values. Arrays are frequently used to store lists of numbers (real or integer) or names (character strings).

In Listing 4.7, the variables Day1$ through Day5$ are all separate string variables storing separate values.

Listing 4.7. Initializing five separate string variables in QBasic.

```
Day1$ = "Monday"
Day2$ = "Tuesday"
Day3$ = "Wednesday"
Day4$ = "Thursday"
Day5$ = "Friday"
```

Like simple variables, an array has a name which you give it. What distinguishes an array from a simple variable is the *subscript*, or *index* number, that comes immediately after the name. The subscript is enclosed in parentheses or brackets. The value of that subscript identifies a single *element* of the whole array. The days of the week could have been stored as Listing 4.8 demonstrates:

Listing 4.8. Initializing five string array elements in QBasic.

```
DIM Day$(1 TO 5)
Day$(1) = "Monday"
Day$(2) = "Tuesday"
Day$(3) = "Wednesday"
Day$(4) = "Thursday"
Day$(5) = "Friday"
```

The difference between Listing 4.7 and Listing 4.8 is that in the first example you have five separate variables, and in the second you have one array variable with five elements. If you wanted to print out a list of the days of the week using the first example you must write a separate output statement for every variable:

```
PRINT Day1$
PRINT Day2$
PRINT Day3$
PRINT Day4$
PRINT Day5$
```

If you had used an array to store the names of the days of the week, you could display the data on-screen without writing an individual PRINT statement for each variable. To print out the days of the week from the Day$() array, you could use the following shortcut:

```
FOR i = 1 TO 5
    PRINT Day$(i)
NEXT
```

After you have declared and initialized the array, it takes only three lines of code to print all of its elements. The loop in the preceding example makes it possible to step through the elements of the array in order. (Loops are discussed more thoroughly in Chapter 6, "Performing Loops.") Because it only took five lines to print the same list in the first example, this probably seems more laborious than timesaving. Now imagine if your array had one thousand or ten thousand elements; you still need only the same three lines of code to print the entire array, as opposed to writing an individual PRINT statement for each variable.

You refer to the individual items in an array by using the name of the array variable, followed by its *subscript*, or *index*. To refer to an element with the subscript 5 in an array named MailList, you would refer to `MailList(5)` in QBasic or Pascal, or `MailList[5]` in C.

One-Dimensional Arrays

You saw in Chapter 3, "Simple Data Types and Elementary Operators," that you can think of a one-dimensional array as a column of items, with each item identified by number. Listing 4.9 is an example of a one-dimensional array, `PizzaTopping`, as written in QBasic. The array has five elements—each initialized to the names of various pizza toppings.

Listing 4.9. Defining the one-dimensional array *PizzaTopping*.

```
DEFSTR A-Z
DIM PizzaTopping(5)        'Make an array with 5 elements.

    PizzaTopping(1) = "Pepperoni"
    PizzaTopping(2) = "Sausage"
    PizzaTopping(3) = "Onions"
    PizzaTopping(4) = "Mushrooms"
    PizzaTopping(5) = "Anchovies"
```

You can refer to the names stored in the array as `PizzaTopping(1)`, `PizzaTopping(2)`, and so forth. To select the fifth item, `Anchovies`, you would specify `PizzaTopping(5)`. Figure 4.1 shows how the contents of each array element is arranged in memory.

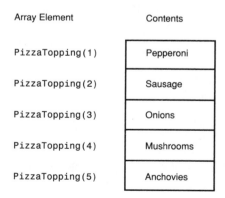

Figure 4.1. An array called *PizzaTopping()*

Multidimensional Arrays

If a one-dimensional array can be thought of as a single column or dimension, a *multidimensional array* can be thought of as two or more of these columns or dimensions.

A two-dimensional array can be used to represent any sort of table. Listing 4.10 creates a two-dimensional array that stores data related to the amount of pizza toppings sold on weekends versus weekdays at a pizza restaurant.

Listing 4.10. A short program to demonstrate two-dimensional arrays.

```
' Program PIZZA.BAS - Listing 4.10

DEFINT A-Z      ' Make default variables of type INTEGER
DIM PizzaSales(2,5) ' Create two-dimensional array

DIM PizzaTopping$(1 TO 5)       ' Create a one-dimensional
                                ' array of strings
PizzaTopping$(1) = "Pepperoni"
PizzaTopping$(2) = "Sausage"
PizzaTopping$(3) = "Onions"
PizzaTopping$(4) = "Mushrooms"
PizzaTopping$(5) = "Anchovies"

Weekdays = 1
Weekends = 2

PizzaSales(Weekdays,1) = 10    ' initialize PizzaSales
PizzaSales(Weekdays,2) = 33    ' array
PizzaSales(Weekdays,3) = 5
PizzaSales(Weekdays,4) = 22
PizzaSales(Weekdays,5) = 1

PizzaSales(Weekends,1) = 17
PizzaSales(Weekends,2) = 41
PizzaSales(Weekends,3) = 9
PizzaSales(Weekends,4) = 28
PizzaSales(Weekends,5) = 1

PRINT , " WEEKDAY SALES"," WEEKEND SALES" ' column heads

FOR Topping = 1 TO 5
   PRINT PizzaTopping$(Topping),
```

```
FOR TimeOfWeek = 1 TO 2
    PRINT PizzaSales(TimeOfWeek, Topping),  'Print table
  NEXT TimeOfWeek
PRINT
NEXT Topping
```

This QBasic code listing actually uses both a one-dimensional array and a two-dimensional array. The one-dimensional array—PizzaToppings—is the list of pizza toppings, and is dimensioned to five elements. The two-dimensional array—PizzaSales—keeps track of how many pizzas of each type are sold throughout a week. Figure 4.2 shows how the arrays can be pictured.

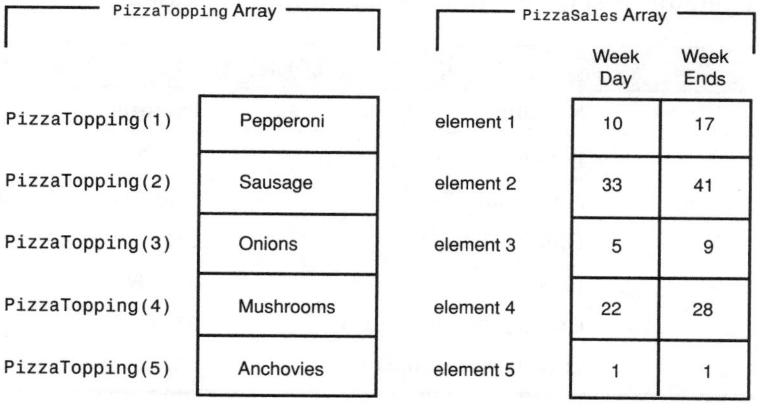

Figure 4.2. The pizza program arrays.

The last section of the program in Listing 4.10 is a short *nested* loop that prints the elements of PizzaToppings followed by the PizzaSales data for the week or weekend. The following is the output of the program:

	WEEKDAY SALES	WEEKEND SALES
Pepperoni	10	17
Sausage	33	41
Onions	5	9
Mushrooms	22	28
Anchovies	1	1

Operators

Operators are symbols that cause a change in an expression.

You saw some simple arithmetic operators (+, -, *, /) in Chapter 3, "Simple Data Types and Elementary Operators." This chapter explains some additional operators that act upon more complex data structures.

In addition to arithmetic operators, there are also relational operators. A relational operator lets your program gather several types of information about a comparison. While the most common comparison operator is the equal sign (=), many programs need to know if something is less than (<) or greater than (>) a certain value. In most languages, both numeric and string information can be compared. Table 4.1 lists six relational operators that QBasic provides for testing expressions.

Table 4.1. Relational operators.		
Symbol	**Meaning**	**Example**
=	Equals	`4 = 2 + 2`
<>	Not equal	`"Apples" <> "Oranges"`
>	Greater than	`300 > 7`
<	Less	`7 < 300`
>=	Greater than or equal to	`25 >= 25`
<=	Less than or equal to	`"Alex" <= "Cindy"`

Table 4.1 lists the symbols and the names of the six relational operators in QBasic, in addition to an example of how each operator is used.

Boolean Expressions and Variables

The term Boolean refers to a special kind of logic. The expressions and variables used in this logic were named for George Boole.

George Boole (1815-1864) was the inventor of Boolean algebra. He became a math teacher at age 16, and published his first book in 1847. Seven years later, he wrote "An Investigation of the Laws of Thought"—the foundation of symbolic logic.

Boole realized that a set of symbols could be applied to logical operators. The symbols could then be manipulated by fixed rules to yield logical results, just as in algebra.

Boolean algebra was used by philosophers such as Alfred North Whitehead and Bertrand Russel in their attempts to explain mathematics on a strictly logical basis.

Boolean variables can only hold one of two values—True or False. You learned in Chapter 1 that binary numbers are represented by 1's and 0's, to reflect the on/off state of bits within the computer's memory.

A Boolean expression is any expression that returns the value True or False. Programming languages use Boolean expressions to test a condition so a decision can be made. (Decision structures will be discussed in detail in Chapter 5, "Making Decisions," and Chapter 6, "Performing Loops.")

Boolean expressions are important in directing the flow of a program. Based on whether an expression evaluates to True or False, program control can follow one direction or another.

QBasic uses the numeric values –1 and 0 to represent True and False, respectively. You can see this in action if you type the following lines of code in QBasic:

```
Salary = 500
Expenses = 1000
PRINT (Salary > Expenses)
PRINT (Salary < Expenses)
```

When you run the preceding program, the output looks like this:

```
0
-1
```

In the preceding example, `Salary > Expenses` evaluates to False, so the output of the first `PRINT` statement is `0` (QBasic's representation of False). The condition `Salary < Expenses` evaluates to True, so the output of the second `PRINT` statement is `-1` (QBasic's representation of True).

Because every expression evaluates to either True or False, you can use an expression to assign the truth value of a Boolean variable, like so

```
GoToGasStation = (GasGauge = 0)
```

Because the statement `GasGauge = 0` evaluates as either True or False, its value can be assigned to a Boolean variable.

The following `IF-THEN` statement contains the Boolean expression `MyAge >= VotingAge`:

```
IF (MyAge >= VotingAge) THEN GoToThePolls
```

If the Boolean expression within the parentheses is true (in other words, if the value of the variable MyAge is greater than or equal to the value of the variable VotingAge) then the subroutine GoToThePolls is executed. (Subroutines are covered more fully in Chapter 7, "Structured Programming.") This example shows the most common usage of Boolean expressions—performing a test on two other expressions to obtain an outcome of True or False. The test is performed with the >= symbol, a relational operator. Expressions can be tested with any of the relational operators shown in Table 4.1. You can also perform a test on two expressions with Boolean operators.

Boolean Operators

Boolean operators are symbols used to specify a logical relationship between two expressions or quantities. The logical operators AND, OR, NOT, and XOR are all Boolean operators.

Logical *AND*

The AND operator is used to make a comparison between two expressions. If both expressions are True, the result of the AND comparison evaluates to True. If one or both of the test expressions are False, the result of the AND comparison evaluates to False.

Because any expression can be evaluated as True or False, when you use AND to compare two expressions you are actually evaluating and comparing two Boolean values, or True-False conditions.

```
IF ((X = 5) AND (Y = 25)) THEN expression_true
```

The terms within parentheses are Boolean statements. X = 5 can only be either True or False. If X really does equal five, then it will evaluate as a true statement. If X equals some other number, then the first expression will be evaluated as a False statement. The same is true for the second expression, Y = 25. It is either True or False.

Using AND, both expressions must be True in order to get a True result. If either expression is False, the result will be False.

Table 4.2 is a truth table. It shows how to determine the truth values of statements that use Boolean operators on expressions. P and Q are expressions (for the purpose of the table). On each line of the truth table you see what the truth value is for the comparison of the statement P AND Q.

Table 4.2. The AND truth table.		
If *P* is...	**and *Q* is...**	**then *P AND Q* evaluates to...**
True	True	True
True	False	False
False	True	False
False	False	False

Logical *OR*

OR is another Boolean operator. You saw above that AND is used to compare two Boolean conditions, and return True only if both expressions are True, and False for all other cases.

OR will return True if either one of the two conditions being evaluated is True.

Table 4.3 is the OR truth table. On each line of the truth table you see what the truth value is for the comparison of the statement P OR Q.

Table 4.3. The OR truth table.		
If *P* is...	**and *Q* is...**	**then *P OR Q* evaluates to...**
True	True	True
True	False	True
False	True	True
False	False	False

Logical *NOT*

NOT reverses whatever truth value it is applied to. It can be used to change the value of a Boolean variable.

If you have a Boolean variable called CollegeGrad which can be either True or False, you can make a statement that says CollegeGrad = TRUE. An equivalent statement would be CollegeGrad = NOT FALSE.

The statement CollegeGrad = FALSE can be expressed as CollegeGrad = NOT TRUE.

You can change the value of the variable by writing CollegeGrad = NOT CollegeGrad. This toggles the variable from True to False or False to True.

73

Table 4.4 is also a truth table. On each line of the truth table you see what the effect of the Boolean operator NOT has on the expression P.

Table 4.4. The NOT truth table.	
If *P* is...	**then *NOT P* evaluates to...**
True	False
False	True

Logical *XOR*

The XOR operator compares two expressions, and returns False if the two expressions evaluate to the same truth value, and True if they are different. In other words, XOR only returns a result of True when the test expressions are opposites. Table 4.5 demonstrates the effect of the Boolean operator XOR on the two expressions P and Q.

Table 4.5. The XOR truth table.		
If *P* is...	**and *Q* is...**	**then *P XOR Q* evaluates to...**
True	True	False
True	False	True
False	True	True
False	False	False

Summary

In this chapter you learned that types, records, and structs are the blueprints for complex variables which refer to one or more related variables of different types. You can refer to the variables that belong to a record by referring to the record's name.

Arrays can be single dimensioned or have two or more dimensions. Two-dimensional arrays are often used for storing information in the form of tables and spreadsheets. It is rare to see an array with more than three dimensions. Arrays are very useful when you have many variables of the same type to keep track of.

Operators are used to change the value of an expression. For every variable that exists, there is an operator to modify its value. Operators are also the means by which we compare variables. It would be impossible to write a program without operators.

5

Making Decisions

by Marcus Johnson

Decisions are the heart of a computer program that produces useful work. Few computer programs operate without making decisions. Decisions can be based on user input, peripheral input (like a comm port), or the result of calculations done by the program itself. Unlike a human, who can waiver on a decision depending on the time of day, season of the year, or phase of the moon, a computer makes concrete decisions. Each decision is the result of comparing two conditions or pieces of data, and acting accordingly. The computer breaks a program down into a series of simple decisions. This chapter presents examples of the types of decision making you can incorporate in your programs.

A Program That Does Not Make Decisions

The program in Listing 5.1 subtracts one number from another and prints the answer:

Listing 5.1. A QBasic program that makes no decisions.

```
' Asks the user for a pair of numbers to compute.
' Displays the difference between the numbers.

INPUT "Enter 1st number: ", FirstNumber
INPUT "Enter 2nd number: ", SecondNumber
Difference = FirstNumber - SecondNumber
PRINT "Difference = ", Difference
```

This program solves a problem that you could solve more easily with a hand calculator. Let's modify the preceding program to make it a little tougher and give it a real-world use—balancing a checkbook.

Rename the original variables FirstNumber, SecondNumber, and Difference to Balance, Debit, and NewBalance. The object of this checkbook balancing program is to determine whether an account is overdrawn (NewBalance is less than zero). The only way for you to know the status at this point is to look at Difference carefully to see if it is negative. The program would better serve its purpose if it could alert you that the Difference is negative by printing OVERDRAWN. The program in Listing 5.2, which reflects these changes, now makes a decision based on the calculation and acts accordingly.

Listing 5.2. The checkbook balancing program rewritten to include a decision.

```
' Asks the user for a pair of numbers to compute.
' Displays the message OVERDRAWN if the result is negative.

INPUT "Enter Balance: ", Balance
INPUT "Enter Debit: ", Debit
NewBalance = Balance - Debit
IF NewBalance < 0 THEN
    PRINT "OVERDRAWN"
ELSE
    PRINT "In Good Standing"
END IF
```

In this example, the program is making a decision based on the result of the calculation in line three. If the resulting new balance is less than zero, the program decides to print OVERDRAWN. Otherwise, it prints a different message—In Good Standing. The program in Listing 5.2 is much more useful than the simple program in Listing 5.1.

IF-THEN-ELSE

Listing 5.1 used a standard mechanism for simple decisions—the IF-THEN-ELSE statement. The following example is the general outline of an IF-THEN-ELSE statement. (The text in *italics* must be replaced with actual conditions.)

```
IF decision evaluates as true THEN
    perform a specified block of instructions
ELSE
```

```
    perform a different specified block of instructions
END IF
```

The exact syntax of the IF-THEN-ELSE statement is determined by the specific language you are programming in. Some languages, such as C, omit the word THEN and immediately execute the command following the condition (if the condition is True). C executes only the first statement immediately following the THEN portion—unless a set of statements are grouped together. In Listing 5.2, the syntax of the QBasic language requires an END IF statement to tell the compiler where the instructions stop. Pascal is similar to QBasic, but does not require the END IF statement.

No matter what the language, IF-THEN statements are not very flexible. The ELSE statement can be used to allow additional comparisons. In Listing 5.2, NewBalance is compared to zero. If the value is less than zero, the overdraft message is printed. If the comparison is False, the statement following ELSE is executed. The statement following ELSE is only used when none of the other conditions is True. Before getting too deep into IF-THEN statements, you need to learn what types of comparisons are available.

The Decisions a Computer Makes

The types of decisions a computer can make are actually a function of the comparisons it can perform. Table 5.1 lists these comparisons.

Table 5.1. The six basic comparisons most computer languages can accommodate.			
Comparison	**BASIC**	**Pascal**	**C**
equal to	=	=	==
less than	<	<	<
greater than	>	>	>
less than or equal to	<=	<=	<=
greater than or equal to	>=	>=	>=
not equal to	<>	<>	!=

The first column of Table 5.1 lists the six types of operators. The three columns on the right illustrate the operator symbols that various languages use. The first three are the primary symbols: less than (<), equal to (=), and greater than (>). The other symbols are combinations of the first three. The only exception is the not equal to symbol in the C language, which combines the NOT operator (!) with the equal sign.

The QBasic program in Listing 5.3 demonstrates some of the comparison decisions a computer can make.

Listing 5.3. A QBasic program that demonstrates the comparisons a computer can make.

```
' Demonstrates comparisons

INPUT "Enter 1st number: ", FirstNumber
INPUT "Enter 2nd number: ", SecondNumber
IF FirstNumber = SecondNumber then
    PRINT "1st number is equal to the 2nd number"
END IF
IF FirstNumber > SecondNumber THEN
    PRINT "1st number is greater than the 2nd number"
END IF
IF FirstNumber < SecondNumber THEN
    PRINT "1st number is less than the 2nd number"
END IF
```

The code in Listing 5.3 performs three comparisons using the simple operators greater than, equal to, and less than.

Any of the comparisons made in the program in Listing 5.3 could have been expressed using the opposite operator: <> rather than =, <= rather than >, >= rather than <. If this had been done, the blocks following the keywords THEN and ELSE would have to be switched. The first comparison could have been written

```
IF FirstNumber <> SecondNumber THEN
        PRINT "1st number is not equal to the 2nd number"
ELSE
        PRINT "1st number is equal to the 2nd number"
END IF
```

Notice the order of the two PRINT statements was switched. Why—and when—would you do this? Better yet, which comparison operator should be used? Every operator shown in Table 5.1 has an opposite operator—which one gets chosen?

You have to use whichever operator makes the most sense in a particular program. A computer program is written to solve a problem. The program should reflect the way the problem is written. One of the major advantages of programming in languages like C or QBASIC is that you can write the program so that it resembles the problem being solved. This helps provide a check that the program is in fact solving the specified problem. For example, faced with the problem "If a person is 18 years old or older, issue a standard driver's license; otherwise, issue a learner's permit," it would be perfectly acceptable for you to write the following code:

```
IF Age < 18 THEN
    ISSUE LEARNERS_PERMIT
ELSE
    ISSUE STANDARD_LICENSE
END IF
```

However, the following code segment

```
IF Age >= 18 THEN
    ISSUE STANDARD_LICENSE
ELSE
    ISSUE LEARNERS_PERMIT
END IF
```

expresses the problem exactly as it was stated. Either version of the code solves the problem, but the second form is preferred because it more closely resembles the stated problem.

Nested *IF-THEN-ELSE*

Many times before making a decision, a program has to look at several conditions—each dependent on another. To make a comparison based on the result of another, you can *nest* the IF-THEN statements. Nesting is the process in which one set of statements is enclosed within another pair of statements.

Listing 5.4 is a simple income tax calculation program. In the program, two types of taxpayers are considered—married and single. Married taxpayers with a combined income under $20,000 are taxed at 10%; married taxpayers with an income of $20,000 or more are taxed at 20%; single taxpayers with an income under $10,000 are taxed at 15%; and single taxpayers with an income of $10,000 or more are taxed at 25%.

Listing 5.4. The QBasic Tax Calculation program.

```
' Simple tax program

SingleThreshold = 10000
MarriedThreshold = 20000
INPUT "Enter 1 if Single, 2 if Married: ", Status
INPUT "Enter income: ", Income
IF Status = 1 THEN
  IF Income < SingleThreshold THEN
    PRINT "Tax = ", Income * .15
  ELSE
    PRINT "Tax = ", Income * .25
  END IF
ELSE
  IF Status = 2 THEN
    IF Income < MarriedThreshold THEN
      PRINT "Tax = ", Income * .1
    ELSE
      PRINT "Tax = ", Income * .2
    END IF
  ELSE
    PRINT "Illegal status: ", Status
  END IF
END IF
```

By following through the code, you can see that the program first tests Status and then branches to the appropriate section. The program then tests the income threshold to determine the amount of taxes due. Status is tested first to see if Status = 1 is True or not. If not, Status is then tested again to see if Status = 2 is True or not. If status is neither 1 (single) or 2 (married), a third condition exists, Illegal status, which is caught by the ELSE statement in the Married section.

Illegal status indicates an error in what the user entered. Ending the program at that point, however, would be unproductive. Instead, you can make it easier for the user to re-enter a mistaken status. Replace the code statement

```
INPUT "Enter 1 if Single, 2 if Married: ",STATUS
```

with the following code fragment:

```
MaritalStatus:
    INPUT "Enter 1 if Single, 2 if Married: ", Status
    IF STATUS > 2 then
        PRINT "Illegal Status"
```

```
    GOTO MaritalStatus
  END IF
```

By adding the early IF-THEN statement, the program catches the incorrect input and enables the user to re-enter the correct Status.

Testing Multiple Conditions with Logical Operators

Another form of nesting IF-THEN-ELSE can be done when more than one comparison is made in the IF statement. By using logical operators—as you saw in Chapter 4, "Sophisticated Data Structures"—you can test several conditions within the IF-THEN construct. Two common logical operators used are AND and OR. The following code fragment illustrates the OR operator:

```
IF condition A is TRUE OR condition B is TRUE THEN
   perform block C of statements
ELSE
   perform block D of statements
END IF
```

The following code fragment illustrates the AND operator:

```
IF condition A is TRUE AND condition B is TRUE THEN
   perform block C of statements
ELSE
   perform block D of statements
END IF
```

In the first example, the block C of statements is performed if either condition A OR condition B is True. If neither condition A nor condition B is True, the ELSE is performed. In the second example, unlike the first, both conditions must be met for block C of statements to be executed. You could have written the income tax example in Listing 5.4 with these logical statements.

QBasic and some other BASIC dialects also support ELSEIF statements that give you the ability to test multiple conditions—similar to OR. The following code fragment shows the syntax for ELSEIF.

```
IF A$ > 'M' THEN
   Do something
ELSEIF A$ = 'M' THEN
   Do something else...
ELSE
   Do something entirely different
END IF
```

There is a point at which complex decisions become too complicated to be understandable and must be broken into simpler decisions. As the programmer, you must decide when to break down decisions. A well structured program expresses the problem to be solved while remaining as close as possible to the structure of the problem statement.

If you decide to break a complex decision into smaller, simpler decisions, you usually can do it easily. When the complex decision is expressed as

```
condition A OR condition B
```

and `condition A` and `condition B` are both simple decisions, the decision might be better expressed as this nested `IF-THEN-ELSE`:

```
IF condition A is TRUE THEN
   perform block C of statements
ELSE
   IF condition B is TRUE THEN
      perform block C of statements
   ELSE
      perform block D of statements
   END IF
END IF
```

When the complex decision can be expressed as `condition A AND condition B`, the decision might be better expressed as the following nested `IF-THEN-ELSE`:

```
IF condition A is TRUE THEN
   IF condition B is TRUE THEN
      perform block C of statements
   ELSE
      perform block D of statements
   END IF
ELSE
   perform block D of statements
END IF
```

The distinguishing feature of the nested `IF-THEN-ELSE` is that selected `THEN` or `ELSE` conditions are handled by yet another `IF-THEN-ELSE` decision.

The Perils of *IF-THEN*

A common trap that you should watch out for is writing `IF-THEN` code without an `ELSE`. Sometimes an unexpected condition occurs that you didn't expect, as you saw in Listing 5.4. Without the `ELSE` on the first example, the user might have paid the wrong taxes due to a slip of the finger. As mentioned earlier, the ELSE statement is a catch all. Anything that does not fit into the other IF statements, is caught by the ELSE condition.

In designing IF-THEN structures, be certain that you do not need the ELSE; without it, anything other than the tested conditions falls through to the next section of code. If the section in question looks ambiguous in the way it works, be sure to comment it appropriately.

Many languages offer additional constructs that give you powerful decision-making capabilities. These decision-making statements include CASE (Pascal), SWITCH (C) and SELECT CASE (QBasic), and are discussed in the following section.

Nested *IF-THEN-ELSE*: An Extreme Case

The IF-THEN-ELSE structure is very powerful and covers most of the decision making that your programs require. Consider the code fragment in Listing 5.5, however, that must test many conditions against one value.

Listing 5.5. An encyclopedia program using nested *IF-THEN-ELSE* statements.

```
' The Encyclopedia Lookup Program.

INPUT "What is the subject? ", Subject$
FC$ = LEFT$(Subject$, 1)
IF FC$ = "A" THEN
        PRINT "Look in Volume 1"
ELSE
        IF FC$ = "B" THEN
                PRINT "Look in Volume 2"
        ELSE
        .
        .
        .
```

The preceding program begins by asking the user for a subject. Using the QBasic LEFT$ function, the program obtains the first character of the subject and uses that character to look up the volume number. The program then does a series of IF-THEN-ELSE tests until it finds the match for the first character. As you can see, this is only the first two lines of 26 possible choices—this is destined to be a terrible program. As it currently is structured, it is a nightmare to maintain and very difficult to read or understand.

A Better Solution

Because all the decisions are based on the same variable (the first character of Subject$—FC$), this program is a good candidate for a SWITCH, CASE, or SELECT CASE statement. This structure is a specialized, nested IF-THEN-ELSE statement in which all the decisions are made based on a single variable. In QBasic this structure is known as a SELECT CASE. Listing 5.6 shows the encyclopedia program from Listing 5.5, rewritten using the SELECT CASE statement.

Listing 5.6. The QBasic encyclopedia program using *SELECT CASE* statements.

```
SELECT CASE FC$
    CASE "A"
      PRINT "Look in volume 1"
    CASE "B"
      PRINT "Look in volume 2"

      .

      .

      .
    CASE "Z"
      PRINT "Look in volume 26"
END SELECT
```

The SELECT CASE statement is an easy-to-read comparison of one value against a list of values. Starting at the top, the value—the variable FC$ in this example—is compared first against A, then against B, and so forth. The program continues down the list until it finds a match and at that point executes the instruction block. Depending on the language, the program might skip to the end or start executing everything from that point on.

In QBasic, when the program finds a CASE, it executes only the instructions immediately following that CASE and before the next CASE. When it has finished with those instructions, it continues with the first instruction after the END SELECT.

In C and C++, the SWITCH statement works similarly to QBasic's SELECT CASE, except that once the program finds a match, it starts executing from that point on, regardless of any other matches. To bypass any further SWITCH statements in the construct, you must use a BREAK statement. The BREAK statement causes the program to break out of the SWITCH structure and continue execution at the end of the list.

Where's the Last *ELSE*?

In the encyclopedia example, everything would go fine as long as FC$ was always one of the choices listed. But again, just as with the IF-THEN-ELSE constructs, the wrong data could cause nothing to be chosen.

To cover all possibilities, the SELECT CASE construct has the CASE ELSE statement to catch anything that does not match the other CASE statements. The following lines could be added at the end of the CASE list to catch bad data, if needed.

```
CASE ELSE
    PRINT "No Volume Exists for That Character, Try Again"
```

In the C and C++ languages, the SWITCH construct has a contingency case called the DEFAULT Case.

It is important to remember that there are certain rules concerning the use of SWITCH and CASE statements. You use the SWITCH and CASE statements to replace a nested IF-THEN-ELSE construct when the nested comparisons compare the same variable to different constant values. You cannot use SWITCH and CASE if any of the comparisons are variable-to-variable.

Summary

In this chapter, you have seen how programs make decisions and why it is important for your programs to be able to make decisions. Three of the most common decision-making constructs were also presented.

- The simple IF-THEN-ELSE construct is the backbone of decision-making. For every THEN there should be an ELSE.

- The nested IF-THEN-ELSE enables you to write programs that can make complex decisions.

- The CASE statement constructs (CASE, SELECT CASE, and SWITCH) provide powerful nested IF-THEN-ELSE decision-making based on a single variable. The SWITCH offers the power of the nested IF-THEN-ELSE, but with a simpler and easier to understand syntax.

With a solid understanding of these constructs, you can tackle virtually any programming task assigned.

Performing Loops

by Marcus Johnson

A computer never gets bored doing the same thing over and over again, and your programs can take advantage of this fact by using loops. A *loop* is a section of code that executes a particular task or set of instructions repeatedly. Code for a loop consists of three parts: the entry point, the body of the loop, and the exit point.

The *entry point* is the location in the program at which the loop starts executing and to which the program returns when the loop is repeated. The entry point can be as simple as a label or, as you'll see later in the chapter, an instruction that conditionally decides whether to continue the loop.

The *body of the loop* is the section of code or set of instructions that is executed repeatedly. Loops are most efficient when the body of the loop contains only what must be repeated. Instructions that are not part of the task are just taken along for the ride. Although they might not affect the results, they do slow down the program.

The *exit point* is the part of the loop that directs program execution back to the entry point. The exit point, like the entry point, can contain statements that conditionally loop back or that just continue to the next section of code. Examples of this are presented later in this chapter.

A Simple Loop

Figuring out when to use a loop is not difficult. If you have identical code lines that are executed more than once, you have an excellent candidate for a loop. The following code fragment is a good example:

```
SUM = 0
INPUT "Enter number: ", NUMBER
SUM = SUM + NUMBER
INPUT "Enter number: ", NUMBER
SUM = SUM + NUMBER
INPUT "Enter number: ", NUMBER
SUM = SUM + NUMBER
PRINT "Sum = ", SUM
```

In looking at the code, notice the INPUT statement and the SUM equation are repeated each time a new number is input. The code is redundant and inflexible. It is redundant because the same two lines are repeated until the sum is calculated. It is inflexible because in order to modify it, you would have to add or remove lines of code.

Infinite Loops

The simplest loop is constructed by placing a label at the beginning of the body and a GOTO statement at the end of the body pointing back to the label. There is no mechanism to stop this loop; it simply runs forever. This is known as an *infinite loop*. Most loops are not intended to run forever. The COMMAND.COM program in MS-DOS is an example of a program that deliberately runs forever; it gets user input and then executes the program. When that program terminates, the loop starts over. There is rarely—if ever—a reason for you to deliberately create a program that can only be terminated by shutting the computer off.

To simplify the code from the preceding example, you can take the two lines of code that are repeated, and put them in a loop. The following code fragment shows a simple loop. The label at the top is the entry point, the two lines of code are the body, and the GOTO is the exit point.

```
SUM = 0                            'clear a variable to collect sum
Start:                             'entry point
    INPUT "Enter number: ", NUMBER 'Body of loop
    SUM = SUM + NUMBER             '  is these two lines.
GOTO Start                         'exit point
PRINT "Sum = ", SUM               'print result
```

What Belongs in a Loop?

As a beginning programmer, it is tempting to place everything inside the body of a loop. This can sometimes lead to slow and cumbersome programs. You must use a little common sense in determining what goes inside the loop.

Suppose a program was written to control a robot window washer. Each window in the house is to be washed from the inside and from the outside. It's tempting to write something like this:

Label:
  Wash inside of window
  Go outside
  Wash outside of window
  Go inside
  If there is another dirty window
    Then
      Move to next dirty window
      Goto Label
    Else
      Robot gets a nice cool glass of 10W40
  Endif
End

This will certainly get the job done—and the robot will eventually wear a path in the carpet and a rut around the house. With a little more thought, the program can be rewritten as follows:

Label1:
  Wash inside of window
  If there is another dirty window
    Then
      Move to next dirty window
      Goto Label1
    Else
      All of insides are clean
  Endif
Go outside
Label2:
  Wash outside of window
  If there is another dirty window
    Then

>   *Move to next dirty window*
>   *Goto Label2*
>   *Else*
>   *All of outsides are clean*
>   *Endif*
> *Go inside*
> *Robot gets a nice cool glass of 10W40*
> *End*

With this program, there is much less wear and tear on the floors and the landscaping, and the robot completes its work much more quickly.

Similar logic applies to any program you write. If a loop seems to be taking forever to execute, examine the body of the loop. If it contains code that does not need to be executed for each iteration of the loop, pull it out of the loop. Remember, if a loop executes 1000 times, every statement in the body of the loop gets executed 1000 times.

This brings up the concept of *optimization*—making your code more efficient. Many of the techniques involved in optimization are beyond the scope of this book. However, often you can optimize your code by working on the bodies of loops. Be discriminating, though, in the loops you choose to optimize. If you work for hours streamlining a section of code that only gets executed once, it isn't nearly as efficient as optimizing a loop that repeats 1000 times.

Controlled Loops

Controlled loops use a conditional expression to control the loop. The loop continues to execute as long as the conditional expression is True and stops as soon as the conditional expression is False.

FOR-NEXT Loops

The FOR-NEXT loop is designed to execute its body a set number of times. The FOR-NEXT loop has three parts: an initialization expression, a conditional expression, and an update expression.

The FOR-NEXT loop is driven by the value of a variable. The *initialization expression* sets the initial value, or starting place. The *conditional expression* is the value that is compared to the driving variable. The *update expression* tells how the driving variable is changed during the loop.

The components of a FOR-NEXT loop are shown in the following QBasic example:

```
FOR X = 0 TO 10        'initialization & conditional expression
    PRINT X            'body of loop
NEXT X                 'update expression
```

QBasic requires the initialization and conditional expressions of the FOR-NEXT loop to be located in the entry point of the loop—the first line. In the preceding example, X is the driving variable. It is initialized to 0. The conditional expression tests X against 10; the loop continues until X reaches 10.

The body of the loop, in this case PRINT X, is the code to be repeated in the loop. In QBasic, the body of the loop is all the code between the FOR statement and the NEXT statement and is executed once for each iteration.

In this example, the NEXT X statement is the update expression. In QBasic, this expression performs an implied increment of X by 1. The NEXT X could also be written (ignoring the proper syntax) as:

```
X = X + 1
GOTO start of loop
```

You can also explicitly state the increment value of the update expression. For example, if you wanted to increment the loop by two rather than one, the loop would look like this:

```
FOR X = 0 TO 10 STEP 2     'initialization & Conditional expressions
    PRINT X                'body of loop
NEXT X                     'update expression
```

The STEP 2 statement tells the program to add 2 to X every time you say NEXT X. The STEP keyword can also step backwards by using a negative number. However, when stepping backwards, the initialization and conditional expressions must be reversed.

```
FOR X = 10 TO 0 STEP -2    'initialization & Conditional expressions
    PRINT X                'body of loop
NEXT X                     'update expression
```

In this example, X is now initialized to 10 and steps backwards by two until the value of X reaches 0. One thing to watch for in a declining loop is that it is initialized correctly. The starting value always has to be greater than the ending value or the loop will never execute.

You use the FOR-NEXT loop when you know how many times to execute the loop. Take another look at the program that added several numbers, shown earlier in this chapter. The following code performs the same task, but is more complex. It asks the user how many numbers to add and, with that information, proceeds to input and add the numbers.

```
'Add numbers with FOR loop
SUM = 0
INPUT "How many numbers? ", HowMany
FOR i = 1 TO HowMany
    INPUT "Enter Number: ", NUMBER
    SUM = SUM + NUMBER
NEXT i
PRINT "Sum = ", SUM
```

The program now asks the user How many numbers? and assigns the value to the variable HowMany. The loop variable, i, is then initialized to 1. The conditional is HowMany. Next, the body of the loop executes until the loop variable (i) is equal to HowMany. When i equals HowMany, the loop ends and the PRINT statement is executed.

DO Loops

There are several types of DO loops. The main characteristic of a DO loop is that you can control the loop based on a condition that *will* happen. Unlike the FOR-NEXT loop, in which the conditional is always a numeric variable that is incremented or decremented, the conditional expression in a DO loop can be a program variable or an event that is expected to happen.

When using a program variable as the conditional of a loop, you can choose either numeric or string variables. The loop iterates until the variable reaches a desired result: an address book program might loop until the string NewAddress equals "stop"; whereas a checkbook balancing program might loop until the variable AccountBalance becomes 0.

Qbasic has four different formats of the DO loop: DO-LOOP UNTIL, DO UNTIL-LOOP, DO-LOOP WHILE, and DO WHILE-LOOP.

DO-LOOP UNTIL and DO UNTIL-LOOP

Most programs allow you to place the conditional before or after the loop. Although this might seem trivial, the placement of the conditional is one of the most important decisions you must make when you write a program. If the body of the loop modifies the driving variable (which is used in the conditional expression), and the loop must terminate after the variable is modified, then having the conditional at the end is right. The checkbook balancing program, which subtracts check amounts from a balance, must exit the loop after the check that zeroed out the account was processed.

With a DO-LOOP UNTIL structure, the body of the loop always executes at least one time. This is the most important reason for having the condition at the end. The following pseudocode loop, the checkbook balancing program, has the condition after the body of the loop:

DO
  Get a check
  Subtract check from balance
LOOP UNTIL balance <= 0

Sometimes, you won't get the desired result if the body of the loop must always execute at least one time. Consider what would happen in the last program if the balance of your checkbook was already in the red. The program would enter the DO loop with a negative balance, and then subtract even more from the account. To avoid this problem, you can move the UNTIL balance <= 0 statement to the top of the loop. This tests the balance before the loop starts. The following pseudocode illustrates this:

DO UNTIL balance <= 0
  Get a check
  Subtract check from balance
LOOP

Now, when the program executes the DO statement, it immediately tests the balance. If it is less than or equal to 0, the body of the loop is not executed.

DO-LOOP WHILE and *DO WHILE-LOOP*

The DO-LOOP WHILE is similar to the DO-LOOP UNTIL structure, except that the loop still executes while the conditional is True. The following pseudocode example illustrates this:

DO
  execute body of the loop
LOOP WHILE conditional expression is TRUE

Looking back at the checkbook balancing example, the DO loop could be written to execute the body of the loop while the balance is greater than zero. The following pseudocode example shows how the loop would be written:

```
DO
  Get a check
  Subtract check from balance
LOOP WHILE balance > 0
```

The WHILE loop is not much different from the UNTIL loop, except that you are testing to see if the balance is still greater than zero. In the WHILE loop, the conditional can be moved to the top of the loop to test before the loop body is executed. The following pseudocode example puts the conditional at the top of the loop:

```
DO WHILE balance > 0
  Get a check
  Subtract check from balance
LOOP
```

As with the DO UNTIL-LOOP example, putting the conditional at the beginning of the loop checks the balance before the loop is executed.

Choosing a Conditional Expression

The question of what to use for the conditional test is something you must deal with. In the previous examples, all the loops have been controlled by actions from within the loop: the loop was monitoring the balance as checks were subtracted.

Another use for loops is to repeat an action until an outside event happens. Many programs give the user the option of cancelling an action, such as printing, after it has already begun. The following pseudocode example could be part of a word processing program.

```
PRINT "Press a key to Cancel Printing"
DO UNTIL key is pressed
  Print a line
LOOP
```

In this example, the program first prints a message that tells the user that pressing a key can cancel the print run. It then begins executing the loop—checking whether a key has been pressed. If a key is pressed, the DO UNTIL condition becomes True, and the loop terminates. Although this example is very simple, a similar mechanism can enable a program to perform useful work while waiting for the user to press a key. In fact, many multitasking operating systems—such as Microsoft Windows—have a system function that can be executed while the program is idle (waiting for user input). The function tells the operating system, "This program is idle—let another program execute while this program waits for user input."

Short-Circuits

Occasionally, a program needs to get out of a loop before the condition is met. This is known as short-circuiting a loop. In the C language, the keyword BREAK stops the loop altogether. It causes control of the program to resume at the point where the loop ends. This is commonly used when—inside the loop—it is determined that something has gone so wrong that there is no point in continuing the loop. In QBasic, the same function is done with the EXIT DO keywords.

Another useful short-circuit statement in C is CONTINUE. This command stops the body of the loop from executing any further and causes control of the program to resume at the point at which the loop's conditional expression is evaluated.

The difference between BREAK and CONTINUE is that BREAK leaves the loop completely and CONTINUE does not. BREAK has the same effect on the loop as meeting the condition would have. That is, the program leaves the loop and execution picks up with the statement that follows the loop. CONTINUE, on the other hand, stops executing in the body of the loop and returns to the conditional test as if the rest of the body had executed.

Short-circuit statements are always used in conjunction with other conditional statements—an IF-THEN statement, for example. In the preceding example, the only way for the word processor program to stop printing would be for someone to press a key. The following pseudocode uses the printing example and adds a short-circuit statement that automatically exits the loop when printing is complete.

PRINT "Press a key to Cancel Printing"
DO UNTIL key is pressed
  Get a line of text
  IF no more text THEN BREAK
  Print a line
LOOP

Now the program loops until the user presses a key or the program runs out of text to print. In effect, this loop has two conditionals. The main conditional is the keypress, which controls the execution of the loop body. The secondary conditional is the test for no more text, which short-circuits the loop if that condition is met. It would be entirely possible to write the loop with no more text as the main conditional and keypress as the secondary. Which conditional to use as the main and which to use as the short-circuit is determined by what the program requires. The keypress should be the main conditional if the body of the loop includes code that must be executed before checking for the end of the text, but never executed if a key is pressed. Both cases require something to be tested, so you will have to experiment to determine the best combination.

Summary

You have seen that loops have three parts: the entry point, the body and the exit point. A loop can be as simple as a label and a goto statement.

Getting more involved with loops, you saw that a loop can have a conditional test to control how many times the loop is executed. A FOR-NEXT loop is the best format for a loop that must execute a finite number of times. If you need to execute a loop dependent on a variable or event, a DO loop is the best format.

Both the DO loop and the FOR-NEXT loop structures share an initialization expression, a conditional expression, and an update expression.

Unlike the FOR-NEXT loop, the DO loop can be made to test the conditional at either the start of the loop or the end of the loop. You can control the execution of a loop by the placement of the conditional expression.

When you need to exit a loop before the condition is met, the loop can be short-circuited. To short-circuit a loop, you must use a statement such as BREAK or EXIT DO, depending on the language.

Overall, loops can save you from having to write many lines of redundant code. Loops can also be used to monitor program events and allow a type of multitasking. By understanding loops, you can create more useful and efficient programs.

Structured Programming

by Lisa Monitto

As any management consultant will tell you, one of the most important things a manager does is delegate authority. The executive in charge of sales for a large company does not single-handedly manage every detail of day-to-day operations. A good manager delegates such tasks as sorting mail, typing letters, answering sales calls, and maintaining office equipment.

One person cannot do every task required to run a successful department. Rather than attempting to accomplish one overwhelming job, a smart manager divides the job into a series of smaller jobs and then assigns each one.

You can use this philosophy when you create a large, complicated program. A good programmer should be like a good manager when it comes to assigning tasks in a program. You can separate the tasks your program must accomplish, then tackle them one by one, making the job less daunting. This approach is the concept behind structured programming.

In structured programming, also called *modular* programming, you break down a large program into small, easy-to-understand *modules*, or subroutines, in a framework you have created. The subroutines you call operate independently to perform specific tasks in the body of your program. Because each task is concentrated in its own section, or module, you can get a shell of your program up and running and fill in the procedures one by one.

To make use of modular programming concepts, you must use a programming language that supports procedures and functions. GW-BASIC, for example, does not provide for modular programming. A program written in GW-BASIC is self-contained and cannot be divided into separate tasks. The entire program must be seen as a unit.

High-level programming languages such as QBasic, Pascal, and C have the capability to split large tasks into structures. Each structure is part of the whole but also functions as a separate entity.

Your computer is equipped with expansion slots that can hold various cards, such as a modem card or a video card. If you remove one of these cards, only one specific function of your computer is affected. This is the idea behind modular programming.

You can write an individual part of the program as a module and tinker with the module as necessary, without tearing apart your entire program. To make this modularization possible, QBasic uses user-defined procedures.

Procedures and Functions

Procedures and functions are the building blocks of modular programming. They are the structures of the program.

A procedure is a series of programming statements that performs a task. This block of code is given a name, and you can pass values to it. By writing procedures, you can extend the language you are working with. In some languages, procedures are called subroutines, which you learned about in Chapter 2, "Introduction to Programming Statements."

Most procedure names read like a phrase in English, for example:

```
CompressTheDataFile
GetInputFromUser
PrintDocument
```

You also learned in Chapter 2 that a function is a type of procedure that returns a value to the calling program. This is different from a procedure that modifies or creates a variable that the calling program can access. Like a procedure, you can pass a value to a function.

You can use a function name in an expression as if it were a variable, because a function returns a value when it has finished executing. Most programmers use short words or phrases to name functions, instead of the sentence-like names of procedures. The syntax used to call a function is similar to the way variables are referred to. For example, you might have a simple function called Sum%(a%,b%,c%) that adds three integers: a%, b%, and c%. You could use the Sum%() function in several ways:

```
PRINT Sum%(a%,b%,c%)
Total% = Sum%(a%,b%,c%)
IF Sum%(a%,b%,c%) = 100 THEN Call AProcedureName
```

As you can see, in all three cases the function name is referred to in the same way as a variable.

Procedures and functions are like mini-programs that can contain their own variables, data types, structures, and even other procedures and functions.

In Chapter 4, you learned how to create sophisticated data structures by putting built-in data types into a record. This is another way of extending the language. In the same way that you create a programmer-defined record by combining different data types, you can create a procedure by combining a series of built-in statements and functions. This is a powerful programming technique.

Where to Start

One way to develop a program is to examine the flowchart or pseudocode you wrote when you initially planned your program. Each broad step you outlined can be used as a subroutine name in the program. The program is easy to follow because it resembles your outline. Your flowchart diagram should indicate the location in your program of each step you have taken and each decision you have made. A sample pseudocode outline follows:

Check the time.
If it is after eleven o'clock, then
  put the cat out,
  brush your teeth,
  turn out the lights,
  go to bed.

This fragment of pseudocode can be used to build the main body of a program. All the details involved in checking the time, putting out the cat, brushing your teeth, and turning out the lights are in the subroutines. To use those details, just call the subroutine by name, as follows:

```
CALL CheckTheTime(AfterElevenOClock)
IF (AfterElevenOClock=TRUE) THEN
        PutTheCatOut
        BrushYourTeeth
        TurnOutTheLights
        GoToBed
END IF
```

If the program is not working correctly, you can easily see which job went wrong and, therefore, which subroutine is responsible.

When you begin programming, you may be tempted to start writing without a plan. Many GW-BASIC and QBasic programmers begin that way. It is easy to write a BASIC program without planning because you do not have to declare variables before using them in the body of the program.

Declaring variables is a chore, but doing so makes it easier to keep track of variables. Declaring variables also eliminates errors if you misspell a variable name. In QBasic, a misspelled variable name simply creates a new variable initialized to 0 (or to "" for a string variable). Such an error is difficult to find.

If you are working in a language that requires you to declare variables, you should have a rough idea of the types and number of variables you plan to use before you begin writing. When you create a complex program in a high-level language such as C++ and Pascal, an outline or a flowchart is a necessity.

Structured and unstructured programming are vastly different. A sample program can help illustrate these differences. Listing 7.1 is a cash register program written in GW-BASIC, a language which does not support structured programming. The program makes change from a total purchase amount.

Listing 7.1. The cash register program in GW-BASIC.

```
10 REM Program Cash Register
20 CLS
30 PRINT "This program calculates how much change"
40 PRINT "should be made for a purchase. You must"
50 PRINT "input two amounts: the total amount due"
60 PRINT "and the amount tendered."
70 PRINT
80 PRINT "Press a key to continue..."
90 WHILE INKEY$ = ""
100 WEND
110 PRINT
120 INPUT "Please enter the amount due: ", TotalDue!
125 IF TotalDue! = 0 THEN GOTO 195
130 INPUT "Please enter the amount tendered: ", Tendered!
140 PRINT
145 Change! = Tendered! - TotalDue!
150 PRINT "Your change is ";Change!;"."
160 PRINT "Please come again."
170 PRINT
```

```
180 INPUT "Run program again (Y/N)? ", Answer$
190 IF Answer$ = "Y" OR Answer$ = "y" then GOTO 110
195 PRINT "Thank you for using CASH REGISTER!"
200 PRINT
205 PRINT "Press a key to continue..."
210 WHILE INKEY$ = ""
220 WEND
230 END
```

The code in Listing 7.1 is inefficient. Code that pauses the program and waits for a keypress is duplicated near the top and bottom of this listing. Additionally, there are two GOTO statements, which cause execution of this program to jump to a line other than the one that comes next.

This program is only decipherable because it is short; a larger program written in the same way would be tangled in an almost impenetrable mess. You would spend a great deal of time trying to understand what the code does and where the GOTO statements were jumping to. This program's flowchart is shown in Figure 7.1.

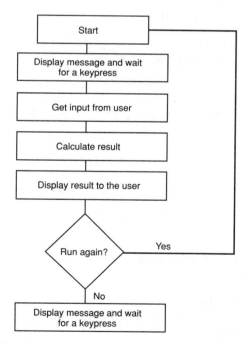

Figure 7.1. The flowchart for the cash register program.

Listing 7.2 is the program rewritten in QBasic. This higher-level language permits the use of subroutines, making it suitable for use in structured programming. This program is easy to read, easy to modify, and easy to debug.

Listing 7.2. The cash register program in QBasic.

```
' Program Cash Register

'MAIN PROGRAM

 Result$ = Message$("CASH REGISTER PROGRAM")
 Result$ = ""
 WHILE (Result$ <> "N") OR (Result$ <> "n")
   CALL DisplayDescription
   CALL GetInput(TotalDue!,Tendered!)
   Call ShowResults(TotalDue!, Tendered!)
   Result$ = Message$("Run program again (Y/N)? ")
 WEND
END


'----  Subroutine and function listings

FUNCTION Message$ (MessageText$)
 ' Function to display a message and wait
 ' for a keystroke

 PRINT
 PRINT MessageText$     ' Display message from parameter

 A$ = ""
 WHILE A$ = ""          ' Wait until any key is pressed
  A$ = INKEY$
 WEND

 Message$ = A$           '  Return whatever key was pressed
END FUNCTION

'-- Subroutine to display introductory text to the user
SUB DisplayDescription
 CLS
 PRINT "This program calculates how much change"
 PRINT "should be made for a purchase. You must"
 PRINT "input two amounts: the total amount due"
```

```
  PRINT "and the amount tendered."
  PRINT
  END SUB

'-- Subroutine to get values from the user
SUB GetInput(TotalDue!, Tendered!)
 PRINT
 INPUT "Please enter the amount due: ", TotalDue!
 INPUT "Please enter the amount tendered: ", Tendered!
END SUB

'-- Subroutine to make calculations and display
'    the result to the user
SUB ShowResults(TotalDue!, Tendered!)
 PRINT
IF TotalDue! <> 0 THEN
     PRINT "Your change is ";Tendered! - TotalDue!;"."
     PRINT "Please come again."
ENDIF
END SUB
```

Listing 7.2 follows the flowchart. You can see how the jobs are divided, and how each job is handled by its own subroutine. Listing 7.1 is more difficult to understand because it is not separated into sections.

To read the GW-BASIC example in Listing 7.1, you start at the top and read through to the bottom. In the structured example in Listing 7.2, the main program begins at the top and shows the major steps the program will take. These steps are then detailed elsewhere, in the subroutines. To follow the details of the subroutines, you must save your place and let your eyes "jump" to the subroutine. This is similar to the way your computer runs the program.

Suppose you added functionality to the cash register program, and it grew to more than a page or two. The GW-BASIC code would be almost impossible to debug. The QBasic program would be simpler to debug because every job takes place out of the main program in its own little cubbyhole of a subroutine.

Subroutines

Subroutines contain the details of the commands that appear in the main program. In Pascal, subroutines are called procedures. In C and C++, subroutines are called functions. QBasic just calls them subroutines.

Subroutines are useful when two or more statements are needed for a repetitive action. Suppose you want to wash your dog. Doing so requires the following steps:

1. Catch the dog.

2. Wet it.

3. Wash it.

4. Rinse it.

5. Dry it.

Now suppose someone washes the dog for you. Instead of requiring five steps, washing the dog becomes one step—asking your assistant to do it. You have delegated the task, saving time and effort.

A subroutine combines a series of individual tasks into one task. If you wrote five lines of code that accomplished a job described as washing the dog, you could place them all into a subroutine and cause the five steps to be executed with one line:

```
CALL WashTheDog
```

Global Versus Local Variables

As long as a program has no subroutines or functions, it has only one *scope* and one set of *global* variables. *Scope* is the range a program or subroutine has to access data. Every program can be considered to have its own scope, or domain, in which there is a set of variables. Variables are said to be *global*, or *public*, when they can be read or altered from all areas of the program.

Every subroutine or function that is added to a program has a scope of its own and a set of variables that is said to be *local*, or *private*, to the subroutine. This means that the data in the subroutine's variables can only be accessed or changed from within the subroutine, and is inaccessible to all other scopes.

Subroutines and their local variables are isolated from the main program and all other subroutines. This isolation is called *encapsulation*. Since data is only accessible within a single scope, other subroutines cannot accidentally alter the local data. Encapsulation is the essence of modular programming and is useful in object-oriented programming as well. Encapsulation is discussed further in Chapter 11, "Object-Oriented Programming."

Passing Parameters

The only way to get data into a subroutine or function is by *passing parameters.* The subroutine or function can then act on and modify those parameters and give them back to the main program.

A parameter can be either a variable or a value, and is "passed" to a subroutine or function by placing it in the parameter list. A *parameter list* is a series of one or more variables or values placed in parentheses directly following the subroutine or function name.

For example, suppose you owned the Petite Poodle Parlor, and people brought dogs to you all day long to be washed. The subroutine you saw in a previous paragraph called WashTheDog washes only one dog, and washes it only once. You could modify the subroutine, however, to accept a parameter that tells it which dog to wash. For example:

```
CALL WashTheDog(Poodle)
CALL WashTheDog(Afghan)
CALL WashTheDog(Chihuahua)
```

Passing information in this way is referred to as passing a parameter. Your subroutine is now good for washing any dog you specify. The subroutine not only combines five steps into one, but also is more flexible.

You could pass irrational parameters, but if you instructed the subroutine to WashTheDog(partyhat), you might not get the results you expect. Therefore, it is a good idea to validate the information sent to a subroutine to make sure it is within logical limits.

Calling Functions

A function is similar in some ways to a subroutine, because it contains a series of statements that can be executed by a single statement. A function, however, returns a value, whereas a subroutine does not.

After you define a function, you call that function in the same way you call a language's built-in functions. You can specify the function name in an expression, in a PRINT statement, or anywhere a built-in function can be used.

Because every function returns a value, you have to designate a type for the function in the same way you designate a type for a variable. Here is a simple function that returns a string value:

```
FUNCTION AskName$
    PRINT "Please enter a name: ";
    INPUT FirstName$
    AskName$ = FirstName$
END FUNCTION
```

This is how you can use the function:

```
DIM Team$(9)
    FOR i = 1 TO 9
        Team$(i) = AskName$
    NEXT

    PRINT "The members of the softball team are"

    FOR i = 1 TO 9
        PRINT Team$(i)
    NEXT
```

Note that the function AskName$ is used on the right side of an assignment statement. Even though invoking the function name executes a series of program statements, the function is used to assign a value to the Team$() array, as though it were a variable.

Debugging Subroutines

Although subroutines and procedures are associated with the main program, they are also isolated from it because they are self-contained units. They do not share variables. For this reason, a procedure cannot accidentally change the value of a variable in the main program or in another subroutine. This compartmentalization is useful when debugging.

An unstructured language such as GW-BASIC has only global variables, which are accessible throughout the program. In a long unstructured program, an error on line 170 could make the program crash at line 6000. You could spend many weekends trying to hunt down the error.

In a properly structured program, each subroutine exists almost unto itself. Other than information passed to and from the subroutine through parameters, the subroutine should be designed so that it is not able to communicate with the rest of the program. The main program "sees" only the parameters that go into the subroutine and the output it returns. Because each subroutine is separate and the variables are also separate, an error in one subroutine does not affect the other subroutines.

This separation means that you can develop and test subroutines one-by-one, outside the main program. You can construct a program shell that calls the subroutine, then test the subroutine with sample data. The shell does nothing in itself. When you test your subroutine in this way, you can be positive that it is not interacting with any other variable or routine in the main program. When you have finished writing, testing, and debugging the subroutine, copy it back to the real program.

This plug-in module approach makes development easier and faster. It also makes it easy to reuse useful subroutines in other programs.

Libraries of Subroutines and Functions

Subroutines and functions are modular, therefore you can collect routines that you have written and save them in a *library* so that they are available for reuse. QBasic, C++, and Pascal all allow a programmer to specify the name of a library, which can subsequently be searched for routines that you haved called in your program. Many companies produce and sell libraries of useful programming routines that you can incorporate into your own programs.

Making Changes

Structured programming is a great advantage when a program must be modified. If subroutines are compartmentalized to handle one task, you can change a malfunctioning subroutine or replace it with one that operates properly, without affecting the rest of the program. It is not necessary to go through the entire listing and untangle everything to locate the flaw.

If you write an unstructured program, making changes can be a nightmare. Any part of the program might be interacting with any other part of the program.

Summary

Plan ahead by making an outline of your program, writing pseudocode, or creating a flowchart.

Make your main program as linear as possible—readable from top to bottom. Avoid the tangled confusion of spaghetti code. Use the same method of linear construction when writing the procedures in your subroutines. An easy-to-read program is also easier to change and debug.

Put the details in the procedures. Keep the main program as short as possible. The main program should be similar to an outline. Delegate all the work to the subroutines and procedures.

If your procedures are getting too long and complex, simply break them into smaller and simpler procedures. Brevity is the soul of readability.

Use local variables as much as possible. Global variables spoil the encapsulation of your procedures and make them less independent. The more local variables you use, the more modular your program will be.

Procedures save you the time and trouble of writing a block of instructions over and over. You write the instructions once, combine them in a procedure, and name it. You can then call your custom-made procedure whenever it is needed.

After you have written a procedure that works well, save it in a library for future use. As you complete other subroutines, add them to your collection. When you create a library of subroutines, your time can be spent tackling new problems rather than reinventing the wheel.

Communicating with the User

by Lisa Monitto & John Tamburo

Whenever you write an ordinary program, you communicate with the user of that program. This communication can take the form of screens, sounds, messages, or printed reports. To the end-user, these tools *are* the program because the user never sees the actual program statements that make up the program.

What you do with the communication tools your program works with determines how good your program is. You may soar to new technological heights in your program's internal design, but if the program is difficult to use, that wonderful technology will be useless. There is nothing more important to your program than good communication with your user.

The Interface

You probably have heard the term *interface,* which has its origins in the language of computers. This term was first used to describe an electronic circuit that governed the connection between two hardware devices in order to help them exchange data reliably.

The serial ports and parallel ports on the backs of most computers are perfect examples of *hardware interfaces.* A serial port enables your computer to "talk" to a modem, and a parallel port lets your computer talk to a laser or dot-matrix printer. A network card lets your computer talk to an interlinked group (a network) of other computers.

A *software interface* is the only means a program has of communicating with the user. The program uses the interface to tell the user what type of input is needed, the way the program accepts the input, and the way the program displays the results of any calculations or manipulations it has made.

An interface, in computer terms, is a *translator* between the computer's view of its data and the human's view of the same data. For example, the integer 128 is stored in the computer as a binary number in 2 bytes. To the computer, the number 128 is 0000000010000000. That's not very easy to read.

To a person not familiar with computers and their internal operation, this number may seem to be ten million, which is grossly incorrect. A *user* interface presents this information to the user in an easy-to-understand manner. Instead of 0000000010000000, the characters 128 are shown on the screen. The information appears in a humanly readable form. Much of this work is done automatically by the program and the computer. However, you need to further organize the data to be used and handled in screens (or windows) and reports.

In addition to showing information to the user, your program must also make it easy to manipulate the information it stores and displays. This is where good screen and window design really matters.

User-Friendly Design

The term *user-friendly* is by far the most abused in the computing industry. Every maker of software sets its own arbitrary guidelines to determine what it considers to be user-friendly. The trouble for users of the product is that these guidelines seldom meet real-world expectations of the term *user-friendly*.

Here are a few guidelines for what is and is not user-friendly, based on common sense and experience:

1. *Intuitive design.* You ought to be able to look at a program screen and make an accurate guess as to what the program does and how you will use it. For example, you can recognize a word processing program because it has a large typing area and some facility to permit typographical control of what you type. You can recognize a data-entry program from the individual fields on the screen or in a window.

2. *Adherence to standards.* Your program should look and work like other programs. For example, your program should use the same keys and codes for the same things, your users should be able to access online help in a consistent way. This sounds much easier in theory than in practice—an issue that is addressed in the next section.

3. *User's manual or help text.* You should provide an easy-to-read reference as a user's manual and as on-line help text. Such a reference is crucial to your program's success. The old saying goes, "When all else fails, read the instructions." If there are no instructions, your user will be helpless when a problem arises.

The Importance of Standards

Standards tell you how a screen should look and how users should interact with screens. In corporate environments, detailed standards tell the programming staff everything from overall design to the exact form of error messages. These standards may differ widely from company to company, and to a programmer they might seem burdensome because they limit creativity.

Standards are useful, however. A family of programs written under the same standard gives end-users the convenience of familiar operating commands. Standards also enable companies to save planning and development time because the programmer does not have to create a new interface for every new program.

Commercial software comes from a variety of manufacturers, and each manufacturer's product marches to the beat of a different drummer where user interface is concerned. This Tower of Babel created by the lack of an industry standard for user interface is evidenced by the many different ways there are to do something as simple as exiting from a program. In WordPerfect, you press F7 and answer No to a prompt. In Lotus 1-2-3, you type a slash (/), move the cursor to Exit and answer Yes to the question Are you sure? In Paradox, you press F10 instead of typing a slash. Furthermore, Exit can be called Exit, Quit, Bye, End, and so on—depending on the program.

SAA

In the middle '80s, IBM released Systems Application Architecture (SAA). SAA was originally intended to make it possible for mainframes, midrange computers, and PCs to exchange data and programs seamlessly. SAA is not a program, but rather a comprehensive set of standards for everything from program language syntax to database access to communications protocols to user interfaces.

SAA's user interface is called CUA, which is short for Common User Access. CUA contains two separate segments: one for character-based program screens, and another for graphical applications such as those that run under Microsoft Windows. CUA specifies comprehensive guidelines on how to construct screens and windows intuitively. Many companies that produce software adhere to CUA, and some companies must adhere in order to receive lucrative government contracts for their products.

CUA provides standards in the following areas:

1. *Look.* CUA describes a generally intuitive architecture for dealing with common business applications. This standard categorizes business programs in one of several types, such as word processing programs, databases, and spreadsheets.

2. *Feel.* CUA sets up terms that refer to certain program actions. For example, to leave a program, the command is Exit. Cancel is used to cancel a pending change or an operation.

3. *Action.* CUA sets up function and accelerator keys, valid for both character and graphical interfaces, to do certain things. An accelerator is a keystroke or combination of keystrokes which is interpreted as a command. Table 8.1 is SAA CUA's list of accelerator keys.

Table 8.1. SAA CUA's list of accelerators and function keys.	
Function Keys	**Action**
F1	Help (context-sensitive if possible)
F3	Exit
F4	Prompt for values
F5	Refresh the screen
F6	Create a new record (certain types of programs)
F7	Scroll backward (character only)
F8	Scroll forward (character only)
F12	Cancel pending operation
Shift-Delete	Cut (also Ctrl-X in Windows 3.1)
Shift-Insert	Paste (also Ctrl-V in Windows 3.1)
Ctrl-Insert	Copy (also Ctrl-C in Windows 3.1)

Function Keys	Action
Alt-Backspace	Undo (also Ctrl-Z in Windows 3.1)
Enter	Process screen or window

These standards are intended to make it easier for a user to switch from one program to another. They also enable the user to move easily from character-based programs to graphical programs because both types of programs work essentially the same way.

Standards Versus Creativity

Some programmers feel that standards are too restrictive and throw them out in favor of some "better way." Most users, however, use a program for a specific purpose and don't want to spend the time learning a new interface. The more closely a program adheres to the standard, the easier it is for a user to understand how to use the program.

In CUA, for example, the F1 key is the help key. No matter which program you are using, if it is CUA compliant, F1 is the help key. F1 will never mean "print document" or "exit without saving."

Without CUA standards, figuring out the interface is like being in a country where the numbers on the telephone are arranged in this way:

    4   3   7

    9   1   5

    2   8   0

         6

You can still make a phone call, but it takes a lot longer to understand the system. Nonstandard interfaces require users to learn how to do the same thing in a different way every time they use a new program.

If, each time you drove a new car, the speedometer, gas gauge, and oil gauge were in different places and the gas and accelerator pedals were swapped, you'd be confused—and perhaps annoyed. At any rate, buying a new car would mean spending a long time learning how to drive. Anyone with a fleet of cars might find that learning to drive them all was a full-time occupation.

Effective Screen Design

To design an attractive and effective screen, you need to decide what the user will do first. For example, if you are writing a program that creates and modifies customer records, the first thing you must decide is how the user will access each record. Does the user have to press a key or type an ID number? Or does the user pick from a list of customers?

If you have the user pick from a list, your program will be much easier to use. It will be even easier if the records are listed in some order other than the ID number, such as the customer's last name. Moreover, the user will find it handy to type just a few characters of the name in order to get closer to the actual choice.

The following sections review the kinds of screens and windows in common use, explain what elements make up each kind of window, and give general guidelines on how a screen is constructed and used. As you will see, the standards adhered to do not constrict designers but instead *focus* their efforts in creating easy-to-use products.

Windows

A *window* is a rectangular area on-screen that is used to frame a display of data. In a window you may view a spreadsheet, a database, a word-processing document, or almost any other application.

A window may be character- or graphics-based. Windows can be sized to fill the entire screen or shrunk to just a small portion of the screen. In programs that allow the user to open more than one window at a time, you can view two or more parts of the same file, or multiple files simultaneously, each in a separate window.

Entry Screens

Entry screens are used to display or enter a full screen of data. You use this kind of screen to create a new record or modify an existing record. Screens that allow viewing only are sometimes called inquiry screens.

Here are some important points to remember about entry screens :

1. You can design an entry screen to display a group of related records at a glance or to show a single record in detail. You can also allow a user to create a new record and update or modify the information being displayed.

2. You need to provide clear labels for all fields on-screen.

3. You should provide the user with a way to cancel any changes that might have been made in error. You can use a Cancel button or the F12 key (for CUA compliance).

4. As a programmer, you can design attractive entry screens in a text-based operating system such as MS-DOS or in a graphical environment such as Windows 3.1 or OS/2.

Pick Lists

A *pick list* is a window on the screen. Inside the window is a list with one or more data items, all of the same type.

The user can move through a pick list by using the arrow keys, the Page Up and Page Down keys, or a mouse. Alternatively, the user can type the first letter of the desired item.

The purpose of a pick list is to provide a quick means of selection of single or multiple data items. There is no need for the user to remember every item on the list; the list can be scrolled and the desired item highlighted. Figure 8.1 shows a pick list that enables the user to select a file from those listed.

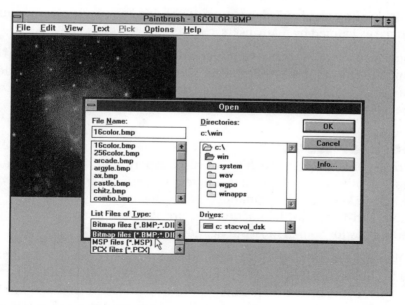

Figure 8.1. A file pick list.

Command-Line Interfaces

Command-line interfaces ask users to input information in response to a prompt. The c:> prompt in MS-DOS is an example of a command-line interface. To use the prompt effectively, you must know what commands can be typed at it.

Many older programs that used command-line interfaces were *modal* in nature. This means that the software operated in different modes. A *mode* is a phase of activity. In a word processing program, the user can be in "entering text" mode, in "command" mode, or in "edit text" mode.

Modal programs allow only one mode or phase of activity to be performed at a time. When you are working with a modal program, you cannot enter a command unless you stop the work in progress and enter command mode. You have to change modes so that the program knows whether it's expecting a command or additional input. Modal programs run more slowly and require more of the user's time than do newer, nonmodal programs.

Pull-Down Menus

Although people used pointing devices before the Macintosh became available, the Mac was the first computer to popularize the use of a mouse. The Macintosh interface, with its windows and pull-down menus, provided an easy-to-learn, point-and-click interface welcomed by many users.

A *pull-down menu* consists of a several elements. A horizontal bar at the top of the screen contains one or more choices, which can expand into a series of vertical pop-up menus that contain more choices. Figure 8.2 shows a pull-down menu from WordPerfect for Windows, a word processing program.

Accelerator Keys

Accelerator keys are shortcuts enabling the user to perform—with just one or two keystrokes—an otherwise complicated and tedious series of commands or menu selections. These keystroke combinations usually include the Ctrl key or the Alt key. (for example, Ctrl-J and Alt-X). Function keys are also used as accelerator keys. F1 is an accelerator key for help in most applications.

Suppose that you are running a program and want to open a file. Most programs allow you to choose File from the horizontal menu bar and select Open File from the pull-down File menu. Instead of going to the File menu and then choosing Open File, your program might provide an alternate way of selecting the Open File command by way of an accelerator such as Ctrl-O.

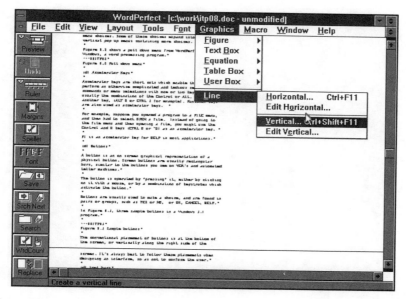

Figure 8.2. A pull-down menu and a pop-up menu from WordPerfect for Windows.

Buttons

A *button* is an on-screen graphical representation of a physical button. Screen buttons are usually rectangular bars, similar to the buttons you see on VCRs and automated teller machines.

You operate, or activate, a button by "pressing" it. To do this, you either click it with a mouse or press a combination of keystrokes.

You usually make choices with buttons. They are often found in pairs such as Yes and No, or in groups such as OK, Cancel, and Help. Figure 8.3 shows three sample buttons in a Windows 3.1 program.

The conventional placement of buttons is horizontally along the bottom of the screen or vertically along the right side of the screen. It is always best to follow these placements when designing an interface so that you avoid confusing the user.

Toolbars

A *toolbar* is a fairly new innovation that belongs mostly to graphical interfaces. Toolbars are sometimes called ribbon bars or button bars.

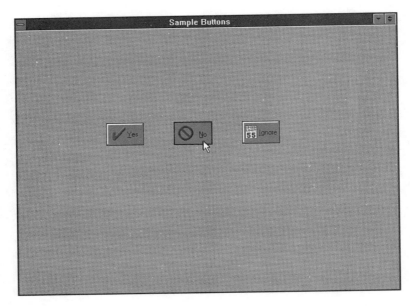

Figure 8.3.   Three sample buttons.

The toolbar consists of one or more rows or columns of miniaturized buttons. Figure 8.4 shows a vertical WordPerfect toolbar on the left side of the screen.

Toolbar buttons are usually used to perform some action, and they can take the place of pull-down menus. Many programs have toolbars that can be customized, enabling the operator to edit the bar and add buttons (such as buttons for the menu choices used most often). Toolbars function as graphical versions of accelerator keys, allowing you to perform an action within a program with just the click of a mouse.

Dialog Boxes

A *dialog box* is a small window that usually takes up less than the whole screen. This box "pops up" when additional input is needed from the user. It is called a dialog box because it allows the program to "talk" with the user, and the user to talk back.

For example, if you choose Print from a pull-down menu, a dialog box opens, asking for further information. The dialog box might ask for the title of the document to be printed, whether you want to print the entire document or selected pages, and whether you want draft- or letter-quality printing. You are given the opportunity to cancel the printing operation at any time. Figure 8.5 shows a Print Setup dialog box from Windows 3.1 for Workgroups.

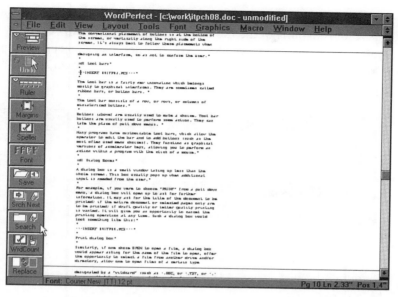

Figure 8.4. WordPerfect's toolbar.

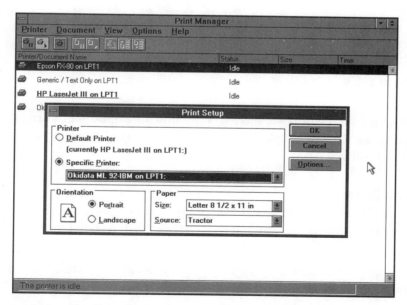

Figure 8.5. The Print Setup dialog box from Windows 3.1 for Workgroups.

Similarly, if you choose Open to open a file, a dialog box like the one in Figure 8.6 appears. It asks for the name of the file to open, offers you the opportunity to select a file from another drive or directory, allows you to open files of a certain type designated by a "wildcard" (such as *.DOC or *.TXT, or even *.* to open all files), and lets you cancel the application if you make an error.

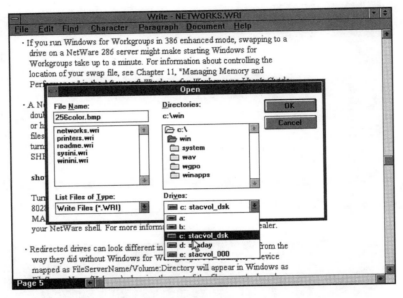

Figure 8.6. The Open dialog box from Windows 3.1.

The dialog boxes in Figures 8.5 and 8.6 communicate important information to the user of the program, and they enable the user to make important choices about how the program will behave.

Check Boxes

You have probably seen check boxes on printed forms. When you create check boxes in your programs, you can implement them with text or graphics.

Check boxes provide the user with a list of choices. The user can "check off" all, some, or none of the choices by using a mouse or a keyboard command. The following example is a daily reminder checklist:

```
        THINGS TO DO TODAY

    [X]   Buy peanut brittle
    [ ]   Renew membership at gym
    [X]   Buy ice cream
    [X]   Buy lard
    [ ]   Walk to work today!
    [ ]   Buy bathroom scale
```

You can also use check boxes to make specific choices within a program, as in this example:

```
    WELCOME TO MEDI-SERVE

Please select areas of interest:

    [X]   Medical Research Library
    [ ]   Names of doctors in your area
    [ ]   Names of good doctors in your area
    [X]   List of physicians by specialty
    [ ]   List of physicians by hospital affiliation
    [X]   List of herbalists
```

Checking boxes instructs the program to display certain information. Again, the user can list one item, all items, or any combination of items on the list.

Radio Buttons

Radio buttons are similar to check boxes but are used when only *one* choice from a number of choices should be selected. Note an example:

```
    Select your Halloween
      costume from our
        vast inventory:

    ( )   Batman
    ( )   Princess
    (●)   Goblin
    ( )   Wicked witch
    ( )   Stand-up comedian
```

Scroll Bars

Scroll bars are conventionally placed on the right side of the screen for vertical scrolling, and at the bottom of the screen for horizontal scrolling. They are used in both character-based and graphical interfaces. The scroll bar appears to be attached to the window, pick list, or list box that it accompanies. The presence of a scroll bar is a clue that there is more information off the screen.

Scroll bars contain a slider, often called a "thumb." This small box indicates where you are positioned in a document and enables you to move quickly through a document. If, for example, a 300-page document is open at page 1, you can move to page 150 by moving the thumb to the middle of the scroll bar. The program then moves immediately to the middle of the document, thus saving the time required to scroll through page-by-page.

Messages

A *message* is a statement your program issues to inform your user about something. Messages fall into three categories:

- *Informational* messages provide information to the user.

- *Error* messages report an error in the way the program is running or in input received from the user.

- *Status* messages inform the user about progress made in long-running operations.

You should issue a message whenever you perform an action significant to the user. For example, when you delete a record, issue a Record deleted message. If you find an error in information typed into a field, issue an error message that describes exactly what the user failed to do, or did incorrectly. The message must always be clearly written, concise, and easy to understand.

Character-based screens frequently display messages in bold type at the bottom of the screen. Microsoft Windows displays messages in a small message window which has one or more buttons and an icon, such as the message box in Figure 8.7. The Microsoft Windows message window uses the following icons:

Circle with an i	Informative
Circle with an !	Error or warning
Stop sign	Fatal error
Circle with a ?	Question

Regardless of how you display the message, make it say what you mean in one or two short sentences. The more you say in your message, the less the user will wonder what went wrong.

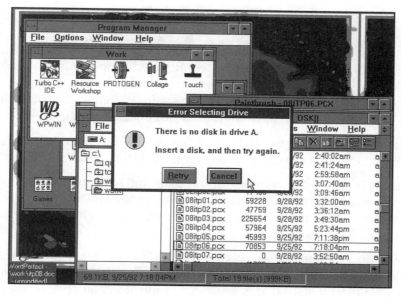

Figure 8.7. A message box from Windows 3.1.

Character-Based and Graphical User Interfaces

Character-based interfaces are generally faster than graphical interfaces. Because characters are stored in a computer's read-only memory (ROM), they are more quickly accessible than graphics.

Graphics have to be drawn. This takes up a lot of the computer's CPU cycles, so a graphics-intensive program or interface can slow down the operation of a program. Graphical user interfaces are prettier, but they take longer to display on-screen. In a graphical user interface, each individual component of the screen must first be calculated and then drawn.

The choice of a GUI (Graphic User Interface) or CUI (Character-based User Interface) depends on which operating system the programmer is using to develop an application. It is up to the programmer to decide which of the two environments is better for a program.

The Growing Popularity of Graphical User Interfaces

The first advance beyond the CUI interfaces appeared in Apple Macintosh computers. Instead of using words and asking the user to type a response to operate a program, Apple devised a graphical user interface for its home computer. GUI programs use small symbols called *icons* to communicate with the user.

Commodore Amiga also has a GUI, and PC users have OS/2, Microsoft Windows, and GeoWorks. Even the multiuser operating system UNIX now has its own GUI.

Graphical user interfaces use a mouse or trackball, and many people find using this method to be much more intuitive than using the keyboard. The user simply points to the icon and clicks it (presses a button on the mouse) to indicate which part of the program should be accessed.

Some programmers prefer a character-based interface, but most personal computer users favor the newer GUIs. Current trends indicate that in a few years almost all interfaces will be graphical—that is, until something newer and better comes along.

It is important to remember that computer technology takes giant strides forward on an almost daily basis. As newer and more powerful computers appear, programs follow, and user interfaces struggle to keep up. As with most technological innovations, today's hottest new interface may be on the trash heap tomorrow.

Effective Manuals and Help Text

Another important facet of communicating with the user is what you provide for instructions. It is critical to give detailed examples; to explain every field, screen, window, and message; and to organize these explanations in a way the user can easily follow. As noted earlier, a user needs two items: a user's manual and help text.

The user's manual should detail the installation of the program and provide instructions on how to get the program up and running. The manual should explain the operation of every part of the program, list all error messages, and tell the user how to correct each error.

Help text is an on-line version of the user's manual. Such text is usually accessed by the F1 key, as a Help menu selection, or as a Help button on the screen. Users have come to expect comprehensive help. It's a good idea to make your on-line help identical to the printed documentation in your user's manual.

General Writing Guidelines

When you write manuals and help text, address the user directly. Avoid silly jokes. Write sentences in the active voice. For example, `Press Enter or click OK to save this record` is an active sentence. However, `These records can be saved by use of the Enter key or the OK button` is a passive sentence. When you write in the active voice, you tend to use fewer words, and the user understands more quickly what you're saying.

Use plenty of pictures to illustrate your points. Include actual copies of program screens in your manual. Most word processing programs and all desktop publishing programs allow you to embed graphics within text.

Programs are available commercially and as shareware that enable you to "capture" or "take a picture" of a screen. These programs are available for both DOS and Windows.

In Windows, pressing Alt+Print Screen copies a picture of the active window to the clipboard. Pressing just the Print Screen key copies the entire screen. You can then paste the contents into a Windows word processing program, or you can use a paint program such as Windows Paintbrush to save the screen image in a reusable format.

Context-Sensitive Help Text

When you are writing help text instead of a manual, you need to decide whether the help text must be *context-sensitive*. This term means that the help the user requests is the help relevant to the part of the program being used when Help was called for. The help you receive can be easy or complex, depending on what kind of help text you have set up.

Summary

In this chapter, you learned the importance of communicating with the user of your program. This kind of communication—called a user interface—consists of screens, windows, a user's manual, and on-line help text. You learned about general standards, and you briefly examined the SAA standard from IBM. Finally, you saw how to create useful manuals and help text.

Data Storage and File Handling

by Lisa Monitto

CHAPTER

The primary unit of data storage is the file. A *file* is a collection of information stored as a discrete unit on a storage medium, such as a disk drive.

In previous chapters, you learned a bit about input and output. Most of the examples showed you how to get input for your programs from the keyboard and how to display the output to your screen. This method of dealing with input and output is useful in some applications, but it has a transient quality. The moment you turn off your computer, all the data you painstakingly entered is irretrievably lost.

When you send output to the screen, there is no way to save or keep your data. If you make a "hard copy" of the data by sending it to a printer, you can read it, but it is still inaccessible to any program until you enter the data all over again. To keep your data so that you can easily access it, you must find a method of storing it. To make your programs more efficient and useful, you must learn to get input from files and write output to files.

Methods of Data Storage

From the day computers were invented, people have been looking for efficient ways to store data. The earliest method was to store information as punched holes in cards or on rolls of punched paper tape. You could then put the cards or tape through a card or tape "reader" and retrieve the stored data.

The next advance in data storage was magnetic tape storage. Huge reels of tape held magnetically encoded data. A magnetic tape storage system was able to hold much more information than punched cards or punched tape could hold. Today, many mainframe computers still use magnetic tape as their primary storage facility.

With the introduction of floppy disks, data storage and the distribution of software became much more convenient and efficient. Floppy disks are smaller, easily transportable and permit faster access to information than does a large reel of magnetic tape. The "floppy" part of the name is a whimsical reference to the way the disk can bend, or flop, because of its thin size and flexible cover. Original floppy disks were 8 inches in size, but the PC market standardized on the 5.25-inch disk and, later, the 3.5-inch disk. In the beginning, a floppy disk could hold approximately 180 kilobytes (K) of data. As floppy technology has improved, the storage capacity has increased. Today, some 3.5-inch disks can hold as much as 2.88 megabytes (M) of data.

Throughout the history of computer development, the trend has been for technology to become smaller, faster, and cheaper. This trend has been reflected in methods of data storage. When the earliest *fixed disk drive* (also called *hard disk drive*) for personal computers was introduced, it had far less capacity for data storage than today's high-speed drive. Slow and expensive, these first fixed disk drives were considered high capacity if they held as much as 10M of data. The interchangeable terms *fixed disk, hard disk,* and *hard drive* are references to the actual disk platter inside the drive, on which the data is stored. This platter is not removable from the drive the way a floppy disk is removable from a floppy disk drive. A hard disk also is not flexible the way a floppy disk is.

Computer owners who were lucky enough to afford one of these dinosaurs couldn't conceive of being able to fill such a disk to capacity. Of course, today's computer owners realize that with the increasing size of commercial applications, a hard disk capacity of 200M or 300M is not excessive.

An emerging technology is the optical magnetic or "floptical" disk that can hold 20M. Additionally, a CD-ROM—a removable, read-only, nonmagnetic storage medium similar to a compact disc—is capable of storing over 600M of information.

Using Data Storage

As a programmer, you are faced with the same issue every time you write an application: how do you get data into your program? Occasionally, it is acceptable to enter data records one at a time as, for example, with an input screen. If, however, you must handle large volumes of data, this method is much too slow.

Suppose that you want to write a program to keep track of a compact disc collection. It wouldn't make much sense to require a person using the program to sit down and type the entire database each time he or she wanted to access a CD title.

The solution is to instruct your program to read this data from a disk file (on a floppy disk or hard disk). Storing the data in a disk file creates a collection of data that remains in existence after the computer is powered-down. This data can be maintained, added to, or modified to fit current needs.

The data in the file you create can often be used in more than one way. It is data that can be read and written to by other programs.

If you have typed any of the sample programs in this book and then saved them, you have used some form of data storage. Your programs were saved as files on either your hard disk or a floppy disk.

Disks and Drives

Without DOS, there would be no disk storage. If you're using a PC, you've already had some interaction with DOS (an acronym for *d*isk *o*perating *s*ystem). If you are using QBasic, you are using MS-DOS (short for Microsoft Disk Operating System).

As you learned earlier in this chapter, a hard disk is a device attached to your computer. It may be located inside the case or it may be a separate piece of hardware attached externally. Floppy disks are small disks that you insert in a drive slot in your computer.

Your computer has one or more disk drives. The magnetic media inside a hard drive consists of one or more spinning platters with a magnetic coating. The platters are inflexible and therefore "hard." Hard disks are also called fixed disks because the disk and the drive cannot be separated from one another.

Floppy drives are the "readers" for floppy disks. Floppy disks, of course, can be removed from their drives, making them suitable for carrying from one computer to another. You use floppy drives for installing new software on your hard disk and for making backup copies of data stored on your hard disk.

Disk drives have letters of the alphabet as names. For most computers with standard configurations, the floppy disk drives are A: and B:. Hard drives have letters starting with C:. You can name drives with letters all the way to Z:. This means that the maximum number of drives you can access at one time is never greater than 26.

A *logical* drive is a partition or section of your hard drive. Early versions of DOS could only recognize 32M on a hard drive. This meant that anyone who had a hard disk with a larger capacity could only use a 32M portion of that capacity, unless the disk was *partitioned* into sections of 32M or less. These partitions are considered by the operating system to be, for all practical purposes, separate hard drives. For instance, you might have logical drives D:, E:, F:, and G: located on the physical hard drive C:.

Current versions of DOS do not have this 32M limitation, but many people like to use logical drives because they speed disk access and help you organize your files. For instance, you might choose to keep business programs and related data on one logical drive and games on another logical drive, or you may choose to keep all program (executable) files on one logical drive and all data files on another logical drive. Using logical drives is no longer a necessity but the practice is still widely used because of the convenience of quick access and file organization.

Naming Files

DOS files can be given almost any name you choose, as long as you follow certain conventions. The filename itself can have a maximum of eight characters. The name can be followed by an extension of three characters, separated from the filename by a period. A typical filename with an extension looks like this:

`FILENAME.EXT`

In naming a file, you can use alphanumeric characters and some symbols and punctuation marks. Certain punctuation marks and symbols have special meaning to DOS and will not be interpreted as part of a filename by your operating system. Although it may be tempting to name an important file `*READ.ME*` or `TEST???`, your operating system will not accept the characters * or ? as part of a legitimate filename. DOS uses these characters as wildcards to hold the place of other characters in a filename. To list on-screen all files with the extension .TXT, for example, you could type

`C:>DIR *.TXT`

When choosing an appropriate three-letter extension for your filename, remember that some extensions have been reserved by convention to indicate the file type. An executable file uses the extension .EXE or .COM. DOS recognizes that these two filename extensions mean that the file is an "executable" or "program" file. For this reason, you should not name data files with the extension .EXE or .COM.

The extension .BAT identifies a batch file for DOS. DOS has a special batch language of its own. You can combine in your batch file some commands that DOS understands, and DOS will execute them in a batch, as if they were an executable program.

The filename extension often provides a clue to what a file contains. A file named DATA.TXT, for example, is likely to be a text file. You can tell this from the extension .TXT.

Many well-known commercial applications reserve extensions, such as .DOC (a document that should be read with a word processor), .WK1 (a spreadsheet), or .DBF (a database file). Extensions such as .ARC and .ZIP mean that the file is compressed and must be uncompressed (or "expanded") before you can use whatever is inside the compressed file. Files often are compressed when data is being archived, because the data requires less disk space in a compressed format.

It's a good idea to use standard extensions to classify files. If you do, it will be easier to see beyond the filename to the type of file you have. A directory crowded with indecipherable extensions tends to be confusing.

If you called your database file FRIENDS.XYZ, someone referencing the file might waste time trying to figure out how to read it. The extension .XYZ does not indicate to a user whether it is a database file, a text file, a spreadsheet file, or some other format. Therefore, it is a great convenience and time-saver to use standard conventions when adding extensions to your filenames.

Using Files

The most common use for a file is to store data as a series of records that can be divided into one or more fields. (Chapter 4, "Sophisticated Data Structures," discusses records and fields in detail.) These records can correspond to data structures you have created. Files can also be used to store unstructured data.

There are several classifications of data files that you can create and use to store your data:

Sequential files

Random-access files

Binary files

Device files

Why are there various types of files? Each type is used for specific purposes. There is no "best" type of file. No matter which file type you choose, there are three things you must do to use the file: open the file, perform I/O (input/output) operations on it, and close it.

To open a file, you must specify the name and path of the file you want to use. You must also specify how you plan to access the file.

At the time you open the file, you must specify a file handle. A *handle* is a unique integer assigned to the file. If you are using QBasic, *you* must choose the integer. If you are using another language, such as Pascal or C, a handle is assigned for you by the compiler. Every time you access the file, you refer to it by the handle you assigned it when you opened the file.

You have to perform I/O operations on the file. Adding or changing information in a file is called "outputting" or writing to the file. Accessing the file to receive information from it is called getting input from the file.

When you are finished working with a file, you have to close it. Because your operating system limits the number of files you can keep open, it's a good idea to close each file before opening the next one. If your program will be run in a multiuser environment, no other program can access the files your program has opened. Therefore, you should close each file as soon as you are finished with it. The action of closing a file causes the operating system to flush all the computer's buffers and ensures that all the data is written to the disk.

Sequential Files

Sequential files in QBasic store data as ASCII text. Writing information to a sequential file is similar to writing the information to the screen with a PRINT statement.

Sequential files are the easiest to program and understand because you enter data by printing it to a file, just as you print to a screen. It's very easy to write data to a sequential file, but writing to (and reading from) the file is slower than with other types of files.

Here is how you would open, write to, and close a sequential file in QBasic:

```
OPEN "SEQFILE.DAT" FOR OUTPUT AS 1
PRINT #1, "This is a test."
CLOSE 1
```

Opening the sequential file for output creates a file if none already exists by that name. If a file already exists, the OPEN statement sets the write location to the beginning of the file, effectively erasing any information it initially contained.

To add information to the end of a file, you must open it in APPEND mode:

```
OPEN "SEQFILE.DAT" FOR APPEND AS 1
PRINT #1, "This is another test."
CLOSE 1
```

As noted, all data within sequential files is stored as ASCII text. A carriage-return character is considered the end of a record, and fields within a record are separated by commas. In sequential files, these records do not have to be of fixed length, so even if you know how many records a file contains, you won't know how long the file is.

The biggest drawback of using sequential files is that you have to read the file just the way you wrote it, which is, of course, sequentially. You start at the beginning, and if you're looking for information that happens to be stored in the last record of the file, you have to read all the previous records to find it. You can't jump to any particular place in the file.

Here is how you would open, read, and close a sequential file in QBasic:

```
OPEN "SEQFILE.DAT" FOR INPUT AS 1
INPUT #1, Text$
PRINT Text$
CLOSE 1
```

These statements open a sequential file, read the first record in it, and assign the record's contents to the string variable Text$. Text$ is displayed on-screen, and the file is then closed.

Reading a sequential file is something like searching a videocassette of your favorite film. If you want to watch a scene from the middle of the movie, you can't access that scene without first going through every scene before it. Even if you use the fast-forward button, it will take a long time to reach the section of tape you want to view.

Sequential files are restricted in another way: You can't open a sequential file for reading and writing at the same time. An additional problem with sequential files is that you can't change information within the file. To change the information, you must write to another file the entire contents of the file you want to change, making appropriate changes in the newer file as you go. You must do this even if the required changes are minor.

Sequential files are simple in function and limited in scope. If you have an application that requires a great deal of data, you should use random-access files instead.

Random-Access Files

A *random-access file* is a collection of identical data types or structures stored in a unit at a specific location on a storage device. Such a file is like a one-dimensional array.

Recall that an array is a collection of data types or structures—so is a random-access file. Whereas the array is memory-based and limited in size, the random-access file is disk-based. The size of a random-access file is limited, therefore, only by the available disk space.

The term *random access* means that you can pick and choose records from anywhere within the file. You can also open a random-access file for reading and writing at the same time. If you make a change in the file, you can modify an individual record without modifying the entire file, as you would have to do with a sequential file.

The programming techniques involved in creating and manipulating random-access files are a bit more complex than with sequential files, but reading a random-access file is faster. You can also find information more easily because each record in the file is the same length.

As noted earlier, you must start at the beginning of a sequential file and read through the entire file until you find the part you are looking for. This is an extremely slow and inefficient method of retrieving data. A random-access file, however, is organized like a compact disc, enabling you to jump to any track without fast-forwarding through all the other tracks to get there. By specifying a record number in the file, you can jump directly to that record. This makes the access time the same whether the record is located at the beginning or end of the file. You cannot do this with sequential files, which contain unstructured data as text.

Modifying a random-access file is also faster because you don't have to close and reopen it in order to write to it. If you were using a sequential file that had 1000 records, to modify record number 920, you'd have to rewrite the entire file.

Random-access files allow you to access only the specific data you want to modify. The only disadvantage is that the file structure is fixed (as with arrays), so you must provide space for the longest record you will ever need. Each record must be long enough to fit the longest one you can think of. This can be a waste of space, and wasted space quickly multiplies if you are adding thousands of records to a file.

If you have a large amount of variable-length data, you may want to use the sequential method, even though it is slower. Hard disk space is a precious commodity, and users tend to resent programs that occupy more space than necessary.

In Chapter 4, "Sophisticated Data Structures," you learned about programmer-defined data structures; you can combine various data types and structures within the structure you define. When you create a random-access file, you must have some type of record structure in mind. You might decide to have a file of simple integers, fixed-length strings, or more complicated data types that combine floating-point numbers with string data.

When using QBasic, you must state the length of the record (in bytes) when you open the file. Look at this sample record:

```
TYPE StudentRecordType
    StudentName AS STRING * 30
    SatScore AS INTEGER
    NetWorth AS SINGLE
    Comment AS STRING * 50
END TYPE
DIM NewStudent AS StudentRecordType
```

You can open a file that holds a record of StudentRecordType with the following statement:

```
OPEN "STUFILE.DAT" FOR RANDOM AS #15 LEN = 86
```

STUFILE.DAT is the name of the file. The FOR RANDOM part of the statement tells QBasic to open the file in random-access mode for both reading and writing. The number 15 is the file handle. LEN = 86 is the length of the record to be stored in the file. This is how the length is figured:

StudentName = 30 bytes

SatScore   = 2 bytes

NetWorth   = 4 bytes

Comment   = 50 bytes

QBasic has a built-in function to calculate the length of a variable so that you don't have to calculate the bytes manually. The LEN function returns the size of any variable or record. Note this example:

```
NameLength = LEN(FirstName$)
```

LEN can be used in the OPEN statement, in place of the byte count, like this:

```
OPEN "STUFILE.DAT" FOR RANDOM AS #15 LEN = LEN(NewStudent)
```

If you use this method to open the file, you don't have to know in advance the exact length of the record, as long as the record type has been defined and a variable of its type declared. You could make the length larger than you need, but that may be a waste of space. If you make the length too small, though, your program will not run properly. It is even possible to leave out LEN =, in which case QBasic provides the file with a default record length of 128 bytes.

Arrays are accessed with subscripts. You can refer to file records by number in the same way. If you had the file from the preceding example, you could retrieve record number 1 from it with the following statement:

```
GET #15, 1, NewStudent
```

This statement accesses file handle #15 (in this case, STUFILE.DAT) and assigns the information from record 1 to the variable you have named NewStudent. The statement assumes that STUFILE.DAT exists and is open, has handle #15 assigned to it, and has record 1 within it.

As noted earlier, when you open a file in a QBasic program, you refer to the file by its handle, not its name. For example, look at the following statement:

```
OPEN "MyFile.Doc" FOR APPEND AS 1
```

In this statement, 1 is the file handle. Because it is a number, you can assign it to a variable with a more descriptive handle, such as MyFile = 1. Later, instead of saying

```
PRINT #1,"Hi there!"
```

you can say

```
PRINT MyFile,"Hi there!"
```

You have assigned the file to a variable with a descriptive name. When you are working with many files, it is much easier to remember a descriptive name than to recall what each number stands for.

When you are working with only one file, it is easy to remember that handle #15 is assigned to STUFILE.DAT. But what if you had 5 or 10 files open, and each had a file handle? It would be difficult to remember which handle belonged to which file. Because the handle is an integer, you should create a descriptive variable name and assign it to the handle. Then your opening statement would look like this:

```
StudentFile = FREEFILE
OPEN "STUFILE.DAT" FOR RANDOM AS StudentFile LEN = LEN(NewStudent)
```

Notice the keyword FREEFILE. This is a built-in function in QBasic that returns the first available unused file handle. In this example, you created a descriptive variable name for a file and made it equal to FREEFILE. There is no reason to know the actual value of the file handle; after you've assigned it to a variable, the variable name is all you need in order to reference the file.

Here is the GET statement shown earlier, with the variable StudentFile substituted for the file handle:

```
GET StudentFile, 1, NewStudent
```

This GET statement does the same thing the other statement does. You access StudentFile (a file handle that refers to STUFILE.DAT), get record 1 from the file, and store it in the variable NewStudent.

When you use a GET statement like this one, you have to make sure that when you try to read the file, the information is actually there. Two functions can help: EOF and LOF.

EOF stands for *end of file*. If you wanted to be sure that information was in STUFILE.DAT before you tried to read it, you would use the following statement:

```
IF NOT EOF (StudentFile) THEN
   GET StudentFile, 1, NewStudent
```

LOF stands for *length of file*. The statement PRINT LOF (StudentFile) prints to your screen the number of records contained in the file assigned to the handle StudentFile.

The other I/O statement you need is the PUT statement. Note the following example:

```
NewStudent.StudentName = "Harvey Johnson"
NewStudent.SatScore    = 1320
NewStudent.NetWorth    = 1320.24
NewStudent.Comment     = "Worth as much as his score."
PUT StudentFile, 1, NewStudent
```

This takes the record variable NewStudent and writes it in record 1 of the file assigned to the handle StudentFile, which, in this case, is STUFILE.DAT.

When you are done reading and writing to StudentFile, it is a sound programming practice to use the CLOSE statement to close the file:

```
CLOSE StudentFile
```

Binary Files

In addition to offering random-access files and sequential files, QBasic offers another type of data file: the binary file. Binary files have no internal structure. They store data as individual bytes. Because the data is stored as a stream of bytes, there is no way to tell what kind of data you are reading from a binary file.

Binary files have the most flexibility but are the most difficult to program. The programmer has to know how many bytes go into each variable, the order of the variables, and how to convert the bytes into the proper format.

Every file, whether created as sequential or random access, is nothing more than a sequence of bytes. When you open a file in binary mode, you can perform I/O operations directly on those bytes. There are no records within the file—in fact, no structure at all. The file is treated as a long stream of bytes.

To read data from a binary file, you must know the original data structure. If you know it, you can access any location within the file as you can with a random-access file, but you can jump to individual bytes rather than records.

Device Files

Device files are input/output devices connected to your computer. Every input/output component of your computer can be considered a device. You can open, read from, write to, and close a device just as you would a file. You open and close such devices as printers, modems, and screens with the same commands you use to open and close files.

The programming statement

```
PRINT "Good Morning!"
```

produces the same output as

```
OPEN "SCRN:" FOR OUTPUT AS 1
PRINT #1, "Good Morning!"
```

Device files give your program the capability to redirect data if necessary. Because you use the same commands in writing from a device file to a disk file, you can easily change the destination of the data. Device names are usually followed by a colon. The printer is LPT1: or LPT2:. The modem might be COM1:, COM2:, COM3:, or COM4:. The screen might be SCRN:. Hard drives and floppy drives are devices too, as you can see from their designations of A:, B:, C:, and so on.

Summary

The primary unit of data storage is a file. The trend of data storage technology has been for storage devices to get smaller, cheaper and faster.

Storing data in a file for later retrieval and/or manipulation by a program is faster and more efficient than entering it by hand.

Your PC (personal computer) can make use of hard disk drives and floppy disk drives, which are controlled by the Disk Operating System (DOS). Logical drives are partitions on a hard drive (fixed disk drive) that can help you organize your data and speed access to the information on your disk.

There are some conventions used when naming files. You should standardize the three-letter file extension so that it indicates the type of file being named.

There are several different types of files: random-access files, sequential files, binary files, and device files. Each file type has its own advantages and disadvantages.

Dealing with Bugs

by Lisa Monitto

Every programmer has to learn how to deal with bugs. This chapter is designed to help you understand where bugs come from, what they do, and how you can fix them.

Bugs are a fact of life for a programmer; so don't get discouraged when the inevitable occurs. Errors happen. The best thing to do is learn from them.

Many first-time programmers are taken by surprise when they discover that most programs do not work correctly the first time they are run. It is comforting to know, however, that even experts make mistakes. The reason the experts know how to fix these mistakes is because they have made so many, so often. You must learn to emulate these expert programmers.

What Is "Debugging"?

Debugging is the process of searching out and fixing errors, or *bugs* in your programs. Debugging is partly a science and partly an art. A good programmer must be skilled in retracing each step of the program in order to find the origin of the problem.

While reading this book, you probably have typed several sample programs. You might have tried to modify these examples or even written one of your own. Chances are very good that at least one of these programs did not work properly the first time you ran it.

This is no reason to feel overwhelmed. Almost no program works right the first time. Everyone makes mistakes—even experienced programmers.

To write a program—longer than 10 or 15 lines—flawlessly on your very first try would probably get you named *Time* Magazine's Programmer of the Year.

Your programs must be written with great care. Because a computer is a machine, and not a human, it is unable to figure out that you mean *Hello* when you type *Helo* or *Helllo*. A simple misplaced comma, colon, or quotation mark, a single space instead of a double space, a transposed letter—any of these can cause a disaster for your program. Therefore, it is extremely important to understand what kinds of errors cause bugs and to learn the methods of debugging.

A "buggy" program can frustrate and infuriate the end-user, fail to perform its functions properly, and cause you, the programmer, to become fretful and anxious until the bug is fixed. It is not easy at first, but as you continue programming, you develop an intuition about the causes of some common errors and how to find and fix them. The more programs you debug, the better you become at targeting the source of problems in your code. You begin to develop your own debugging technique.

What Is a Bug?

There's a well-known cartoon showing a small boy in a library. His face is sooty, his hair askew, his eyeglasses are hanging from one ear, and his clothes are ripped and smoky. He is in the process of returning a book to the librarian entitled *Introduction to Basic Chemistry*. The caption reads: "I want to report an error on page 245."

Programming errors are known as *bugs*. Although they are usually less likely to cause physical damage than the error in the chemistry book, programming errors are certain to cause anguish and consternation when they are discovered. In some extreme cases, if a computer program is used to land an aircraft, to move a medical laser in a series of delicate steps, or to report the location of a fire, the results of a bug can be fatal.

Taking the broad approach, a bug is anything that the end-user of a program perceives as an error. Debugging is not just making your program run correctly; it's getting your program to run the way the end-user expects it to run.

This is not always easy; it involves a certain amount of mind reading. A poor or non-standard user interface can make a program seem buggy. If all your users expect the F1 key to show them a help screen, they might perceive it as a bug if your program uses F1 to mean "Exit without saving."

Why are errors called *bugs* in the first place? One story dates from the early days of computers.

In the late 1940s, at an East Coast Naval installation, one of the enormous vacuum tube computers began to malfunction. The operators tried everything they could think of to get the computer running again. Nothing worked, and finally, they made an extensive tube-by-tube examination. After days of inspection, they found a dead moth in the circuitry. When they removed the moth, the computer worked once again. The removal of the moth is said to be the first computer debugging job.

Although this first bug was a hardware problem, the term is now also used to describe software that doesn't work properly.

Think about other usages of the word bug. *Buggy* is a slang word for crazy. *To bug someone* is to be very bothersome. An infestation of bugs—as in *a buggy sack of flour*—is unpleasant and renders the food useless.

In computer terms, buggy incorporates all these meanings. A buggy program is a program that simply does not work the way it is supposed to.

In computer terminology, *glitch* means a flaw in logic that either causes unexpected results or prevents a program from working at all. Perhaps bug is merely an acronym for Big Ugly Glitch.

Where Do Bugs Come From?

Bugs are introduced by you, the programmer.

There are rare cases in which your program does not work due to a flaw in the language, the compiler, or the hardware. But in almost every instance, program bugs are there due to some oversight or error on the part of the programmer. That's why it is important to spend adequate time in the design phase of programming.

Bugs can come from inadequate planning, design, and testing—and sometimes from plain carelessness.

Many bugs can be eliminated with planning and forethought in the early stages of writing your program. Some programmers prefer a get-in-there-and-start-writing approach that frequently leads to sloppy spaghetti code that is inefficient and hard to follow.

The term *spaghetti code* refers to quickly written, haphazard programs that have little or no structure—that do not make use of functions and subroutines. The lines of code are as difficult to follow as the tangled strands on a plate of spaghetti. To keep from writing spaghetti code, sit down and make an outline or flowchart of how you want your program to run. It makes your job much easier later, and your users appreciate it!

Outlines

In Chapter 2, "Introduction to Programming Statements," you read about flow charts and pseudocode. It doesn't matter whether you use a flow chart or a pseudocode outline to plan your program, both work fine. Breaking your program into steps and diagramming the steps in a flow chart help you see whether you have made any logical errors. Because you see each step in order, you are able to see the whole program at a glance. This overview is helpful for discovering any obvious mistakes you made when writing the program.

Types of Bugs

There are two categories of bugs: those specific to the particular language in which you are programming and those common to any language.

Bugs can be caused by typographical errors, mismatched parameters in subroutines and functions, poorly designed loops, illegal variable values, errors in logic, or any other error that causes your program to behave in a way you did not intend.

How Can You Write a Bug-Proof Program?

You probably can't write a bug-proof program.

You certainly can try to guard against bugs during the design stages of your program. A simple guard is to have your program check all the input it gets—as it is input—to make sure it is within the prescribed limits.

For example, if a user enters a string value when the variable is a numeric type, QBasic displays a cryptic `?Redo from start` error message. Other languages such as C and Pascal stop running and display an uninformative runtime error message.

Users perceive this as a bug because it is unexpected and confusing. A program that halts with an error can cause your users to lose valuable data.

One way programmers can get around this is to validate input as it is received. Validation of input is a step that should be part of your design phase.

The program in Listing 10.1 prevents a runtime error if the wrong type of data is entered. This program inputs one character at a time and checks each character to see if it is a digit. Digits are appended to the string UserInput$; other characters are discarded. When an illegal character is entered, the program beeps to warn the user. After the user has entered the numeric string, the string is converted to an integer value to be used in calculations.

Listing 10.1. A program that prevents runtime errors.

```
DO                          ' Loop until the user
                            ' enters a carriage return.

     Digit$ = INKEY$        ' Keyboard input

' If the character entered is numeric, add it to
'   the string that accumulates the numeric characters,
'   UserInput$. If the character is not numeric, beep
'   the speaker.

     IF (Digit$ >= "0") AND (Digit$ <= "9") THEN
          UserInput$ = UserInput$ + Digit$
          PRINT Digit$;

     ELSEIF Digit$ <> "" THEN
               BEEP
     END IF
LOOP UNTIL Digit$ = CHR$(13)

' Convert UserInput$ string to an single value
NumberEntered! = VAL(UserInput$)

PRINT                               ' skip line
PRINT "The number entered was: ";
PRINT NumberEntered!                ' display result
```

When Should You Debug a Program?

Every program longer than a few lines needs testing and debugging. It is important not to get discouraged and frustrated when first starting out. Even professional programmers have to spend time finding and correcting bugs. It comes with the territory.

When you first begin planning your program, plan for the debugging phase. Writing your programs using structured programming pays off in the debugging phase.

Chapter 7 explained the idea behind structured programming. Structured programs divide your program's tasks into separate compartments, or subroutines. Each subroutine can be debugged separately from the main program. This makes debugging much simpler because you can isolate the area where the bug occurs.

How Do I Find a Bug?

To write a successful program, you have to go through two steps—testing and debugging. *Testing* refers to observation of how your program runs with different data. *Debugging* is the actual process of locating and removing the bugs.

Every time you run a program, you are, in effect, testing it. No single test you run can unearth all the bugs that may be lurking in your program. As the debugger, you should plan on running your program with lots of test cases. Use a variety of data to test your program.

You should know the minimum and maximum values the variables in your program will hold. Test your program with those values.

You can also use *control data,* a set of data that will produce results you have predetermined and are expecting. Run your program with different sets of control data to make sure the output is what you expect it to be.

You should also run your program with unreasonable data. Enter values you know are highly incorrect to make sure your program can recover without crashing. This is called *error trapping.* The programmer must "trap" errors and display some informative error message to the user, rather than allowing the program to "crash."

Once you've ran your program and corrected any errors you have discovered, let others test your program for you. Using other people to test your program after you're sure it is bug-free is sometimes called *beta testing*. (Your own test was the *alpha test*).

These outside testers usually enter things you never dreamed of and almost certainly find some bugs you overlooked.

Beta testing is important; the end-users of your program almost always expect different things from the program than you anticipate. The more people who beta test your program, the better—more bugs and glitches are likely to be discovered.

When bugs are found, you might use a debugging program to trace the steps your program takes while it is executing. Some integrated development environments' (IDEs) have a built-in debugger that allows you to set breakpoints, inspect and change values, and trace execution.

The debugging program you use enables you to locate the cause of the problem and where it is located in your program.

How Do I Correct a Bug?

A bug is sometimes easier to find than to fix. If the bug is merely a typographical error, it is easy to correct. If you have made an error in logic, however, locating and repairing the problem becomes much more difficult. In some cases, a logic-flaw bug compels the programmer to take everything apart and start over. Listing 10.2 contains a language-related bug.

Listing 10.2. A program containing a language-related bug.

```
NumberOfLightBulbs% = 100
DIM LightBulbs%(1 to NumberOfLightBulbs%)
BurnedOut = 0
BulbOk = 1
 .
 .

 .
FOR i = 1 to NumberOfBulbs%
   IF LightBulb%(i) = BurnedOut THEN CALL ReplaceBulb
NEXT i
```

How many times does the FOR-NEXT loop in Listing 10.2 run? Zero. This loop never executes for two reasons. Look carefully at the variable names. NumberOfLightBulbs% is equal to 100, which is probably the value we wanted to use in the FOR-NEXT loop. But we have carelessly entered NumberOfBulbs% instead.

This is a language-related error. Unlike most other languages, QBasic permits the programmer to refer to a variable within the body of a program without explicitly declaring it first. In Listing 10.2, a new variable NumberOfBulbs% is created and initialized to the value 0 without generating a warning. Consequently, we are specifying that the FOR-NEXT loop should run for all values of i from 1 to 0. Listing 10.3 shows the correct code.

Listing 10.3. The program from Listing 10.2 with the variable name corrected.

```
NumberOfLightBulbs% = 100
DIM LightBulbs%(1 to NumberOfLightBulbs%)
BurnedOut = 0
BulbOk = 1
    .
    .
    .
FOR i = 1 to NumberOfLightBulbs%
    IF LightBulb%(i) = BurnedOut THEN CALL ReplaceBulb
NEXT i
```

Now what happens when you try to run your program? If you typed it the way it appears above, you get the error Subscript out of range. What does that mean?

Array elements are referred to by their subscripts. The array in the example, LightBulbs%(), has NumberOfLightBulbs% elements in it. So why does the code generate a Subscript out of range error? The error is generated because the array LightBulb%() is not the array LightBulbs%().

C or Pascal programs would not compile with such an error because both languages require a declaration of each data structure and variable before it can be used in a program. However, QBasic does allow you to refer to an array you never explicitly defined, so you can create an array simply by referring to it—just like a variable. But an array created in this fashion is given, by default, only 10 elements. Therefore, when i is incremented to 11, we are trying to reference element 11 of the array LightBulb%(), which does not exist. Spelling counts in programming.

Knowing the characteristics and meaning of error messages in each language helps you chase down bugs.

Why Use a Debugger?

Using a debugging program can make your life easier. A debugger allows you to peek into your program while it is running so that you can see exactly where problems occur.

It is much easier to use a debugger than to manually review every code statement, which is both tedious and time consuming. With a debugger, you are able to step through your program line by line. This helps you identify exactly which line was being executed when the bug occurred. You can spy on variables and watch how their values change during program execution. You can even change the variables' values to see how the changes affect the outcome.

Where Do I Start?

Begin at the beginning.

The first thing is not to panic. Remember that most programmers—even professionals with years of experience—seldom write a bug-free program.

You can't begin debugging until you realize something has gone wrong with your program. Many errors are obvious—your program fails to run, freezes while running, enters an endless loop, or seems to "explode" on your screen, displaying strange, meaningless characters you never included.

Other bugs might not be so obvious. Your program might run perfectly, but the output is askew—all your checking account figures have a misplaced decimal point, your mailing list has mismatched names and addresses, or your grade-point average is half what it should be.

Start by using a debugging program. Some compiled languages such as Pascal, C, or C++ must be debugged with a separate debugging program such as CodeView, Turbo Debugger, or Soft Ice.

QBasic has an integrated debugger. This means the debugger is built into the QBasic development environment, and a separate debugging program is not needed.

Why Use Comments?

Chapter 2, "Introduction to Programming Statements," stressed the need for extensive comments in your code. It also mentioned the importance of descriptive variable names. If your program proves to be buggy and you did not follow this advice, it is much more difficult to identify and remove the bugs.

Assume you have a program that balances your checkbook. After entering the data, you are surprised to discover that your balance is significantly higher or lower than you anticipated. Is someone depositing money into your account without your knowledge? Is a dishonest teller appropriating it? Or, more likely, is it a bug in your program?

Now, imagine if you ignored the advice in this book and wrote your checkbook balancing program without comments and descriptive variable names. You open your program to debug it and see the code in Listing 10.4.

Listing 10.4. The original checkbook balancing program.

```
DIM A%(1 TO 100)
INPUT B
FOR T% = 1 TO 100
    PRINT T%;
    INPUT A%(T%)
    IF A%(T%) = 0 THEN
        EXIT FOR
    END IF
NEXT

T% = T% - 1

FOR I% = 1 TO T%
    PRINT A%(I%)
    B = B + A%(I%)
NEXT I%

PRINT "Total: $"; B
END
```

The preceding program is confusing and difficult to discern. What is B? What is A%()? It's difficult to tell why this program produces inaccurate figures. It would be much easier to locate the problem if you had written extensive comments and used descriptive variable names, such as the code in Listing 10.5.

Listing 10.5. The rewritten checkbook balancing program with comments and descriptive variables.

```
DEFINT A-Z                       ' Make all numeric variables
                                 '  integers by default.
NumberOfTransactions = 100   ' Set maximum # of entries.

DIM Amount(1 TO NumberOfTransactions) ' Data structure
                                 '  to hold
                                 '   transactions.


  ' Get your account's starting balance:
CLS                              ' Clear the screen.
INPUT "Type starting balance, then press <ENTER>: ", Balance!

' Get transactions. Continue accepting input until the
'  input is zero for a transaction, or until
'  NumberOfTransactions have been entered:

FOR TransactionNum = 1 TO NumberOfTransactions
   PRINT TransactionNum;
   PRINT ")  Enter transaction amount (0 to end): ";
   INPUT "", Amount(TransactionNum)
   IF Amount(TransactionNum) = 0 THEN
       TransactionNum = TransactionNum - 1
       EXIT FOR
   END IF
NEXT
' Print the list of transactions. If a transaction
'  is greater than zero, print it as a "CREDIT"; if a
'  transaction is less than zero, print it as a "DEBIT":

FOR I = 1 TO TransactionNum
   IF Amount(I) > 0 THEN
      PRINT USING "CREDIT: $$#####.##"; Amount(I)
   ELSEIF Amount(I) < 0 THEN
        PRINT USING "DEBIT: $$#####.##"; Amount(I)
   END IF
  ' Update balance:
   Balance! = Balance! + Amount(I)
```

continues

153

Listing 10.5. Continued

```
NEXT I

' Print the final balance:

PRINT
PRINT "--------------------------"
PRINT USING "Final Total: $$######.##"; Balance!
END
```

The liberal use of comments, PRINT statements, and informative variable names in Listing 10.5 has made the same program much easier to understand and follow.

In this version of the program, all numeric variables were defined as integers unless referred to as a specific numeric data type. Balance! is a single-precision floating-point variable. We forgot to make the array Amount() single-precision as well; therefore, any amounts such as 6.33 or 14.12 are rounded off to the nearest integer. The program calculates the balance correctly if the third statement is changed to read:

```
DIM Amount!(1 TO NumberOfTransactions)
```

so it can store floating-point values.

Understanding Error Messages

If you have a bug that prevents your program from running to completion, the result is most likely an error message. This message helps you identify the source of the error and is a good starting point for your detective work.

As a programmer, you should plan for every contingency. Users who aren't computer knowledgeable can make mistakes that cause your program to crash—unless you have planned ahead so your program traps the errors caused by these mistakes. A very common mistake users make is trying to read a floppy drive without a disk in the drive. If your program does not specifically check for this particular error, the program will stop running with an error message like:

```
Error reading drive A; Abort, Retry, Ignore?
```

An experienced programmer may have run into this error before and will include programming statements that will check the condition of the drive to determine whether it is possible to access the drive without causing an error and a program crash.

Syntax Errors

When you have used a keyword incorrectly, made a typographical error, or combined keywords in a way that makes them incomprehensible to the compiler or interpreter, it is said that you have made a *syntax error*. QBasic has a built-in syntax checker that can catch many errors at the time you enter them. An example of a syntax error might be:

```
PIRNT "Please enter your name:"
```

The misspelling of PRINT as PIRNT causes the compiler or interpreter to report a syntax error when you attempt to compile or run your program.

FOR without *NEXT, DO* without *LOOP,* and Block *IF* without *END IF* Errors

FOR-NEXT, DO LOOPS, and IF-THEN-ELSE statements are convenient ways to control the flow of a program, but you must take care to match the start and finish of each statement. A mismatched statement end can cause unpredictable results, so it can be difficult to track down the cause of error messages having to do with mismatched statements.

FOR-NEXT, DO LOOPS, and IF-THEN-ELSE statements are all considered block statements. You must provide each with a beginning and ending statement—depending on the rules of the language in which you are writing your program.

The QBasic code fragment in Listing 10.6 produces a surprising NEXT without FOR error message.

Listing 10.6. This code fragment produces a *NEXT* without *FOR* error message.

```
DEFINT A-Z              ' All variables integers by default
.
.
.
For i = 1 to NumberOfMembers    ' Check all members
                                '   for late dues owed
```

continues

Listing 10.6. Continued

```
CALL AreDuesPaid(Member(i),AmountOwed!,DaysLate)

                                ' Send letter if dues late
IF (AmountOwed!>0) AND (DaysLate>90) THEN
    CALL SendDunLetter(Member(i))
PRINT "Member "; i; " owes $"; AmountOwed!

NEXT i                          ' end of loop

END
```

You can clearly see the FOR statement and its matching NEXT statement; there appears to be no problem. The trouble is the IF statement.

When the IF-THEN statement is written on more than one line, it automatically becomes a block. When it is used as a block, you must end it with END IF. There is no END IF statement in Listing 10.6, so the QBasic interpreter counts everything after the IF to be part of the block. Because there is no FOR statement inside the IF block, the NEXT is assumed to be an error.

Listing 10.7 shows the code from Listing 10.6 with the END IF statement added.

Listing 10.7. The program from listing 10.6 with an *END IF* statement.

```
DEFINT A-Z      ' All variables integers by default
.
.
.
For i = 1 to NumberOfMembers      ' Check all members
                                  '  for late dues owed
   CALL AreDuesPaid(Member(i),AmountOwed!,DaysLate)
   ' Send letter if dues are late
   IF (AmountOwed! > 0) AND (DaysLate>90) THEN
       CALL SendDunLetter(Member(i))
   END IF        ' END IF closes this statement block
   PRINT "Member "; i; " owes $"; AmountOwed!
NEXT i                            ' end of loop
END
```

Any block of statements that begins and ends with a keyword can be nested—but you must remember to match the pairs correctly.

In Pascal, blocks of statements are marked by the keywords BEGIN and END. In C, blocks of statements are marked by curly braces: { for BEGIN and } for END. Accidentally mismatching, omitting, or misplacing a brace or a BEGIN or END can cause your program to run improperly or stop running altogether. It also can cause misleading error messages to be generated. For example, an error message may point to a section of code that has nothing wrong with it. Because a BEGIN or END was mismatched, however, code is included in a section where it doesn't belong, and the program generates an error message.

Mismatched BEGIN and END statements, mismatched parentheses and quotes, and open loops can all cause errors.

Summary

In this chapter, you learned what bugs are, how to start looking for them, and how to find them. You also learned that debugging is the process of searching out and finding errors in programs, and that it is virtually impossible to write a bug-free program the first time.

This chapter also showed you that bugs are almost always due to programmer error or oversight, rather than a failure of the programming language or hardware, and that outlines and generous comments can be of great help when debugging a program. This chapter emphasized the importance of planning ahead for the debugging phase while writing your program so that you are, effectively, writing and debugging at the same time.

You learned the importance of testing your program with all kinds of data, including the minimum and maximum your variables can hold, as well as testing with control data. You learned the importance of using descriptive variables and subroutine names and the importance of using comments liberally in your program script. This chapter also encouraged you to anticipate and trap for errors that can cause your program to stop.

In many ways, debugging skill is as important as programming skill; a buggy program is no good for the author or the end-user. Once you become comfortable with debugging, you will have greater confidence as a programmer—when something goes wrong, you will be prepared to correct the errors.

Object-Oriented Programming

by Lisa Monitto

Introduction to Object-Oriented Programming

You learned about sophisticated data structures in Chapter 4. You learned that you can combine variables of different types and sizes in a programmer-defined record. These records, or structures, extend the programming language you are working with to include the data types you have defined, as if they were built into the language.

In Chapter 7, you were introduced to the concept of structured, or modular, programming. When you are writing a structured program, you break down a large program into small, easy-to-understand modules, or *subroutines,* in a framework you have created. Each subroutine operates independently to perform specific tasks in the body of your program. Because each task is encapsulated in its own section, or module, you can get a shell of your program running, then fill in the procedures one by one.

Object-oriented programming brings together the concepts of structured programming and sophisticated data structures, offering programmers the ability to permanently bond data to the routines that manipulate that data. The result of this bonding is called an *object.*

When you bond a data structure to the routines that manipulate it, you have created an *intelligent data structure*—one that knows how to take care of itself.

The two most popular object-oriented programming languages are C++ and Turbo Pascal. The terms that these two languages use to describe objects and their properties differ. In Turbo Pascal, objects are referred to as *objects,* and the procedures and functions that the objects contain are referred to as *methods.* In C++, objects are referred to as *classes,* and the procedures and functions that classes contain are referred to as *member functions.* The way you refer to the objects you create when you are programming depends on the language you use.

Chapter 4 showed you that data structures and records contain one or more fields. The fields in a record can be the same type, or many different types. A record can even contain other records.

Study the two code fragments shown in Listings 11.1 and 11.2. At first glance, the object definition in Listing 11.2 looks like the record definition in Listing 11.1. But in addition to *data members* (variables contained in the object definition), the object definition includes procedures and functions to deal with that data.

Listing 11.1. A sample record definition in C++.

```
struct stars_struct_sample {
    int luminosity;
    int location;
} starfield;
```

Listing 11.2. A sample object definition in C++.

```
class star_class_sample {
   public:
     int luminosity;
     int location;
     void StarCatalogue();
     void CalculateMagnitude();
};
```

The concept of encapsulation was introduced in Chapter 7, "Structured Programming." The autonomy of a subroutine is preserved because the data variables in its scope are local, or *private,* to the subroutine. In a similar way, the data variables in an object are considered to be private to the object. In the object defined in Listing 11.2, the only way to access the data fields `luminosity` and `location` is through the two methods, or member functions, `StarCatalogue()` and `CalculateMagnitude()`, contained in the object. Because the data is *protected* by encapsulation in the `star_class_sample` object, it cannot be altered accidentally by any external means.

In Turbo Pascal, an object is referred to as an object. In C++, an object is referred to as a class. These objects or classes exist only as definitions. In Chapter 4, "Sophisticated Data Structures," you learned that a record definition creates a blueprint, or template, for a data structure. You can't use the data structure that you have defined until you create a record variable of the type in your record definition by declaring it in your program. Similarly, in order to use an object, you must create an object definition.

Then, just as you would with a record, you must create a variable that uses the object's template by declaring an object variable.

Why Use Object-Oriented Programming?

Object-oriented programming, or *OOP*, is a new way to think about programming. Using object-oriented programming languages saves many coding steps because of a feature called *inheritance*. Inheritance makes it possible for different objects to inherit, or share, characteristics with other objects. Inheritance is discussed in greater detail later in this chapter.

After you define useful objects, they can be saved in a library, like subroutines. A *library* is a collection of code that can be reused in other projects and can save the programmer from rewriting the same code for every project. Many companies sell libraries of predefined objects that can help you write programs quickly and easily.

Structured or Object-Oriented Programming?

In a structured program, all the data is passive. A record of information is passed from one subroutine to another. In order to do anything with the data in the record, you must write an external subroutine and pass the record to it as a parameter, as you learned in Chapter 7, "Structured Programming."

In an object-oriented program, you can define an object that holds data fields in a similar way that you define a record that holds data fields. You can then include, in the object, the procedures and functions needed to manipulate the data. Functions and procedures in an object are also called *methods*. The result is an object similar to a sealed "capsule" that includes all the data fields and methods it needs. This encapsulation of data and methods is one of the key concepts of object-oriented programming.

In Turbo Pascal, you define an object type with the reserved word OBJECT, followed by the data fields and methods of the object. In C++, you define an object by using the reserved word CLASS, followed by the list of data members and member functions. In C++, the words CLASS and STRUCT are interchangeable when creating an object definition.

The procedure headers are listed in the body of the object definition. Methods that operate only on data members within the object do not require that the data members be passed as parameters. There is no need to pass an object's variables as parameters to the object's methods, because the data members are public, or global, to these methods in the class's scope. (Global and local variables, along with the concept of scope, were discussed in Chapter 7, "Structured Programming.")

In the class star_class_sample defined in Listing 11.2, there are two data fields: luminosity and location. These two data fields are inaccessible to the program outside of the object, or class. The two member functions, StarCatalogue() and CalculateMagnitude(), have direct access to the class's data, because they are included in the class. A programmer who wants to access luminosity or location must use these two member functions.

Inheritance

In object-oriented programming, the capability to create an object or class that has all the functions, data, behaviors, and properties of its parent is called *inheritance*.

Pretend for a minute that you are in the hotel business. You and your investors build a hotel. The product you are offering to the public—with the anticipation of a solid return on your investment and the prospect of a comfortable retirement—is lodging.

It's fairly safe to assume that most rooms in the hotel, from broom closets to board rooms, will share some basic characteristics. A simple definition of a room is a cube-shaped space with four walls, a ceiling, a floor, and a door at floor level in one of the walls. This is a fairly generic definition of what a room is, defining only those characteristics that all rooms are certain to share.

With this definition in mind, you can think of the generic room as your base object. It will be the fundamental concept for the space your company will rent. The generic room, which you will refer to as "Generic Room," will serve as the *parent* room from which *child* rooms will be *descended,* or *derived.*

As a test case, you can take your generic room and derive a more useful room from it. In other words, you create a "child" object of which generic room is the "parent" object. The child object inherits all the characteristics of the parent object. The child object consists of a cube-shaped space with four walls, a ceiling, a floor, and a door at floor level in one of the walls. All these elements are part of the "parent" generic room, however the broom closet will also contain a shelf and a sink, as shown in Figure 11.1. From your base object, you've just derived your first useful room.

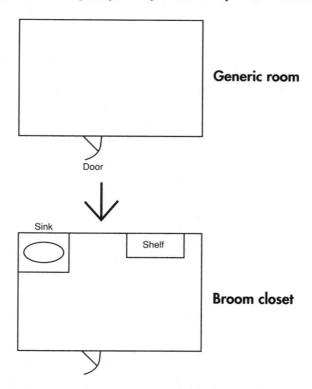

Figure 11.1. Child broom closet derived from parent generic room.

Now that you've seen how a child can inherit a parent's characteristics, you can begin building your hotel. Derive an economy room from the generic room; it will have all the characteristics of the parent generic room: four walls, a ceiling, a floor, and a door. To make this bare-bones room inhabitable and attractive to guests, add a bathroom, a rug, a double bed, and a window (so your guests can have a view of the parking lot).

Your economy rooms have been so successful that you decide to expand. You want to cater to a new class of clientele, so you upgrade the rooms to first class.

You want the first-class rooms to have all the features the economy-class rooms have, plus an extra bed, a color television, a writing desk, and another window (for an even better view of the parking lot). In this generation of inheritance, a second child is derived from the first child. It has all the characteristics of the base object and the first child, with more, unique features.

Once again, your success has emboldened you to venture even further. You decide to expand to the luxury market and create a more exclusive class of rooms. The fundamental concept is still in existence: a cube-shaped room with four walls, a floor, a ceiling, and a door. The new luxury rooms, however, will offer all the features in the economy and first-class rooms, plus cable TV, a jacuzzi, a marble sink, a returnable bathrobe, and a view of the highway instead of the parking lot.

Your hotel has grown to the point where you now want to construct a parking garage for your guests. This parking garage has all the characteristics of your generic room: It is cube-shaped, with four walls, a floor, a ceiling, and a door. Because the garage shares these characteristics, you are able to derive a new "child" from generic room, adding parking spaces, elevators, and ramps.

All these classes of rooms are derived from the parent, generic room. This derivation is called inheritance. A chart of successive generations of rooms is shown in Figure 11.2.

Object-oriented programming enables you to create an object that contains or "inherits" every data field and method from another object. The newly created object is called the child or *descendant* and the original object is called the parent or *ancestor*. The power and flexibility of inheritance is the heart of object-oriented programming, making program development easier and faster than it would be with structured programming.

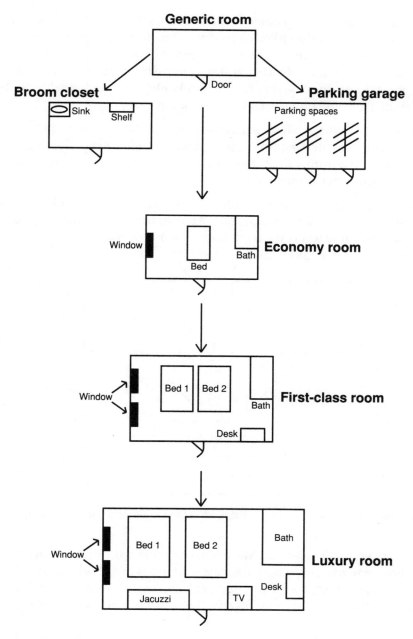

Figure 11.2. Generations of descendants from generic room.

The object will contain all the characteristics of its parent object. You can add unique characteristics to the child, such as new data fields and new methods. You can change or override methods that were inherited from the parent. These children can become parents of new objects, creating successive generations all based on the original parent. Every descendant can add another layer of functionality, and the generations can become progressively more complex.

The Turbo Pascal language allows *single inheritance.* The hotel example showed you how child objects were derived from a parent object called generic room. Each child room was descended from a single parent room. In other words, each child object inherited characteristics from only one parent object.

C++ features *multiple inheritance.* An object can have one parent or it can inherit characteristics from multiple parents. An ice cream truck, for example, combines the characteristics of two very different things—a motor vehicle and an ice cream shop, as you can see in Figure 11.3.

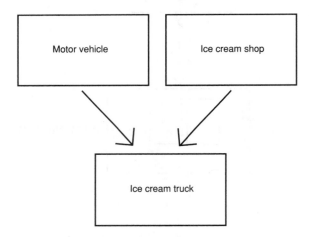

Figure 11.3. An ice cream truck as an example of multiple inheritance.

An important feature of object-oriented programming is the opportunity it affords the programmer to override a parent object's methods in a child object. When you derive a new child object from a parent object, you can create methods that have the same names as those in the parent object. The new methods override the parent's methods.

For example, in a consumer mailing list program, you can create a parent data type that contains the basic consumer information, such as name, address, and telephone number. Based on this parent type, you can then create multiple specialized consumer types without duplicating the code from the parent type. Every derived object (the child or descendant) inherits everything from the parent object.

Polymorphism

Polymorphism is a feature of object-oriented programming languages that enables you to create several versions of the same function or operator. The term comes from the combination of two Greek words: *poly*, meaning many, and *morph*, meaning form. So, to say that something is polymorphic is to say that it takes many forms.

Consider the three function prototypes in Listing 11.3.

Listing 11.3. C++ function prototypes.

```
int AddSum(int a, int b, int c)
float AddSum(float a, float b, float c)
double AddSum(double a, double b, double c)
```

Each of the functions shown in Listing 11.3 is designed to accept and return a particular data type, but each one has the same name, AddSum. In C, you can have only one function with a given name, but in C++, functions can be "overloaded" as long as the parameters differ between the overloaded functions bearing the same name.

The function AddSum is present in more than one form in Listing 11.3; this is what is meant by polymorphism. The version of AddSum from Listing 11.3 that is actually called by the compiler, depends on the values being passed as parameters. For example, if AddSum is called with three integer parameters, it will return an integer value. AddSum(4, 3, 19) would return the integer value 26. If AddSum is called with two floating point values, the float version of AddSum is invoked. AddSum(27.1, 3.8) would return 30.9, a floating point value.

Constructors and Destructors

There are special methods referred to as *constructors* and *destructors* that determine how objects are created, initialized, copied, and destroyed. When an object is created, memory is allocated in the constructor for all the data fields it contains and for the methods in it.

A *constructor* is a special kind of member function or method that is used to set up and initialize the object. The programmer must insure that all data members in the object are initialized to avoid unexpected results. Uninitialized data fields are uninitialized variables. When a variable is created, a part of your computer's memory is reserved for it. This memory is not automatically cleared, or set to zero. That area of memory might hold data from the last variable to make use of that space, or might simply hold random values that are far out of the range of values your program can operate on.

Such random values can cause unexpected results in your program, or even cause your program to stop running. This is why a variable should be initialized before it is used, preferably immediately after it is created. This initialization is normally done in the constructor.

In Turbo Pascal, the keywords CONSTRUCTOR and DESTRUCTOR are used instead of PROCEDURE or FUNCTION to distinguish these important functions from the other methods. In C++, constructor and destructor names are distinguished from all other member functions by bearing the same name as the class they belong to. The destructor's name is preceded by a tilde (~).

If a class has one or more constructors, one of them is invoked each time you define an object of that class. The constructor creates an object and initializes it. Destructors reverse the process by destroying the class objects created by constructors.

Constructors also are invoked when local or temporary objects of a class are created. Destructors are called when these objects are not needed anymore.

Constructors and destructors have many of the characteristics of normal member functions. You define a constructor or destructor in the same way that you would define a regular member function. However, they have some unique features and differ slightly in the way they are implemented between Turbo Pascal and C++.

The following features are unique to constructors and destructors:

1. Constructors and destructors do not return a value in the way that normal functions do.

2. A child can't inherit a constructor or destructor from its parent. Although a derived class can call the base class' constructors and destructors, every object must define its own constructors and destructors.

3. Constructors and destructors can be generated by the C++ compiler if they haven't been explicitly defined. They also are invoked on many occasions without explicit calls in your program. Any constructor or destructor generated by the C++ compiler will be public, or global, to the rest of the program.

4. You cannot call C++ constructors the way you call a normal function because of the special purpose that constructors serve. You can call destructors if you use their fully qualified name.

5. The C++ compiler automatically calls constructors and destructors when defining and destroying objects. In Turbo Pascal, the programmer must explicitly call both.

When there is no further need for an object, a special method called a destructor is invoked to release the memory that was allocated for this object and all of the data fields in it. This is done so the memory is freed and can be used by other parts of your program. If the destructor does not free the memory used by the object, then each time you create this object you use more of your computer's memory. Eventually, you will use all available memory and your program will stop running.

Summary

Darwin once said "Biology is destiny." Inherited traits determine functionality in living things, and (to stretch an analogy) in the classes and objects you define using object-oriented programming techniques. Every successive descendent of a base object can add new behaviors, and make use of established ones.

Object-oriented programming is an immensely powerful technique. It greatly reduces the amount of time and labor required to write a program. The larger and more complex the project, the more object-oriented programming can help to reduce that complexity.

An object is an intelligent data structure. It encapsulates all the data and methods that it needs in order to operate on that data. Any object type can have descendants that inherit all of its data members and methods. Inheritance is a powerful feature of OOP languages that enables you to design your program in a modular way.

Polymorphism, along with inheritance, helps you customize and extend functionality of base-class (parent) objects.

Constructors and destructors are special types of methods or member functions which, respectively, allocate memory and free memory used for the object.

Object-oriented programming allows greater flexibility than ever before. Many companies offer libraries of useful ready-made objects that can be used in your own programs. By using the encapsulation, inheritance, and polymorphism features, your code will be more modular and, therefore, more reusable and easier to maintain.

II

Programming Languages

Overview of Batch Files

by Jay Munro

The batch file originated in the days when computers were largely time-shared. To be cost effective, computers had to process the most information in the least amount of time, so computer tasks were grouped, or *batched*.

Batch files on the personal computer work in a similar way. A *batch file* is a group of DOS commands executed one after the other. The group of DOS commands can be useful, but the developers of DOS have added batch commands to extend the use of the batch file. Modern batch commands make up a simple, yet dynamic interpreted programming language and are available to users of any DOS-based computer. The batch command set contains programming elements (variables, remarks, statements, functions, conditionals, and input and output commands) usually associated with languages, such as BASIC, Pascal, and C. Because of this similarity, it is treated as a language in this chapter. Some batch file programs are as functional as those written in other "real languages."

The Batch File

A *batch file* is a simple ASCII or text file that you create using a word processor, the DOS editors EDIT or EDLIN, or the DOS command line. The file has a .BAT file extension, which is recognized by DOS and passed to the command interpreter for execution.

When a batch file is executed, the command interpreter reads the first command in the file and executes it. Then the interpreter reads the file again and executes the next command, and so on. The technique has both advantages and disadvantages.

A batch file's primary disadvantage is speed. The execution time of a batch file depends on the access speed of the disk drive: slow drive, slow execution. If a RAM disk is used, you can increase the access speed.

The major advantage of a batch file is that it can be modified "on the fly." A program that can change its own code as it executes is called *self-modifying code*. Writing self-modifying code is an advanced programming technique that can be used to customize the execution of a program at runtime. An early menu program, the IBM Fixed Disk Organizer, used self-modifying code to modify a user's AUTOEXEC.BAT file to run applications.

Modifying a batch program works because the batch processor keeps track only of its current position in the file. Consequently, the programmer can change subsequent lines as needed. The changes can be made either by programmatically writing the file or by copying alternate versions of the file to the version currently running.

DOS uses a special batch file called AUTOEXEC.BAT to initialize and load programs. AUTOEXEC.BAT is a reserved name that DOS looks for when it loads. The AUTOEXEC file can be run like any other .BAT file, but you should be careful not to rerun utilities that only have to be run once.

A batch filename can be any DOS filename—up to eight characters—followed by the .BAT extension. The name can describe the action the file performs. For example, a file that runs a menu can be called MENU.BAT.

In naming batch files, you must be careful not to use names that exist as .COM or .EXE files. DOS uses a hierarchy for running executable files by the same name. When you type a filename without an extension on the command line, DOS first tries to find a .COM file by the same name. Failing that, it searches for an .EXE program, and finally looks for a .BAT file. The only way around this problem is to enter the full filename, including the extension.

Why Program with Batch Files?

When you are considering writing a program in the batch language (or in any language), your first question should be: "Does the language provide the functionality I need?"

A good use for the batch language is writing programs that execute other programs. On the simplest level, an efficient DOS menu system can be built using batch files. Some shell menu systems leave a portion of the menu program in memory, using up to 80K of memory. A batch file, however, uses only a small portion of the PC's memory (50 to 100 bytes).

In addition to executing a program, a batch file can make decisions based on the result of the program. When some programs are run, they can return an ERRORLEVEL value (up to 255) that is stored by DOS. A batch file can retrieve this value and use it to select the commands in the file to run. This subject is described in more detail in the "Conditional Statements" section later in this chapter.

Output Statements

The output statement in the batch language is a command that sends text output to the screen, to the printer, or to a file. Normally, output is sent to the Standard Output device—usually the screen. If you use the redirection command (discussed later in this chapter), the standard output can be sent to a file or to the printer.

Printing to the Screen (*ECHO*)

The batch language has several ways to produce output. The ECHO command prints a message to the screen. The syntax is

```
ECHO message string
```

The output of the ECHO command goes to the standard output and is executed in the TTY mode. (The TTY mode is named after the old teletype machines that printed a line of text, moved down a line, then printed the next line.)

TTY output is line oriented, so the only supported formatting commands are space, backspace, tab, carriage return, and linefeed. Formatting characters are entered as control characters. With certain text editors, you may have trouble entering control characters into a batch file. Sometimes the key is interpreted by the editor as an editing command, rather than a character being input. Many text editors require you to use a command that tells the editor to just send the code for the key to the text and not to interpret it. In the DOS 5 Edit program, you can press Ctrl-P, and then the Ctrl or Alt key combination you want to send to the file.

Not all editors enable you to enter all keys, so check the documentation on your particular editor. If you're entering control codes from the command line, most (not all) codes can be entered by holding down the Alt key and entering the code on the number pad. For example, to put the character for a page feed into a file (ASCII 12), press Alt followed by 12 on the number pad. In an editor, the symbol will be the female graphic character, on the command line, it will be a ^L.

One useful control character is the BELL character, or Ctrl-G. When echoed to the screen, this character makes a beep sound. A program can signal the end of a process by echoing several Ctrl-G characters. For example, the batch file shown in Listing 12.1 uses Ctrl-G to indicate when it has finished copying a set of files.

Listing 12.1. The SAMPLE1.BAT program.

```
ECHO OFF
COPY A:*.* B:
ECHO ^G
ECHO Finished!
```

The ECHO command also controls whether other batch file instructions are printed to the screen. If you use the ECHO OFF command in the first line of a batch program, when the ECHO command is used later in the program, the word ECHO is not dis-played—only the output of the ECHO command is printed on-screen.

If you don't include the ECHO OFF command, the SAMPLE1.BAT file would show the following on-screen:

```
C:>COPY A:*.* B:
COPY A:*.* B:
C:>ECHO ^G

C:>ECHO MESSAGE STRING
ECHO MESSAGE STRING
```

When a program is run, the ECHO command prints on-screen unless the ECHO OFF command is specified beforehand. Most programmers put ECHO OFF as the first statement in the batch program. To turn the echoing of commands back on, you use the ECHO ON command.

Clear Screen (*CLS*)

For neater output, most programmers send a CLS after the ECHO OFF at the start of a program to provide a clear screen for any upcoming output. The CLS command clears the screen and places the cursor in the upper-left corner. Subsequent printing starts at that point. The CLS command can be placed anywhere in the program.

Text Files (*TYPE*)

Sometimes it is easier to create a screen in a word processor, and then store it in a file for display by a batch file. The TYPE command accepts a filename and sends that file to the screen in the same way the ECHO command prints hard coded text.

One use of the TYPE command is to display a list of choices for a menu. For this example, you create two files: MENU.TXT containing the text of the list to choose from, and MENU.BAT containing the commands to display the list of choices.

The MENU.TXT file contains the following:

```
1 - Lotus 1-2-3
2 - Microsoft Word
3 - Microsoft Flight Simulator
Enter the number of your selection and press <ENTER>
```

The MENU.BAT file contains

```
ECHO OFF
CLS
TYPE MENU.TXT
```

If the user selects choice number one, the 1.BAT file is executed. The 1.BAT file might contain the following code:

```
CD\LOTUS
123
CD\
MENU
```

If the user selects choice number two, the 2.BAT file is executed. The 2.BAT file might contain the following code:

```
CD\WORD
WORD
CD\
MENU
```

Finally, if the user selects choice number three, the 3.BAT file is executed. The 3.BAT file might contain the following code:

```
CD\FLIGHT
FS
CD\
MENU
```

The MENU.BAT program clears the screen using the CLS command, and then displays the MENU.TXT file for the choices. MENU.BAT then ends, and the user is sitting looking at the choices. If the user selects the second menu option, for example, DOS executes the 2.BAT batch file. When the batch file finishes, it reruns the original MENU.BAT program to display the menu again.

Keyboard Input (*PAUSE*)

The PAUSE command is essentially a simple input routine. It can accept two kinds of input: a keypress or a Ctrl-Break. The PAUSE command is useful when the batch program must stop so that the user can do something, such as change disks or read a message.

A time-honored use for batch files is in installation programs, which copy program files from a floppy disk to a hard disk. The following batch program shows a simple installation that copies files from the floppy in drive A: to the hard disk, and then pauses for a disk change:

```
ECHO OFF
ECHO Insert Disk 1 in Drive A:
PAUSE
COPY A:*.* C:
ECHO Insert Disk 2 in Drive A:
PAUSE
.
.
.
```

When the PAUSE command is executed by the batch interpreter, it prints the message

```
Press any key to continue . . .
```

and then waits for a keypress. When the user presses any key—except Ctrl-Break—the batch file continues. The Ctrl-Break combination stops execution of the batch file and displays the following message:

```
Terminate batch job (Y/N)?
```

Pressing Y stops the batch file. This action can be useful in an AUTOEXEC batch file that runs a program that might need to be aborted occasionally. For example:

```
ECHO To continue and do your tape backup for the night,
ECHO press any key. If you do not want to back up,
ECHO press Ctrl-Break to stop and answer yes to
ECHO terminate the batch job.
PAUSE
.
.
.
```

File Output (> and >>)

Although the batch language does not have a direct file access command like that found in higher-level languages, file output can be accomplished using the redirection commands. The redirection character (>) redirects standard output to another DOS device. A DOS device is one that can be accessed by name, such as a file, a printer (LPT1) or a comm port (COM1).

When a batch command uses the > character to direct standard output to a file, a file is created each time the command is executed. Most DOS commands send their screen output through standard output, so the following batch command could be used to keep a catalog of filenames on a disk:

```
DIR > CATFILE.TXT
```

The DIR (directory) command by itself sends its listing to the screen. With these additions, however, the output is sent to the CATFILE.TXT file. If the command is executed again, the old CATFILE.TXT file will be overwritten with a new one.

You can also add to an existing file. The redirection command >> creates the file if it does not exist, or adds to the file if it already exists.

The batch file language also supports *piping*, in which input and output are piped through other utilities. The MORE utility is used with the pipe character (¦) to provide a paged listing of directories, text files, and the like.

Branching (*GOTO*)

In Chapter 5, "Making Decisions," you saw how the most efficient programs do not always work in a linear fashion. The batch language supports only one branching command, GOTO.

The GOTO command unconditionally jumps from the current line to a specified label. The syntax for the GOTO statement is

```
GOTO label
```

The *label* can be anywhere in the program, before or after the current position. A *label* is a name or group of characters that identifies a part of a program and acts as the target of a GOTO. The following batch program could be used to copy files from one floppy to another, until you press Ctrl-Break:

```
ECHO OFF
:StartHere
ECHO Insert source in drive A: and destination in drive B:
```

```
ECHO Press Ctrl-Break when finished
PAUSE
XCOPY /s /e A: B:
GOTO StartHere
```

This is a simple program, but it can save you keystrokes when copying several disks.

A label must always begin with a colon. Labels are not case sensitive, so you can be as creative as you want. Also, as with most languages, the label cannot contain spaces. Following are some examples:

```
:EXIT
:END
:Start_Here
:Read_Disk_A
```

Conditional Statements

In Chapter 5, you learned that programmers use conditional statements to control the logical flow of a program. The batch language also provides support for making decisions within your programs.

The *IF* Statement

The power of the batch file may well lie in its ability to make a decision based on input. The IF batch statement says "If condition is true, then do something."

The condition can be the result of a program running—error level—or an explicit comparison of two values or variables. When two things are compared, the computer stores a True or a False value. If the condition to be tested is a function, such as EXIST, it returns the True or False value, which the IF statement can act on. If the condition is a comparison of two variables and the two are the same, the condition is True. If the two are not the same, the condition is False. Variables are discussed in detail later in this chapter.

The following example uses the EXIST batch function to copy a file:

```
IF EXIST TODAY.TXT COPY TODAY.TXT B:
```

This one line of batch code tests whether the TODAY.TXT file is present; if the file exists, it is copied to drive B:. A batch file with hardcoded conditionals is limited to doing only what was specified when the batch file was written. Later, if you need to copy a different file, the batch file must be rewritten. However, if you add the preceding line to your AUTOEXEC.BAT file, the TODAY.TXT file would automatically be backed up each time the computer is rebooted.

Executing a single command or function such as COPY is not always useful in itself. Adding the GOTO command and a label makes the COPY command more functional. The following code fragment could be used in a software installation batch file:

```
:CHANGEDISK
IF EXIST DISK2.ID GOTO NEXTLABEL
ECHO Put disk 2 in drive A
PAUSE
GOTO CHANGEDISK
:NEXTLABEL
COPY
.
.
.
```

This batch file is getting complicated. If DISK2.ID is present, the code goes to the NEXTLABEL label and continues working. If DISK2.ID is missing, the batch file drops down to the next line and executes the ECHO command. The ECHO command prints the message asking the user to insert the disk that contains the .ID file.

Now that the user has been prompted to change disks, the batch file stops at the PAUSE statement. The PAUSE command prompts the user to press a key to continue and waits for the user's response. After the user complies, the batch file executes GOTO CHANGEDISK, which brings the program back to the original test for the file.

Caution:

A batch file is executed one line at a time. DOS reads each line as if someone typed it on the command line. The batch processor in DOS keeps track of the line in the batch file that it is executing and opens and reads the next line every time it finishes with the previous line. If the file is removed or erased in the process, DOS displays the BATCH FILE MISSING error message. If you want a batch file to work over several disks, as in an installation program, put a copy of the installation batch file on every disk to be installed prior to running. DOS does not care whether it reads the original file or a copy, as long as the file has the same name and length as the original batch file and is located in the same drive.

The *NOT* Operator

The NOT operator can be used with the IF statement to test the opposite condition or when a condition fails. For example, IF EXIST tests whether a file exists and IF NOT EXIST tests whether the file does not exist. The following example illustrates how NOT EXISTS could be used in the code fragment shown in the preceding section:

```
IF NOT EXIST DISK2.ID GOTO NEXTLABEL
```

Adding this statement makes your batch program more flexible by letting you test either condition easily. IF and IF NOT may be used with functions, such as EXIST, or with string or variable comparisons, as described in the next section.

Using Variables for Comparisons

You can input up to ten variables or parameters at a time in your batch program. The variables are numbered 0 through 9 and are represented by the symbols %0, %1, %2, and so on. Variable %0 is a special case; it represents the name of the batch file that is currently running. The other variables are replaced by parameters that you type after the batch filename on the command line.

For example, suppose you want to copy a series of files (each with a different extension) to different directories and then erase them from the current directory. Your batch file, called SRCCOPY.BAT, is shown in Listing 12.2.

Listing 12.2. The **SRCCOPY.BAT** file.

```
COPY %1.C   D:\SOURCE
ERASE %1.C
COPY %1.H   D:\HEADERS
ERASE %1.H
COPY %1.OBJ D:\OBJECTS
ERASE %1.OBJ
```

Now, suppose the incoming parameter is PROJECT, a filename without an extension. On the command line, you type

```
SRCCOPY PROJECT
```

and press Enter. DOS starts executing the SRCCOPY batch file and replaces the %1 variables with the name PROJECT. The program runs as if the filename PROJECT was hard-coded:

```
COPY PROJECT.C   D:\SOURCE
ERASE PROJECT.C
COPY PROJECT.H   D:\HEADERS
ERASE PROJECT.H
COPY PROJECT.OBJ D:\OBJECTS
ERASE PROJECT.OBJ
```

Variables can also be used to add flexibility to IF statements. The SRCCOPY.BAT file works as long as you give it a filename without an extension. If you did give the batch file a file with an extension, the filename would end up with two extensions (for example, PROJECT.C.C.) and DOS wouldn't know what to do with the file.

To avoid this, you could test whether the specified file exists, as follows:

```
IF EXIST %1 GOTO END
COPY PROJECT.C   D:\SOURCE
ERASE PROJECT.C
COPY PROJECT.H   D:\HEADERS
ERASE PROJECT.H
COPY PROJECT.OBJ D:\OBJECTS
ERASE PROJECT.OBJ
:END
```

The test at the beginning checks whether the file exists, before the batch file tries to copy it. A programmer should always try to make programs as well behaved as possible. The term *robust* is used to describe how well a program can handle errors.

Variables can also be compared using the == operator. When used in an IF statement, an expression using two variables and the == operator creates a conditional that provides a true or false result.

For example, FILECMP.BAT compares the contents of two files, but will abort if one or the other variable is not provided (see Listing 12.3).

Listing 12.3. The FILECMP.BAT file.

```
IF "%1"=="" GOTO ERRORMSG1
IF "%2"=="" GOTO ERRORMSG1
  FC %1 %2
GOTO EXIT
:ERRORMSG1
ECHO Syntax  FILECMP [File1] [File2]
:EXIT
```

FOR Loops

The FOR loop is a powerful but often overlooked feature of the batch file language. When a DOS command must be executed repeatedly, it is a good candidate for inclusion in a FOR loop.

A FOR loop has the following format:

```
FOR placeholder IN (set) DO command
```

The FOR loop puts the items in *set* one-by-one into the *placeholder*. The following example is a batch file that finds a filename that matches a certain type, or mask, and puts it on the screen:

```
FOR %%A IN (*.EXE) DO ECHO %%A
```

The FOR command instructs DOS to look for files that match the *.EXE specification and put the matching files one-by-one into the %%A placeholder. The ECHO statement then prints whatever follows it to the screen. When used in a FOR command, the variable is a single letter and is prefaced by two % signs.

This example is unimaginative; it could easily have been accomplished with a DIR *.EXE command. By using the FOR command with the %%A variable, however, you can execute programs that do not normally accept wildcards (many compilers do not allow wildcards). For example:

```
FOR %%A IN (*.BAS) DO BC %%A
```

In this example, the program loops while it finds files with a .BAS extension, which signifies a BASIC file. The matching BASIC file is assigned to %%A in the program. The compiler (BC.EXE) is executed by the batch file with the %%A command-line argument, which contains a filename. The BC compiler normally accepts only a full filename, not wildcards.

Subroutines

As mentioned earlier, the batch command language supports labels and GOTO, but those result in one-way jumps. There is no formal GOSUB RETURN convention for the batch language, but DOS 3.2 and later support the CALL statement.

In a batch language program, an .EXE or .COM program always returns to the batch file when completed. However, because DOS can have only one batch file running at a time, you cannot run a second batch file and return to the first. When the second batch file starts executing, it becomes the currently running file; the first file is forgotten.

To overcome this limitation, the designers of DOS started supporting the CALL command. With the CALL command, you can begin to execute a batch file, and then branch or CALL a second batch file. When the second file terminates, control is returned to the first batch program.

Batch programs can be written to execute as subroutines to the main program. You can pass parameters on the command line from the main program to the subroutine, just as if the subprogram was executed by itself. For example, consider the following batch program, called MAIN.BAT:

```
ECHO OFF
ECHO Running the XYZSort batch with %1 datalist
CALL XYZSORT %1
ECHO Finished with sort
PAUSE
.
.
.
```

The MAIN.BAT program is executed with the MYFILE command-line argument. The ECHO line is just a user-friendly prompt to tell the user which file is being used for the sort. In the CALL XYZSort line, the %1 parameter passes the MYFILE name to the XYZSort batch file. When XYZSort has finished its work, it returns control to the MAIN.BAT program, which then continues.

Summary

The batch command set contains many basic components found in more sophisticated languages. By using thought and creativity in writing batch programs, you can automate many mundane tasks. As with any language, the batch command language should be used for appropriate tasks. You would not think to write a spreadsheet program as a batch file. You could, however, create a batch file that runs Lotus 1-2-3, for example, then copies the files to a backup disk when you have finished.

Many magazines have featured utilities for enhancing batch files. Shareware packages are also available to provide your batch files with special input routines, color, file handling, date and time handling, and many other programming tasks.

13

Overview of Database Languages

by Dave Linthicum

Many database management systems (DBMS) on the market today come standard with a built-in programming language. These high-level languages assist database programmers in the creation of custom database applications by automating the functions and facilities of the DBMS. Chapter 18, "Database Products," presents several major players in the PC database industry—dBASE, FoxPro, Clipper, and Paradox. All four database systems support special programming languages for the creation of custom database applications.

Most businesses today prefer to use the development environment built into database systems, thereby decreasing the amount of time required to develop applications. These built-in development environments, however, have not always been an option. In the past, database applications were programmed using a low-level programming language such as COBOL or FORTRAN. These applications were time-consuming to build because the complex database operations had to be developed along with the functions of the application. Database sorts, queries, appends, edits, and reports had to be written from scratch using the limited constructs of the more primitive languages. Fortunately, times have changed, and thousands of computer consultants now earn their living programming in languages provided by DBMSs, such as dBASE, FoxPro, Clipper, and Paradox.

The high-level application programming languages that come with these database products are known as *fourth-generation languages,* or *4GLs.* 4GLs are built on more generalized languages, such as C, which is a third-generation language (3GL). 4GLs are usually created for particular purposes, such as statistical analysis, artificial intelligence, or database applications development. By using 4GLs for database application development, you can create entire accounting systems, inventory control systems, and other complex business applications much more quickly than using C, Pascal, or BASIC.

In this chapter, you learn the fundamentals of two of these fourth-generation languages: xBASE and PAL. The *xBASE* language is supported by dBASE IV, FoxPro, and Clipper and is considered by many to be the "industry standard" database programming language for microcomputers. Although there are differences in the xBASE language from product to product, its general look and feel remains the same.

The Paradox DBMS supports its own proprietary language called *PAL* (Paradox Application Language). PAL and Paradox, although used by a smaller community, have maintained a consistent following over the years. Many consider Paradox and PAL the preferred database platform. This chapter covers both PAL and xBASE and illustrates the key features of both languages.

The primary advantage in using a 4GL—such as xBASE or PAL—over a 3GL is in the power of the language. Sort routines, search routines, and other standard database operations are built directly into the xBASE and PAL languages. More complex operations and problems of low-level file input/output are handled by the DBMS. This means that as a programmer, you can spend more of your time on the function of the application.

Introduction to xBASE

Ashton-Tate's dBASE DBMS products brought a sophisticated and powerful method for creating database applications to the small but growing number of microcomputers. Small businesses that could only afford microcomputers now had a method to create custom database applications using hardware and software at only a fraction of the cost of a mainframe or minicomputer.

dBASE became the standard database development environment. Although other products were developed to compete in the million dollar DBMS market, Ashton-Tate remained dominant. These other products, sometimes called "dBASE clones," could run or compile dBASE applications with little or no modifications and, in some cases, looked almost identical to the dBASE user interface. These clones provided not only an alternative to dBASE, but also additional features and enhancements not offered by the Ashton-Tate product, including greater speed, a better development environment, and above all, a cheaper price tag.

As you might have guessed, the presence of these products made Ashton-Tate nervous. In the late 1980s, Ashton-Tate filed lawsuits to protect its rights to the dBASE language. To make a long story short, Ashton-Tate lost on the grounds that the dBASE language was originally created for a government concern (NASA's Jet Propulsion Lab) and therefore was not the soul property of Ashton-Tate or anyone else. That historical court decision turned the dBASE language into the xBASE language, removing the ties to Ashton-Tate and dBASE products. Today, most database programmers refer to the standard database language that was dBASE as xBASE.

The Concept of xBASE

Today, the xBASE language is considered to be the standard for programming database applications on microcomputers. The xBASE language is supported by several different DBMS products, including dBASE IV, Clipper, and FoxPro. It is important to mention that although the basics of the language are generally the same from product to product, most of the products have their own enhancements to the xBASE language. If you write a program in one product and utilize specific product enhancements, you might have some compatibility problems if you run the program on a different DBMS product.

The concept that a program written in xBASE is portable among all xBASE products is limited. If a programmer utilizes commands only supported by a particular product, the program is then tied to that product and portability is diminished. By not using product-specific enhancements, it is possible to create xBASE programs that are able to move from product to product; but most programmers take advantage of the advanced features of their xBASE interpreter or compiler.

It also is interesting to note that the xBASE language is not limited to microcomputers or MS-DOS. Several database management systems—including dBASE IV—have moved to other operating systems, such as UNIX. xBASE compilers and interpreters can even be found on mini- and mainframe computers.

The xBASE language is here to stay. Its survivability is greatly enhanced by the number of database products that utilize it. Organizations that utilize xBASE can be assured that programs they develop using xBASE will have a product available to run the application in the future. Even if the product that the application was originally developed in is no longer available, other interpreters and compilers can certainly be found. The xBASE language has become a standard language for database programming on microcomputers.

xBASE Interpreters and Compilers

In order to run an xBASE application, you must select an interpreter or compiler (see the "Compilers and Interpreters" discussion in Chapter 14, "Overview of BASIC"). As mentioned earlier, there are several xBASE products from which to choose. Some of these products are compilers, which create an MS-DOS executable file (.EXE) that you or your user can execute from the DOS command line. The remaining xBASE products are interpreters. An interpreter is a software program that "interprets" each line of program code as the program runs and immediately performs the specified action. In the xBASE world, Clipper is considered to be a true compiler, whereas dBase and FoxPro are considered to be interpreters. The Paradox DBMS is also considered to be an interpreter; it is discussed later.

Selecting an xBASE interpreter or compiler is much like buying a car—it requires some research to make an educated decision. Do not let reviews in computer-related magazines make your decision for you. You first must define your requirements and then select the best product to meet those requirements.

xBASE Programming

This section introduces you to the general programming concepts of xBASE. It covers the basic program syntax and structure, including the following basic functions:

- Database operations
- Program branching and operators
- Looping
- Screen writing
- Printing

The xBASE Program

First, let's look at a simple xBASE program. Don't be overwhelmed by the details right now, just try to understand the general concepts presented. xBASE programs usually have the extension .PRG and are executed from interpreters with the DO command. For example, to execute the program from Listing 13.1 using dBASE IV, you would type

DO XBASE

The program in Listing 13.1 displays a menu with four options. The program performs a few simple database functions or exits from the program to MS-DOS, depending on which item is selected.

Listing 13.1. An xBASE program that creates a menu.

```
****************************************************************
*    XBASE.PRG   Sample xBASE program                         *
****************************************************************
* Setup the Environment
SET ECHO OFF                        && Commands not displayed
SET TALK OFF                        && Command results not displayed
SET STATUS OFF                      && Turn the status bar off
SET COLOR TO +W/N                   && Change the screen colors

DO WHILE .T.                        && Program Menu Loop
   CLEAR                            && Clear the screen
   @ 8,30 SAY  "M A I N    M E N U" && ---|
   @12,30 SAY  " (A)ppend the Clients" &&     |
   @14,30 SAY  " (E)dit the Clients" &&       > Write to the screen
   @16,30 SAY  " (P)rint the Clients" &&    |
   @18,30 SAY  "e(X)it"              && ---|
   STORE "X" TO ANSWER              && Store a default value
   @20,37 GET ANSWER                && Prompt the user
   READ                             && Read the information

   DO CASE

   CASE UPPER(ANSWER)="A"           && If user presses A
      USE CLIENTS                   && Open the database file
      APPEND                        && Add records
      CLOSE DATABASE                && Close the database file

   CASE UPPER(ANSWER)="E"           && If user presses E
      USE CLIENTS                   && Open the database file
      EDIT                          && Edit the database
      CLOSE DATABASE                && Close the database file
```

continues

Listing 13.1. Continued

```
CASE UPPER(ANSWER)="P"          && If user presses P
    USE CLIENTS                 && Open the database file
    LIST TO PRINT               && List records to the printer
    EJECT                       && Eject to the top of page
    CLOSE DATABASE              && Close the database file

CASE UPPER(ANSWER)="X"          && If user presses X
    QUIT                        && Quit to DOS

ENDCASE

ENDDO                           && Loop
```

Comments

xBASE uses the asterisk (*) to denote a comment. When the xBASE interpreter or compiler reads an asterisk at the beginning of a program line, that line of code is ignored. Alternatively, you can use a double ampersand (&&) to place a comment directly after a command, on the same line. The && tells the compiler or interpreter where the command ends and the comment begins.

Functions and Expressions

Just as C provides built-in functions for many general tasks and user-defined functions so that you can encapsulate specific tasks, xBASE provides built-in functions that do a variety of things. Most xBASE products also enable you to define your own functions, which are called *user-defined functions*, or UDFs. Like most languages you have seen so far in this book, xBASE functions are easily recognized by the parentheses (()) that follow the function name. Functions generally have the following format:

FunctionName(Argument)

An argument is a parameter or a set of parameters required by the function. An argument can be a data field, another function, or anything that the particular function may require. For example, Listing 13.1 included the following line:

UPPER(ANSWER)="A"

The function UPPER()—one of many xBASE string functions—converts to uppercase the entire contents of the string stored in the variable ANSWER. Therefore, if the user entered a lowercase *a*, it would be converted to uppercase *A*. In contrast, xBASE provides a LOWER() function to convert the entire contents of a string to lowercase and a TRIM() function to delete the blank spaces from a string variable.

Several functions, referred to as *database-oriented functions*, do not require that you supply an argument. They are called database-oriented functions because they provide information to the program pertaining to the status of the database file. You can use these functions to get valuable information from open database files. Some examples are shown in the following:

Are we at the end of the file?	EOF()
How many records are in the current database?	RECC()
What is the current record number?	RECNO()
Is this database record marked for deletion?	DELETED()

Expressions enable you to represent data fields, memory variables, constants, or any combination of these. The types of expressions supported by xBASE can be divided into arithmetic expressions and alphanumeric expressions.

Arithmetic expressions contain values, memory variables, or numeric data fields. These values must be joined by one or more arithmetic operators (+, -, *. /, and others). For example:

```
STORE .10 TO SALES_COM
STORE 10000 TO SALES
TAX_RATE = .30
GROSS_PAY = (SALES_COM*SALES)
NET_PAY = (GROSS_PAY-(GROSS_PAY*TAX_RATE))
```

Alphanumeric expressions enable you to modify the way in which alphanumeric information is displayed. You can use alphanumeric strings enclosed in quotation marks, alphanumeric memory variables, and alphanumeric data fields—or any combination of these—in an alphanumeric expression. These items can be joined by the plus sign (+). For example,

```
STORE "Linthicum" TO LAST_NAME
STORE "Dave    " TO FIRST_NAME
?"The Writers name is :"+FIRST_NAME+" "+LAST_NAME
```

The question mark (?) forces the expressions to be evaluated and displayed on-screen. As you can see, the xBASE expressions provide the necessary functions to display data in any way you desire. You can even combine functions and expressions to get a desired effect. For example:

```
?"The Writers name is :"+TRIM(FIRST_NAME)+" "+LAST_NAME
```

This expression uses the TRIM() function to strip the blank spaces from the variable FIRST_NAME.

Database Operations

Several database operations are supported directly by the xBASE language. As shown in Figure 13.1, the APPEND command places the user directly in a data-entry screen. The user can append data to the database until he or she presses either Esc or a set of keys defined by the xBASE product. In contrast, the EDIT command places the user at a similar screen where he or she can edit the data already in the database. The USE command connects the program to a particular database file. After the file is attached, the information in the database can be read, altered, and deleted by the program.

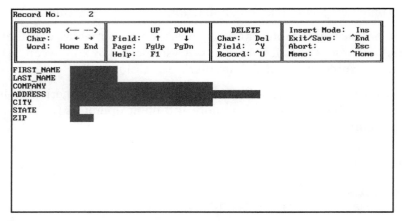

Figure 13.1. A sample *APPEND* screen.

Another command supported by the xBASE language is the BROWSE command. Like EDIT, the BROWSE command enables the user to modify data already in the database. Unlike the EDIT command, however, BROWSE displays data in a tabular format, allowing the user to edit several records at one time (see Figure 13.2). The BROWSE command is not supported by the Clipper DBMS, but Clipper does have its own command which emulates BROWSE.

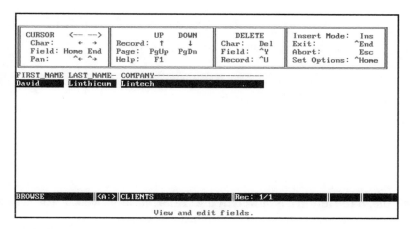

```
CURSOR    <-- -->        UP    DOWN      DELETE         Insert Mode:  Ins
Char:      ←  →   Record:  ↑     ↓    Char:   Del    Exit:        ^End
Field: Home End   Page:  PgUp  PgDn   Field:  ^Y     Abort:        Esc
Pan:      ^←  ^→  Help:   F1           Record: ^U     Set Options: ^Home

FIRST_NAME LAST_NAME- COMPANY-----------------------------------------
David      Linthicum  Lintech




BROWSE          |<A:>|CLIENTS             |Rec: 1/1
                    View and edit fields.
```

Figure 13.2. A sample *BROWSE* screen.

Displaying the Data

Just as a database can add and edit data in several ways, it can also display the information in several ways. You can use the LIST command to simply list the contents of the database to the screen. For example, the following set of commands lists the entire contents of the CLIENTS database on-screen:

```
USE CLIENTS
LIST
```

The DISPLAY command works in a similar way, although only one record is displayed on-screen. You often find two or more commands in xBASE that do basically the same thing. This was brought about by the evolution of the xBASE language. Commands that were supported by dBASE II are still supported today. This provides *upward compatibility,* or the ability to run older programs under newer compilers or interpreters. The dBASE II DBMS was the first version of dBASE, followed by dBASE III, and then dBASE III PLUS. dBASE IV is the most current version available.

Program Branching and Operators

As with most other programming languages, the xBASE language supports IF-ELSE, or Boolean logic, enabling you to make decisions within the program. For example:

```
IF Condition
    .
    .                  && If condition is met, do this
    .
```

```
ELSE
   .
   .                    && If condition is not met, do this
   .
ENDIF
```

The actual xBASE code might look like this:

```
IF ANSWER="Y"
   APPEND
ELSE
   EDIT
ENDIF
```

In this example, if the letter *Y* is stored in the xBASE variable ANSWER, the APPEND command is invoked; if not, the EDIT command is invoked.

The DO CASE-ENDCASE command provides multiple-condition checking for a multiple-condition section. In the following xBASE program, the DO CASE statement is used to check the menu selection that was entered by the user. When the user enters a selection, that selection is evaluated by the DO CASE statement. If *condition* is True, the commands under the DO CASE statement are executed. For example:

```
DO CASE
CASE UPPER(ANSWER)="A"              && If user presses A
    USE CLIENTS                     && Open the database file
    APPEND                          && Add records
    CLOSE DATABASE                  && Close the database file
    ENDCASE
```

Generally, DO CASE-ENDCASE commands are used for menu processing as demonstrated in the sample xBASE program, but all types of conditional operations can be applied to this command.

Logical operators enable you to add complex decision-making capabilities to the commands provided by xBASE. The basic operators are .AND., .NOT., and .OR. For example, if you would like the APPEND command to execute only when a check variable is set to *Y*, and you are at the end of the database file, you might use the following code:

```
IF CHECKVAR="Y" .AND. EOF()
   APPEND
ELSE
   EDIT
ENDIF
```

You can also use logical operators in loops. For example:

```
DO WHILE .NOT. EOF() .AND. AMOUNT> 0 .OR. BALANCE < 0
.
.
.
ENDDO
```

This command would loop as long as you are not at the end of the database file and one of the following is True: the database field AMOUNT is greater than 0, or the database field BALANCE is less than 0.

Variables

The xBASE language provides several types of variables that enable you to temporarily store string, numeric, date, and logical information. Variables do not have to be predefined, or *allocated*. Within a program, variables can be assigned values using the STORE command or using an equal sign (=). For example:

```
STORE "DAVE" TO FNAME        && Stores word Dave into FNAME
TODAY = DATE()               && Stores todays date in TODAY
AMOUNT = 800                 && Stores number 800 to AMOUNT
ACCOUNT = "10201"            && Stores String "10201" to ACCOUNT
ISRIGHT = .T.                && Stores logical true to ISRIGHT
```

The information is retained in the variables while the program executes. When the program is completed, the information stored in xBASE variables—and the xBASE variables themselves—disappear.

Looping

The xBASE language has looping capabilities that provide you with the ability to easily perform a given operation over and over. The DO WHILE, and ENDDO commands provide this functionality for xBASE.

```
DO WHILE Condition
.
.                    && If condition is met, do this
.
ENDDO
```

As you saw in Listing 13.1, a loop can be utilized to redisplay a menu after each menu selection is processed. Other uses for a loop include performing some sort of repetitive database operation that needs to proceed until a predefined condition is met. For example, if you wanted to move through a database record-by-record, you could do the following:

```
DO WHILE .NOT. EOF()
   SKIP
ENDDO
```

The SKIP command skips to the next record in the database. When the .NOT. EOF() condition is False after a SKIP command is issued, the program loop is terminated. The loop command used in Listing 13.1,

```
DO WHILE .T.
```

continues looping until the program exits the loop—usually with an EXIT command. In Listing 13.1, the QUIT command is used to exit from the program loop and return to DOS.

Screen Writing

Several xBASE commands write information to the screen. The most popular is the @SAY command, pronounced "at say." @SAY not only enables you to display words and numbers on-screen, but also enables you to dictate exactly where on-screen the information should be placed. For example,

```
@ 10, 12 Say "Hello World!"
```

would display Hello World starting on line 10 at column 12. In Listing 13.1, the @SAY command is used to create the menu. The @SAY command provides a facility to custom design screens.

Getting Data from the User

Just as you can display data using the @SAY command, you can get information from the user with the @GET command. As demonstrated in Listing 13.1, you can use the @GET command to tell the program the screen location of the information being retrieving. For example, from Listing 13.1, @GET is used to prompt the user for a menu selection:

```
STORE "X" TO ANSWER        && Store a default value
@20,37 GET ANSWER          && Prompt the user
READ                       && Read the information
```

The user is prompted for a menu selection—at line 20, column 37—to be stored in the variable ANSWER. This variable must first be created. In this example, the STORE command is used to place the character X into ANSWER. The @GET command is then issued, but the command doesn't actually work until the READ command is invoked.

@GET is implemented in this way so that additional @GET commands can be utilized, if required.

The @SAY and @GET commands are used to display information to, and get information from, the terminal. If you run the program from Listing 13.1, the screen would display the menu selections and prompt the user for input (see Figure 13.3).

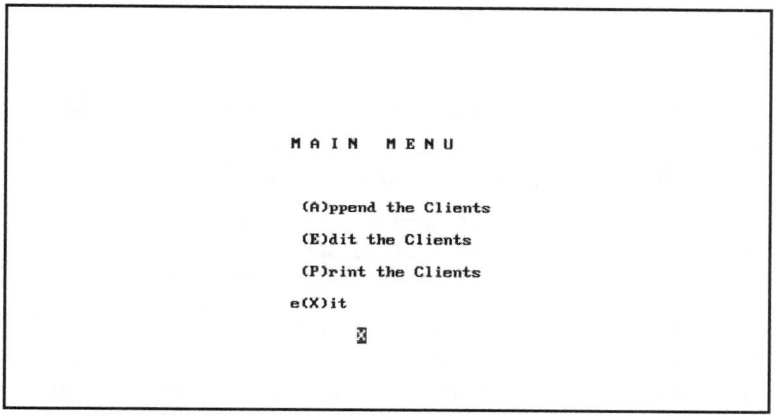

```
        M A I N    M E N U


        (A)ppend the Clients

        (E)dit the Clients

        (P)rint the Clients

        e(X)it
               ▨
```

Figure 13.3. Using *@SAY* and *@GET* to create a menu.

Setting the Environment

The xBASE language uses the SET command to set up the program environment. There are several things that you can control, including the screen color, sound, whether or not program commands are displayed on-screen, and whether a status bar is displayed on-screen. To invoke the SET command, enter:

SET *feature*

where *feature* is a specific program environment feature that can be altered.

The following code example illustrates several items that you can control with the SET command.

```
SET ECHO OFF              && Commands not displayed.
SET TALK OFF              && Command results not displayed.
SET STATUS OFF            && Turn the status bar off.
SET COLOR TO +W/N         && Change the screen colors.
```

This code lets xBASE know that you do not want the program commands displayed on-screen as they execute (SET ECHO OFF), that you do not want the results of those commands to be displayed (SET TALK OFF), that you do not want a status bar at the bottom of the screen (SET STATUS OFF), and that you want the foreground color set to an intense white and the background color to black (SET COLOR TO +W/N).

Printing

Printing in xBASE is fairly straightforward. For example:

```
USE CLIENTS
LIST
```

prints the entire contents of the CLIENTS database on-screen. If you wanted to send that same listing to the printer, you would add TO PRINT to the end of the LIST command. The following is a print command from Listing 13.1:

```
USE CLIENTS          && Open the database file
LIST TO PRINT        && List records to the printer
EJECT                && Eject to the top of page
```

The EJECT command moves the print head to the top of the page. The basic idea in xBASE is that if you can display information to the screen, that information can also be sent to the printer by adding the TO PRINT command option after the LIST command. Several other methods of printing are also available, here are a few examples:

```
SET PRINTER ON
SET PRINTER OFF
```

When the SET PRINTER ON command has been invoked, all the information normally displayed on-screen using @SAY is also sent to the printer. When SET PRINTER OFF is invoked, the information is no longer sent to the printer.

```
SET DEVICE TO PRINT
SET DEVICE TO SCREEN
```

As in the preceding example, when SET DEVICE TO PRINT is invoked, all information normally displayed on-screen, with the exception of @SAY output, is directed to the printer. The SET DEVICE TO SCREEN diverts the information back to the screen.

You can create custom reports using the report-generating facilities provided with most xBASE products. For example, you can send an xBASE report to the printer with the following code:

```
USE CLIENTS                && Open the database file
REPORT FORM CLIREP TO PRINT   && Print out report "CLIREP"
```

Structured Programming with xBASE

As with other high-level and low-level programming languages, you can call an xBASE program from within another xBASE program. This is done by simply executing the DO *ProgramName* command from within an xBASE program. xBASE programs can call other programs, which in turn can call other programs, and so on.

There are limits pertaining to the number of times you can *nest,* or call one program from within another program. These limits are defined by the xBASE product that you use. You use the RETURN command to tell xBASE when to return to the calling program. When the RETURN command is issued from the called program, the control is returned to the calling program, and the program resumes execution from the point following the DO statement.

This ability to *modularize*—separate larger xBASE programs into smaller component programs—enables you to neatly divide different operations into separate program files. This modularization assists you in troubleshooting an xBASE system and makes the xBASE system easier to understand and maintain.

Introduction to PAL

The Paradox Application Language (PAL), like xBASE, provides developers with a robust and easy-to-use database-oriented programming language. You can use PAL to create custom database applications by automating the functions and facilities of Paradox. Just as xBASE is used by an xBASE database, PAL relies on Paradox as its database engine. PAL programs are called scripts (not programs). These scripts usually have the extension *.SC.*

PAL can be separated into two distinct areas: the PAL programming language itself and the facilities that provide support for PAL. This first area—PAL itself—includes the commands, functions, and constructs. A few of these are briefly discussed here. The second area—the facilities that are provided to support PAL—include a PAL menu, a script editor, a built-in debugger, and several methods of executing or "playing" scripts.

What Is PAL?

Basically, anything that you can do with Paradox, you can do with PAL. PAL also provides a set of programming features and tools to support the requirements of most database programmers. A few of the more notable features include:

- *The Paradox query language.* This powerful *query-by-example* (QBE) user inter-face provides you with the ability to create queries using a user-friendly inter-face. In a database query, the DBMS user provides the DBMS interface with a set of criteria. Using this criteria, the DBMS retrieves information from the database. This information can be displayed, printed, or saved. (See Chapter 18, "Database Products," for a full explanation of the Paradox query language.)

- *Validity checking.* Certain values—dates, picture formatting, and table lookups, for example—are verified automatically.

- *Multitable forms.* Using multitable forms, the program can create sophisticated data entry applications allowing data to be entered in several database files at once.

- *Report generator.* A sophisticated report generator is provided with PAL. With this report generator, you can create attractive custom reports to support any application.

- *Graphics.* Presentation-quality graphics have been built into PAL and Paradox. This facility provides the ability to create pie, bar, and line charts that represent the data in the database files. Database programs that utilize graphics are much more effective than database applications that just provide reports—more fun too.

PAL (Script) Programming

As with an xBASE program, the PAL script is a sequence of commands. PAL pro-grammers can put together a set of scripts to create a complete database applica-tion. The PAL script controls the application, on-screen output, and printed output. When scripts are executed, they are "played." To play a script, simply invoke PLAY from the Paradox menu.

Database Operations

As with xBASE, PAL provides several methods of performing database operations. You can build the standard PAL methods of adding, editing, and deleting data directly into your scripts. As a programmer, you might find the methods employed by PAL a bit more forgiving than xBASE.

Two of the more important database operations to mention here include the EDITKEY and DEL commands. These commands are important to the PAL programmer because they enable the PAL script to allow the user to edit or delete information in the database. Remember, with xBASE you create programs that interface directly with the database without going through a menu; with PAL, you are still operating the Paradox menu. PAL simply automates the menu selection procedures so the user does not have to understand Paradox. The EDITKEY command simulates pressing F9 to enter the database edit mode, and the DEL command simulates pressing the Del key.

Commands

PAL commands can be divided into three categories: programming commands, keypress interactions, and abbreviated menu commands.

With programming commands, you can do things you cannot do directly with Paradox. The most important of these are IF-THEN-ELSE, ENDIF, and WHILE.

Keypress interactions are recorded from inside Paradox. These commands simulate the keystrokes that you would enter to directly control Paradox.

The abbreviated menu commands emulate Paradox menu selections that you would make from the standard Paradox menu.

Conditional Branching

The branching commands let the PAL script select one set of commands to be invoked from among other commands that may be in your program. As in xBASE, PAL makes these selections by evaluating a condition you specify. Consider the following PAL script:

```
IF retval>100
THEN Over = True
ELSE
    BEEP
    MESSAGE "I beeped"
    Over = False
ENDIF
```

This is an example of how these commands are utilized by PAL. The IF statement works the same in PAL as it did in xBASE. Other related commands include THEN, ELSE, and ENDIF, which you can use to make logical decisions within the program. The IF-THEN-ELSE structure in PAL resembles the following:

```
IF Condition
    THEN          ; Perform this set of commands
    ELSE          ; Perform this set of commands instead
ENDIF
```

Just as the DO CASE-ENDCASE statement is used in the xBASE language to perform conditional branching within the program, PAL utilizes a command called SWITCH. (The semicolon (;) tells Paradox where a command ends and a comment begins.) Using the SWITCH command is like using multiple IF-THEN statements to branch to locations in the PAL script or to call additional PAL scripts. The SWITCH command is often used with menus. The SWITCH command includes CASE statements that will execute the commands directly under that CASE statement when predefined conditions are met. The SWITCH command has the following structure:

```
SWITCH
    CASE Condition1 :       ; These commands are executed
    CASE Condition2 :       ; These commands are executed
    OTHERWISE:              ; These commands are executed
ENDSWITCH
```

Here is an example of a SWITCH statement:

```
SWITCH
    CASE answer = "A"
        PLAY "addrec"
    CASE answer = "E"
        PLAY "editrec"
    OTHERWISE:
        BEEP
ENDSWITCH
```

Command Structure

The PAL programming commands are structured to allow one keyword and some-times several parameters. For example, the BEEP command—presented earlier in the chapter—is just one keyword, and does not require a parameter. The MESSAGE command is a bit more complex, and requires at least one argument. PAL pro-vides all the necessary commands that you may require to complete a database application.

PAL Expressions

Parameters to PAL commands are called expressions. The MESSAGE command must be passed a string in order to display that string on-screen. Other expressions can be added to that command. For example:

```
MESSAGE "Today's date is", TODAY()
```

In this example, two expressions are passed to the MESSAGE command: the string to be displayed on-screen, and an expression that displays today's date after the message. Expressions can return alphanumeric, numeric, currency, short number, data, or logical values.

Looping

A loop is a set of PAL commands that is invoked over and over again. There are three loop commands provided by PAL: FOR, WHILE, and SCAN.

The FOR loop uses a numeric variable called Countonme to control the number of times the loop is repeated. You can name your counter variable with any valid PAL variable name. You set the counter to a starting value, and as the loop executes, the counter's value is incremented by an amount you predetermine. The following is the general outline of the PAL FOR loop:

```
FOR  Countonme
.
.              ; Commands go here
.
ENDFOR
```

You set the number of loops by providing an argument to the FOR command, such as:

```
FOR Counter FROM 1 TO 100
```

The WHILE loop is used to repeat a series of PAL commands an indeterminate number of times. As with the xBASE DO WHILE, the PAL WHILE loop continues until a certain condition is met. The command is structured as follows:

```
WHILE Condition
.
.              ; Commands go here
.
ENDWHILE
```

The SCAN command moves through the current database and executes a group of commands each time it finds a database record that meets the specified condition. The SCAN command is structured as follows:

```
SCAN [FOR  condition]
.
.              ; Commands go here
.
ENDSCAN
```

Sample PAL Program

Listing 13.2 is a very simple PAL script that demonstrates many of the topics just discussed. Note some of the similarities and differences between PAL and the xBASE program shown in Listing 13.1 The PROC command enables Paradox to name a script. After being declared, a procedure is always available in main memory until it is released from memory by Paradox. This procedure naming scheme is used to permit Paradox to load the script directly without having to rerun it line by line if the script is needed again. This allows Paradox to play scripts faster.

Listing 13.2. A simple PAL script.

```
PROC PALSCRIP()                    ; Header contains name of proc
PRIVATE name, password, username   ; variables that are private to proc
VIEW "USERS"                       ; places USERS table on workspace
MOVETO FIELD "last_name"           ; makes "last_name" field current
FOR i FROM 1 TO 4                  ; loop 4 times
   @4,6 ? "Enter your last name:"  ; prompt the user for a Name
   ACCEPT "A10" TO username        ; get input
   @4,6 CLEAR EOS
   CURSOR NORMAL
   LOCATE username                 ; is the supplied name in the table?
   IF retval                       ; If Yes
   THEN nameok = True              ;
      QUITLOOP                     ;
   ELSE                            ; If No
      BEEP                         ; Beep
      MESSAGE "Name not in database"
   ENDIF
ENDFOR
ENDPROC                            ; end of procedure definition
```

Comparing the xBASE Language to PAL

By now, you probably are thinking "xBASE or PAL"? As with most things, you can't have your cake and eat it too—you must choose one or the other. It is now time to compare the xBASE and PAL programming languages. To many programmers, the question is a matter of personal choice. Many PAL programmers would not even consider writing xBASE programs, and xBASE programmers generally do not even consider Paradox and PAL as an option. You, as a beginner, can make an unbiased decision.

As with any software purchase, you must consider all factors when deciding to buy a database programming language. With database-oriented 4GL languages such as xBASE and PAL, you should consider the usability, performance, portability, and maintainability of the language, what the future looks like for the language, and the price. You can examine prices at your local software vendor (some prices are also provided in Chapter 18, "PC Database Products"), but this chapter covers the other considerations. The remainder of this chapter offers some of the good and bad points of each language.

Advantages and Disadvantages of xBASE

Lets begin with xBASE. There are several advantages and disadvantages to using the xBASE language over PAL. Some of these advantages or disadvantage may not be such a big deal to you, and some may. Again, consider which language is best for the application you are writing and who is going to use that application.

Usability

The single most common complaint of xBASE programmers—especially xBASE programmers who have used other database-oriented 4GLs (even PAL)—is that the xBASE language is not as easy to learn and to use as other database languages. This, of course, is a matter of opinion, but most agree that xBASE is not as easy to learn and to program as it could be. This might be attributed to the fact that xBASE evolved over a period of several years, and all the commands that were supported in earlier releases of the dBASE language are still supported today in xBASE. These obsolete commands are considered by many programmers to be overly complex and especially confusing to beginners—definite considerations if you must learn the language.

Performance

Obviously, performance in the xBASE world is directly related to the product that you select to drive your xBASE application. In general, the fierce competition in the xBASE interpreter and compiler industry has provided an array of products including the ones listed at the beginning of this chapter. These products are among the fastest in the business.

For example, FoxPro (an xBASE interpreter) is considered by many to be the fastest database running on a PC (see Chapter 18), although programmers using dBASE IV sometimes find FoxPro's performance lacking. The xBASE product manufacturers are improving their products constantly, and faster and faster products are inevitable. Ask your software vendor for benchmarking information before you purchase an xBASE product. *Benchmarking* information is database performance data and enables you to compare the performance of other xBASE products with the product you are considering.

Portability

If there is a single most significant advantage to using the xBASE language, it is *portability*. When your application is portable, you can move it from one xBASE product to another. This portability even enables you to move an xBASE application residing on an MS-DOS based personal computer or LAN, to another operating system, such as UNIX or VMS running on a mini- or mainframe computer. This is the area in which the xBASE language shines. Much like C and Pascal, there are several products that can drive an xBASE application—on both MS-DOS and non-DOS environments.

An application created in dBASE III PLUS several years ago can be run without modification under both dBASE IV and FoxPro. With only a few modifications, that same application can be compiled in Clipper or moved to non-DOS systems if an xBASE product is available—and usually one is. This portability enables an application to move from product to product as companies go out of business or their products become obsolete, and it also allows for hardware and operating system technology changes.

Maintainability

After an application is created using xBASE it may require maintenance. This maintenance usually comes in the form of program and database changes to meet the changing needs of the user. Programs written in the xBASE language are considered very maintainable—if the programs are initially written so that others can read them. Some xBASE programmers can make an xBASE program look much like a C program, but the xBASE constructs do not enforce a particular kind of structure. As previously mentioned, the inclusion of primitive xBASE commands can also complicate the maintainability of xBASE programs.

The maintainability issue becomes even further complicated because the xBASE programs look a bit different from xBASE product to xBASE product. A system written in Clipper cannot be completely understood by an xBASE programmer who primarily uses FoxPro. Clipper supports (and requires) some commands and functions that are not supported anywhere else.

Third-Party Products

The popularity of xBASE has led not only to the availability of a wide selection of xBASE compilers and interpreters, but to a wide selection of other products that support the xBASE system development process. These products are called third-party or "add-on" products. Some of the more popular products are the following:

- *Code generators.* A code generator is a software product that enables you to easily design screens, menus, and other parts of an application. After you have defined a menu, screen, report, or other application component, the code generator can create the correct xBASE program code that, when run, creates the desired functions. The code generator is a program to create programs. Generally, programmers use code generators to create the basis of a system before they begin to define the details. Using a code generator, programmers are able to save hundreds of hours of programming time that normally would be required to create certain pieces of an application.

- *Report writers.* A report writer replaces the generic report writers that come with most xBASE products. The most popular is a product called Relational Writer from Concentric Systems. A report writer enables you to create more complex reports than you could create with the standard report writer.

- *Graphics products.* The xBASE products do not provide graphics. There are several products that work with xBASE products, however, to enable you to add graphics such as pie, bar, and line charts to your applications.

The Future

The future of the xBASE language is assured. The number of products and companies that support it virtually affirm its viability. With the competition fighting it out in the xBASE marketplace, users can be confident that xBASE products will continue to provide high quality application development environments.

Advantages and Disadvantages of PAL

Paradox is thought of in the database world as an underrated and under-used product. It is the database that everyone loves, but no one uses. There may be some truth to this, but its survival over the past years, while other database systems struggled, is a testimonial to its overall quality. The fact that the software power-house Borland purchased Paradox is an indication that it and PAL are not fly-by-night products.

Usability

PAL gains points over the xBASE products in terms of usability. As you can see from the examples presented in this chapter, PAL is extremely easy to use. Its close inte-gration to the Paradox menu system does not tend to leave you in a lurch; Paradox guides you through complex database operations with ease. After using Paradox and PAL, you can easily see that the product provides an attractive and powerful user interface and programming language.

Performance

Although the debate continues, Paradox has outdistanced most of the xBASE database systems in terms of speed. Although FoxPro seems to have given Paradox a run for the money, the Paradox database system consistently performs like an industry leader (see Chapter 18).

Portability

One of the major drawbacks of PAL is the fact that you can only run its scripts under Paradox. This ties you and your scripts exclusively to Paradox. If you have to move an application to another database system, either DOS-based or non-DOS, the application must be rewritten in a new language—probably xBASE. PAL is Paradox and nothing but Paradox. The fact that Paradox is a time-tested and accepted product takes most of the danger out of selecting PAL—but there is always the possibility that Paradox might not be around in the future.

Maintainability

PAL provides simplicity and structure to programming code, making it very easy to understand and modify scripts—even easier than xBASE. This maintainability is built into PAL and the Paradox database engine. In addition, PAL code is only executed using Paradox; there are no derivations from product to product, as is the case in the xBASE world.

Third-Party Products

There are a few third-party products for PAL and Paradox, but certainly not as many as with the xBASE products. Paradox provides the PAL developer with all the tools required: A report generator, code generator, and graphics support. Its report generator is considered one of the best in the business, and its internal support for graphics makes it a more rounded system than those found in the xBASE world.

The Future

With Paradox safely in the hands of Borland, the product is surely going to be around for awhile. The Paradox and PAL users are fiercely loyal to their database—and more and more database application developers are finding that Paradox may be the right selection for their applications. As the products in the xBASE world chase a "standard," it is nice to see a product that still sets its own standard.

Other Considerations

Besides the topics of usability, performance, portability, and maintainability of the language and its prospects for the future, you should consider two other items that also are important to database developers: xBASE and PAL support for networks and client/server applications.

Networks

An ever increasing number of organizations are using local-area networks (LANs). It is an easy way for small companies to link several computers together and share data. On a network, several users can share files, printers, and other devices. Networks are the home to more and more xBASE and PAL applications, giving them the ability to service several hundred to several thousand users at one time.

All the products discussed in this chapter support networks, but in different ways. The xBASE products vary greatly in the way they support network applications, especially in price-per-user. In Chapter 18, "Database Products," you'll discover that dBASE IV and FoxPro provide automatic file and record locking. Clipper requires that you build it into your xBASE code.

Paradox does a good job of supporting network users and providing automatic file and record locking in network environments. Paradox also provides a quick-lock algorithm to speed record locking and unlocking.

Client/Server

One of the newest technologies in PC-based database systems is the *client/server* architecture. Simply put, client/server applications operate using two computers that are connected on a network. One computer is considered the *client,* or the computer that is used by the application program and the user. The second computer is considered the *server,* or the computer that processes the database request.

Client/server architecture is used to create faster database applications by splitting up the tasks between two CPUs. Although still in its infancy, some xBASE products can act as client front ends to available database servers, such as Microsoft Database Server and Oracle Database Server. This means that all database operations are not handled by the local xBASE DBMS but are transmitted over a network to a server where the database operation is processed.

Many database systems, including those presented in this chapter, either currently support or have announced plans to support available database servers and act as a client to those servers. As time goes by, more and more microcomputer database systems will be able to put client/server architecture to work.

Summary

This chapter presented you with a brief overview of the xBASE and PAL programming languages and concepts. Both xBASE and PAL provide novice and advanced programmers with an easy and effective way to create database applications quickly. Both languages are certainly survivors in the competitive database management industry.

The xBASE language certainly seems to have the advantage of application portability over PAL. Several DBMS vendors currently support the xBASE standard. This support has provided the xBASE world with a heavy portion of the personal computer database market and, therefore, a little more job security for xBASE programmers and consultants. The Paradox PAL language, which provides its developers with an easy-to-use command structure and a quick and efficient database, may have the usability advantage over the xBASE language and its associated products. Whether you select xBASE or PAL, you should be able to start creating database applications quickly with these powerful high-level languages.

14

Overview of BASIC

by Greg Perry

The BASIC programming language is one of the most well-known programming languages in the world. One reason for its popularity is that it has been around for so long; BASIC is one of the oldest microcomputer programming languages still in use today. Makers of microcomputers provide BASIC with every computer sold. To use other PC languages such as Pascal, C, and C++, you must pay additional money to buy them. BASIC, on the other hand, comes with your computer purchase.

BASIC also offers another distinct advantage: It is the language of choice for beginning programmers. Because of its easy-to-understand interface, its interpreted nature, and its English-like commands, BASIC is a great way to start programming.

This chapter provides an overview of BASIC so you can better understand how BASIC began as a programming language and see its strengths and weaknesses. The chapter also teaches you several common BASIC commands and shows several programs you can follow to learn a little about using BASIC.

BASIC's Background

Although today BASIC is considered to be a microcomputer programming language, it predated microcomputers, originally running on large mainframes. BASIC was developed at Dartmouth College in the 1960s. Some professors needed a programming language for students that was not as stodgy and cryptic as FORTRAN. FORTRAN was the programming language for engineering students (its name stands for FORmula TRANslator), but the business students were not always comfortable with the inflexibility of FORTRAN.

The professors "watered down" FORTRAN into a simpler language they called BASIC. Enamored with the FORTRAN acronym, they decided to use BASIC as the name for their new language, which stands for Beginner's All-Purpose Symbolic Instruction Code—a name that is more difficult to remember than the BASIC language commands themselves!

Through the years, many versions of BASIC have come and gone. Many other programming languages also have been written since BASIC's inception, but more people continue to learn BASIC than any other programming language. When beginners want to learn to program, they learn BASIC first. Many college curriculums require BASIC as a prerequisite to other programming language classes. The simple nature of BASIC, as well as its availability—being supplied on virtually every computer in the world—makes it a common language for almost every programmer in the PC programming world.

BASIC's Evolution

BASIC began as a simple and small programming language. To keep the language easy for beginners, designers kept the early versions simple, with only a few keyword commands. As BASIC's popularity grew and its use expanded to more and more computers, programmers began wanting more power than BASIC could provide.

Designers of BASIC languages began adding more commands and *constructs* (language control statements) to BASIC. BASIC has gone through many iterations and has had many names (such as BASIC, BASICA, GW-BASIC, QBasic, QuickBASIC, and others), all of which are based on the same BASIC language.

The early versions of BASIC had limited *structured programming* capabilities. Structured programs are easier to maintain than programs written without structure. When a program is structured, its code is organized in a straightforward style that is easy to change when the program's requirements change. This ever-changing world requires that businesses change the way they do business from time to time. The changes also mean that programs written for yesterday's business needs no longer suffice for today's and tomorrow's requirements.

When a program contains many *branches,* that is, when a program's execution jumps back and forth in an unordered manner, that program is not considered well-structured. BASIC implements branching through the use of a GOTO statement. Unlike a structured program, a nonstructured program's flow jumps around so much that you often lose your place when trying to follow the program's logic.

214

Although GOTO is not a bad statement in itself, its overuse almost always signals a poorly written, nonstructured program.

During the 1960s and 1970s, programmers recognized the need for structured programs, and the BASIC language evolved to adapt to structured code. The program you see in Listing 14.1 is a sample of an early BASIC program. Early BASIC programs required line numbers to the left of each line (usually numbered in increments of 10 so you could easily insert up to nine lines), and early BASIC programs allowed only limited use of character data manipulations. Notice that the program contains several GOTO statements. GOTO was required more in the early versions of BASIC than in current versions because the language had a more limited command vocabulary.

Listing 14.1. An early BASIC program.

```
10 REM BASIC program that asks the user for
20 REM his or her age and prints a message
30 REM based on how old the user is.
40 PRINT "How old are you";
50 INPUT AGE
60 IF (AGE > 21) THEN GOTO 100
70 IF (AGE > 18) THEN GOTO 120
80 PRINT "You look old for your age!"
90 GOTO 130
100 PRINT "You look young for your age!"
110 GOTO 130
120 PRINT "You can now vote! Congratulations!"
130 REM All statements get here to wind down the program
140 PRINT "Thanks for taking the time to answer my question!"
150 END
```

The following is the output of a sample execution of the program in Listing 14.1:

```
How old are you? 19

You can now vote! Congratulations!

Thanks for taking the time to answer my question!
```

Although you might know very little about programming, this program is relatively simple, and yet it can be much improved. The early versions of BASIC, although simple to learn, did not lend themselves to readable programs. This caused BASIC to be characterized in the professional programming community as a language for beginners and children and not one to be taken seriously by real-world applications.

BASIC was a language that never seemed to get enough credit from the experts. Even its early versions were better than the experts gave it credit for. Despite its bad publicity, BASIC's use continued to grow and new features were added. Today, BASIC is finally getting serious attention from programming experts. BASIC contains as many structured commands and is as powerful as just about any programming language on the market.

To give you an idea of today's BASIC, Listing 14.2 contains a modern version of the AGE program shown in Listing 14.1. The remaining sections of this chapter discuss the specifics of the language, but Listing 14.2 gives you a good idea of how the language has matured. Even if you are a new programmer, you should find that Listing 14.2's program is much easier to follow than the one in Listing 14.1.

Listing 14.2. A sample of today's BASIC language.

```
' BASIC program that asks the user for
' his or her age and prints a message
' based on how old the user is.

INPUT "How old are you"; AGE

IF (AGE > 21) THEN
    PRINT "You look young for your age!"
  ELSEIF (AGE > 18) THEN
        PRINT "You can now vote!  Congratulations!"
      ELSE PRINT "You look old for your age!"
END IF

PRINT "Thanks for taking the time to answer my question!"
END
```

Modern-day BASIC programs are *free-form*; that is, you can add as many blank lines and as much indentation as you want to make the program easily readable. As you program, you should always consider the future; make the program as readable as possible because someday either you or someone else will probably have to make changes to the program.

As you can see from Listing 14.2, the line numbers to the left of each line are being phased out of BASIC programs. Although it still is possible to use line numbers and to write a nonstructured BASIC program with too many GOTO statements, you now can structure BASIC programs so they are easy to maintain and require less jumping from place to place. You need line numbers only when you want to branch from one line to another. Because this version of the program has no GOTO statements, the program does not need the line numbers cluttering up the program.

Interpreted Ease

BASIC is one of the few programming languages that you can run interpreted or compiled. BASIC began as an interpreted language so beginning programmers did not have to mess with the compilation details but could concentrate on the actual program. As BASIC became more powerful and as more people began using it, language vendors started offering compiled versions of BASIC to speed the program execution and bring BASIC into the mainstream of programming languages.

Many BASIC programmers still write and test their programs using an interpreted BASIC because they can test and interact with their programs more easily than if they compiled the programs. Once they test the final program, however, they compile the program into an executable file used as the final product.

Another advantage of compiling BASIC programs that you sell is that your customers cannot change the programs. Being able to change the original BASIC code increases the likelihood that errors will creep into the program and you will lose some of the control you have over the programs you sell.

Compilers and Interpreters

Your computer cannot actually understand BASIC or any of the other computer languages. Your computer is nothing more than an electronic machine that understands only electrical impulses.

Something has to convert your program's instructions to the electrical impulses, called *machine language*, that your computer can comprehend. Two tools are available in computers that convert a high-level programming language such as BASIC to the machine's native low-level machine language. These tools are *compilers* and *interpreters*.

A compiler converts your entire program into machine language before it executes one program statement. The compilation takes a while, and you must take on the added responsibility of compiling the program before you can see any results from it.

An interpreter converts your program, one statement at a time, as it executes each statement. Therefore, if a statement repeats, the interpreter must reinterpret that statement as many times as it executes.

Although the end result is the same—the program executes and produces the output you need—the two methods of computer language conversion differ in the programmer's responsibility. If you have an interpreted language, as many BASIC languages are, you have to do very little to see the results of the program. This is one reason BASIC is the beginner's language choice. If you have a compiled language, such as Pascal, you must learn how to use your compiler as well as the language itself, placing more responsibility on compiled language programmers.

The BASIC Language

Although mastering any programming language takes a while, you can learn the fundamentals of BASIC in a relatively short time. The following sections explain the key language elements of BASIC and guide you through an overview of BASIC. After you finish the chapter, you will have a good idea of what BASIC programs look like and will be able to read and understand simple BASIC programs.

Readable REMarks

Because readability is important for any programming language, the designers of BASIC included a documentation command in the first version of the language. In BASIC, a *remark statement* is a statement for people, not for computers. Whenever you see a line in a BASIC program that begins with REM, you are looking at a remark.

Remarks are useful for describing, in English, exactly what the program is doing. Straight programming code, even well-structured programming, is difficult to follow at times. Remarks help explain what is going on throughout the program. If someone has to make changes to the program, he or she can use the remarks to get a feel quickly for what is happening in different areas of the program. Programmers often put their names at the top of a program in a remark. If someone later has a question about the program, he or she can track down the original programmer.

Most versions of BASIC support a shortcut for the REM statement: a single quotation mark. The following lines are identical:

```
REM Print a paycheck

' Print a paycheck
```

BASIC ignores everything on a line following REM or '. Remarks do not have to be on lines by themselves. Often, programmers put remarks to the right of valid BASIC statements, such as the following:

```
FOR CT = 10 TO 1 STEP -1      ' Count down from 10 to 1
```

You must admit that Count down from 10 to 1 is much easier to understand than FOR CT = 10 TO 1 STEP -1, and yet the computer understands only the FOR statement. If computers could understand English, you would have little need for a programming language. Computers, however, are not advanced enough at this point to understand English as people do; programming languages such as BASIC are therefore designed with strict rules and *syntax* (grammar and spelling guidelines) so machines can grasp the commands. Remarks help people better understand what is happening in the program.

BASIC Data

As with most programming languages, BASIC enables you to work with *variables* and *constants.* A variable is a location in memory that holds some data (either a number, character, or a string of characters). A constant is a number, character, word, or phrase that does not change. All variables have names and variable names must be unique.

You, the BASIC programmer, determine the names for variables you need. Therefore, you should learn the naming rules for variables. When you learn how to create valid variable names, you can use them in your own programs. Here are the variable naming rules for most versions of BASIC:

1. All variable names must be from 1 to 40 characters long.

2. All variable names must begin with a letter of the alphabet.

3. The remainder of the name can be a mixture of letters, numbers, and periods.

The following are valid variable names:

```
SALES

Payroll93

AcctRec

Volume.DECEM
```

These, however, are not valid variable names:

93Payroll	*Variable names cannot begin with a number.*
Total Amount	*Variable names cannot contain a space.*
Dept$@#$Mktg	*Variable names cannot contain special characters.*

BASIC does not distinguish between uppercase and lowercase variable names. Therefore, the following are all the same variable name to BASIC:

```
Sales

sALES

SALES

sales
```

BASIC variables can hold different types of data, which can be either numeric or character data. Table 14.1 describes the types of data that variables can hold and gives an explanation of each type.

Table 14.1. Variable data types.		
Type	**Examples**	**Description**
Integer	45, -7	Whole numbers, without decimal points, from 32,768 to –32,767
Long Integer	1456787	Extremely large or extremely small whole numbers
Single-precision	956.534	Real numbers, with decimal points, significant to six places
Double-precision	-2.3211221	Real numbers, with decimal points, significant to 15 places
String	"Sally said"	Strings of 0 to 32,767 characters

Following are the two formats for placing values in variables. Both ways use the assignment operator: the equal sign (=).

```
LET var_name = value

var_name = value
```

The LET keyword is optional, so very few programmers use it. The equal sign works just like a left-pointing arrow, that is, BASIC stores whatever is to the right of the equal sign into the variable on the left side.

Here are some more examples:

```
LET Sales = 2323.45

Sales = 2323.45    ' Same as the previous because LET is optional

CostOfSales = Sales * .36

NetSales = Sales - CostOfSales
```

When you put character data (called *string data*) into variables, you must enclose the data in quotation marks, and you must add a dollar sign to the end of the variable name. The dollar sign signals to BASIC that the variable holds character data and not numeric data. For example, to store a name in a string variable, you make the following assignment:

```
Employee$ = "Goodwin, Kim"
```

Character data are data strings on which you perform no calculations. For instance, a phone number contains all numbers, but you never add two phone numbers together. Therefore, a phone number makes a good candidate for a string variable, as follows:

```
Phone$ = "555-3421"
```

Simple Math Operators

As you saw in the earlier examples, BASIC uses math symbols that are similar to those used in elementary math. Table 14.2 shows the four regular math operators.

Table 14.2. BASIC's primary math operators.		
Operator	**Example**	**Description**
+	23 + 34	Addition
-	545.54 - 29.8	Subtraction
*	4 * 8	Multiplication
/	28.0 / 4.2	Division

You don't have to understand complex math to be a good programmer. BASIC computes all the mathematical answers for you. You must, however, understand the way BASIC performs its computations. BASIC, as well as most programming languages, does not evaluate math computations in a left-to-right order. Rather, BASIC evaluates math results based on a hierarchy of operators, sometimes called *operator precedence*.

Given the following simple assignment statement, what value do you think BASIC stores in ANS when it reads this statement?

```
ANS = 3 + 2 * 3
```

If you thought 15, you are incorrect. BASIC stores 9 in ANS. BASIC performs all multiplication before it performs addition, even if the multiplication appears after the addition in the formula. Table 14.3 shows the order in which BASIC performs calculations.

Table 14.3. BASIC's hierarchy of operators.	
Precedence	**Operator**
1	( )
2	*, /
3	+, -

As you can see in Table 14.3, multiplication and division appear before addition and subtraction. In the previous statement, therefore, BASIC first evaluates the 2 * 3, producing an answer of 6. It then adds 3 to 6, resulting in 9. BASIC stores the 9 in ANS.

Because multiplication and division appear on the same level in the hierarchy of operators, they have equal precedence. For example, BASIC evaluates the following statement from the left:

```
RESULT = 25 / 5 * 2 - 5 + 3
```

BASIC evaluates the formula and stores an 8 in RESULT. Because division and multiplication appear on the same hierarchy level, BASIC evaluates the formula from the left.

Because parentheses have a higher precedence than any of the other four operators, you can override the regular operator precedence by using parentheses in certain calculations. For example, the following statement stores a 15 in ANS:

```
ANS = (3 + 2) * 3
```

Input and Output

Although you can now store data in variables and you understand the way BASIC performs calculations, you still have to know how to produce data on-screen and to send it to the printer. The primary command you use to send data to the screen is PRINT. You can print characters, words, and sentences to the screen with PRINT statements like these:

```
PRINT "I can program in BASIC."
PRINT "BASIC is great for beginners."
```

You also can print numeric values to the screen with statements such as the following:

```
PRINT 25.8
PRINT 14.5 + 10.76      ' Prints the answer
```

You can combine words and numbers by separating them with a semicolon, as in the following:

```
PRINT "I am"; 23; " years old."
```

When BASIC executes the program that contains the preceding PRINT, it sends the following output to the screen:

```
I am 23 years old.
```

If you separate the values with a comma rather than a semicolon, BASIC prints the values a little farther apart. The comma instructs BASIC to print values in the next 14 spaces on the screen. For instance, the following command

```
PRINT "I am", 23, " years old."      ' Uses a comma separator
```

prints the following output to the screen:

```
I am       23            years old.
```

You can use a comma if you want to separate values, for example in a table, and use a semicolon if you want to print values that are consecutive.

When printing variables, BASIC prints the values of the variables, not the names of the variables. Consider the program in Listing 14.3.

Listing 14.3. Salary computing program.

```
' This program computes pay based on the
' hours worked and the pay rate per hour
Hours = 43
```

continues

Listing 14.3. Continued

```
Rate = 4.75

GrossPay = Hours * Rate

PRINT "My salary is $"; GrossPay
```

When you run this program, you see the following output produced by PRINT:

```
My salary is $ 204.25
```

The quotation marks inform the PRINT statement that you want everything inside the quotation marks printed literally. If you do not include quotation marks, BASIC prints the value of the variable or number listed.

Language Spotlight

BASIC offers a shortcut from which even beginning programmers can benefit. Instead of typing PRINT for all your screen display commands, you can type a question mark. Both of the following statements are exactly the same:

```
PRINT "To program is to impress thyself.
```

and

```
? "To program is to impress thyself."
```

Because PRINT is such a common statement, you can save typing time by using the shortcut. The question mark does not remain in your program. BASIC changes it to PRINT so, when you list your program, it appears as if you typed PRINT instead.

If you want results to go to a printer, BASIC supplies a statement named LPRINT. LPRINT works just like PRINT, except all output goes to the printer and not to your screen. Listing 14.4 is the same program as Listing 14.3 except the PRINT is now LPRINT.

Listing 14.4. Salary computing program with *LPRINT* statement.

```
' This program computes pay based on the
' hours worked and the pay rate per hour
Hours = 43
Rate = 4.75

GrossPay = Hours * Rate

LPRINT "My salary is $"; GrossPay
```

When you run this program, be sure your printer is on and has paper. The output beginning with My salary goes to the printer.

You've just seen how to ouput values from your program, now you need some way to get data into your program. The INPUT statement is BASIC's way of asking you for keyboard values when you run a program. Whenever BASIC runs into an INPUT statement, it displays a question mark and waits for you to type something. For example, the following statement produces only a question mark:

```
INPUT Amount
```

The question mark is the user's signal that he or she must type something in response to the INPUT. If the user were to type 450 and press Enter, BASIC would store the 450 in the variable named Amount, and then continue execution of the program at the next statement.

Because BASIC produces only a question mark in response to INPUT, you should print a prompt message before INPUT, so the user will know the kind of data needed from the INPUT statement. In other words, the following two statements make more sense than the preceding single, obscure INPUT:

```
PRINT "What is the amount";
INPUT Amount
```

The semicolon at the end of the PRINT statement forces the INPUT statement's question mark to appear on the same line. When the program gets to these two lines, the user sees the following:

```
What is the amount?
```

Because the printed message explains what kind of INPUT is desired from the program, the user knows exactly what to type.

BASIC's designers knew early on that the PRINT-INPUT combination was important. After all, programmers do not want question marks popping up all over the screen

225

without messages appearing as well. Therefore, BASIC's designers added power to INPUT so that you can combine the prompt message directly with INPUT. The following single INPUT statement does the same thing as the two previous PRINT-INPUT statements:

```
INPUT "What is the amount"; Amount
```

The program in Listing 14.5 combines the concepts you learned in this section into a single program. The program asks the user for his or her name and then asks for three numbers. The program then prints the average of those three numbers.

Listing 14.5. Number averaging program.

```
' Program that averages three of the user's numbers
'
INPUT "What is your first name"; First$

' Now, get the three values
INPUT "What is the first number to average"; Num1
INPUT "What is the second number to average"; Num2
INPUT "What is the third number to average"; Num3

' Compute the average
Avg = (Num1 + Num2 + Num3) / 3

PRINT "The average is"; Avg
PRINT "Thanks for stopping by, "; First$
END
```

Some BASIC programmers choose to add the END statement to the last line of the program. END is optional, however; BASIC knows when the program finishes with END. Many programmers prefer to include the optional END so users looking at the code know the program is complete.

The following is an example of output for Listing 14.5, assuming a user named George has responded:

```
What is your first name? George
What is the first number to average? 10
What is the second number to average? 30
What is the third number to average? 50
The average is 30
Thanks for stopping by, George
```

If you are following along but are having a difficult time getting these programs to work with your version of BASIC, you might have to put line numbers before each line, as shown in Listing 14.1.

Comparing Data

Computers are not only for calculating and printing results. They also quickly compare data and produce output based on those comparisons. Computers can compare data much faster than people can. By quickly comparing data, your computer can sort through a list of 1,000 names searching for someone's address or arranging those names and addresses in alphabetical order or ZIP code order. Programs can also respond to the user's input, performing one of several actions depending on the user's response to a question.

In addition to the math operators you learned about in a previous section, *relational operators* compare data in BASIC programs. Table 14.4 lists the relational operators and their descriptions.

Table 14.4. BASIC's relational operators.	
Operator	**Description**
=	Equal to
>	Greater than
<	Less than
>=	Greater than or equal to
<=	Less than or equal to
<>	Not equal to

These six operators always appear with two numbers, strings, variables, expressions, or a combination of such, on each side. Many of these relational operators might already be familiar to you. As you program in BASIC, you will learn them as well as you know the +, -, *, and / mathematical operators.

The six relational operators perform a series of True-False comparisons. For example, assume a program initializes four variables as follows:

```
A = 5
B = 10
C = 15
D = 5
```

Given these assignments, the following relational tests are True:

A is equal to D	A = D
B is less than C	B < C
C is greater than A	C > A
B is greater than or equal to A	B >= A
D is less than or equal to B	D <= B
B is not equal to C	B <> C

The following relational tests are not True; they are False:

```
A = B

B > C

A <> D

C <= B
```

You deal with relational logic in everyday life. Think of the following statements you might make:

"The apples cost less than the oranges."

"Jim is older than Ed."

"The cars are not the same type."

Before using the relational operators, you must understand the IF statement. BASIC uses IF to test data using the relational operators and make comparisons. IF has several formats. The primary one is

```
IF condition THEN
    .
    .            ' One or more BASIC statements go here
    .
END IF
```

You use IF to make a decision. The statements that follow THEN occur only if the decision (the result of the condition) is True. You use IF logic in everyday life; consider the following statements:

"If the day is warm, then I will go swimming and camping."

"If the light is green, then go."

"If I make enough money, then we will build a new house."

Each of these statements is conditional. That is, if and only if the condition is true, do you complete the statement.

The program in Listing 14.6 asks the user a question and prints a message based on the response. BASIC calculates and prints the employee's bonus if sales are greater than $5,000. Otherwise, a bonus of 0 is printed.

Listing 14.6. A bonus computing program.

```
' Compute a bonus based on sales figures
'
Bonus = 0

INPUT "What are your sales for the month"; Sales

' Compute the bonus only if the sales are more than 5000
IF Sales > 5000 THEN
    Bonus = 25
END IF

PRINT "Your bonus for sales of $"; Sales; " is $"; Bonus
END
```

Following is one possible output from the program:

```
What are your sales for the month? 4356.54
Your bonus for sales of $ 4356.54 is $ 0
```

Here is another possible output from the program:

```
What are your sales for the month? 6093.01
Your bonus for sales of $ 6093.01 is $ 25
```

Notice that the bonus is different depending on the value of Sales. The program conditionally displays a $25 bonus if the sales are more than $5,000 but displays a bonus of $0 if the sales are $5,000 or less.

Another form of the IF statement is more powerful and enables you to write programs that can determine more conditional results. You can add an ELSE statement to the IF statement when your program logic is more complex than a simple IF can handle. Following is the format of an IF-ELSE statement:

```
IF condition THEN
    .
    .          ' One or more BASIC statements go here
    .
```

229

```
ELSE
    .
    .          ' One or more BASIC statements go here
    .
END IF
```

Here is the way IF-ELSE works: If the conditional test is True, the block of state-ments following the IF executes. If the conditional test is False, the block of statements following the ELSE executes.

Listing 14.7 is the bonus display program using an IF-ELSE. Notice that the logic becomes clearer and more outcomes are possible due to the ELSE. You can custom-ize the display message depending on the sales.

Listing 14.7. Revision of Listing 14.6 using the *IF-ELSE* loop.

```
' Compute a bonus based on sales figures
'

INPUT "What are your sales for the month"; Sales

' Compute the bonus only if the sales are more than 5000
IF Sales > 5000 THEN
    Bonus = 25
    PRINT "Your bonus for sales of $"; Sales; " is $"; Bonus
ELSE
    PRINT "Your bonus is zero for sales of $"; Sales
    PRINT "Get those sales up next month!"
END IF

END
```

The indented lines following the IF and ELSE simply make the program more read-able—the extra spaces are not required. By indenting those lines, the logic that goes with IF and the logic that goes with ELSE are both easier to spot. Following is a sample output from the program:

```
What are your sales for the month? 2343.45
Your bonus is zero for sales of $ 2343.45
Get those sales up next month!
```

The statement following ELSE can even be another IF. Therefore, you can combine powerful logic by putting one IF in another. The first program in the chapter, repeated in Listing 14.8, combines one IF statement in another.

Listing 14.8. The age program.

```
' BASIC program that asks the user for
' his or her age and prints a message
' based on how old the user is.

INPUT "How old are you"; AGE

IF (AGE > 21) THEN
    PRINT "You look young for your age!"
ELSEIF (AGE > 18) THEN
        PRINT "You can now vote!  Congratulations!"
      ELSE PRINT "You look old for your age!"
END IF

PRINT "Thanks for taking the time to answer my question!"
END
```

This program prints a message based on one of three answers from the user. If the user is over 21, the program prints You look young for your age! If the user is between 18 and 21, it prints You can now vote! Congratulations! If the user is 18 or younger (the only remaining option), the program prints You look old for your age!

Looping Statements

The repetitive capability of the computer makes it a good tool for producing large amounts of information quickly. Often, you have to program a *loop*, which is the repeated, circular execution of one or more statements. The two primary means by which a BASIC programmer creates a loop are with the FOR statement and with the WHILE statement. There are several variations of each. This section attempts to familiarize you with their concepts.

A FOR statement in a program always has a matching NEXT statement. If you see one, you should see the other. The FOR statement begins a loop and the NEXT ends it. The format of FOR is

```
FOR counter = start TO end [STEP increment]
    .
    .          ' One or more BASIC statements go here
    .
NEXT counter
```

in which *counter* is a numeric variable you supply that controls the loop. The *counter* variable is initialized to the *start* value before the first iteration of the loop. The *start* value is typically 1, but it can be any numeric value you supply. Every time the body of the loop repeats, the *counter* variable increments by the value of the *increment*. If you supply no STEP statement (the brackets indicate the STEP statement is optional; never type the brackets), the increment is always 1.

The value of *end* is a number that controls the end of the looping process. When *counter* reaches the *end* value, BASIC stops repeating the loop and continues execution at the statement following NEXT.

The FOR statement sounds more difficult in theory than it is in practice. Here is a simple three-line program, comprised entirely of a FOR loop:

```
FOR ctr = 1 TO 10
    PRINT ctr
NEXT ctr
```

If you type this program and run it, you see the following output:

```
1
2
3
4
5
6
7
8
9
10
```

The loop repeats by printing the value of ctr until ctr reaches the *end* value of 10. You can count down as well, as the following program demonstrates:

```
FOR ctr = 10 TO 1 STEP -1
    PRINT ctr
NEXT ctr
PRINT "Blast off!"
```

In this program, ctr begins at 10; the negative STEP value forces ctr to be one less each time through the loop. Here is the output:

```
10
9
8
7
6
```

```
5
4
3
2
1
Blast off!
```

FOR loops are useful for applications other than simple number displays. A teacher can use the program in Listing 14.9 to track grades in a class. If there are 15 students, the program loops 15 times, each time asking the teacher for the next student's grade. When the teacher has entered all 15 grades, the loop finishes (because the *counter* variable becomes more than 15) and the class average then prints.

Listing 14.9. The grade-averaging program.

```
' Grade-averaging program
'
total = 0    ' Before getting any grades, the total for the class is 0

PRINT "** Class Average Program **"     ' An opening title message
PRINT        ' Prints a blank line

FOR std = 1 TO 15
   INPUT "What is the next student's grade"; grade
   total = total + grade     ' Add this student's grade to the total
NEXT std

PRINT "All grades have been entered."
PRINT                          ' Prints a blank line
average = total / 15

PRINT "The class test average is"; average
END
```

Here is what the output looks like when you run Listing 14.9:

```
** Class Average Program **

What is the next student's grade? 88.6
What is the next student's grade? 56.7
What is the next student's grade? 100.0
What is the next student's grade? 99.5
What is the next student's grade? 90.4
What is the next student's grade? 75.6
What is the next student's grade? 94
What is the next student's grade? 72.3
```

233

```
What is the next student's grade? 78.5
What is the next student's grade? 92.3
What is the next student's grade? 89.0
What is the next student's grade? 45.6
What is the next student's grade? 100.0
What is the next student's grade? 78.6
What is the next student's grade? 82.4
All grades have been entered.

The class test average is 82.9
```

The FOR loop causes the program to request and accept only 15 grades.

Another BASIC loop statement is WHILE. WHILE enables your program to loop, repeating the same statements over and over, while a certain condition is True. When that condition becomes False, the WHILE stops and execution continues through the rest of the program.

There are many variations on the WHILE. One of the most common is the WHILE-WEND set of loop control statements. As with FOR and NEXT, you rarely see a WHILE without a WEND. The format of WHILE is

```
WHILE conditional test
     .
     .            ' One or more BASIC statements go here
     .
WEND
```

Unlike FOR loops, WHILE loops are controlled by a conditional test and not by a specified number of iterations. The *conditional test* is any relational operator. You can use the same types of tests you used with the IF statement. As long as the conditional test is True, the body of the WHILE-WEND loop repeats.

The following example helps clarify the WHILE-WEND loop. The program in Listing 14.10 converts a Celsius temperature to a Fahrenheit temperature. It first asks the user for a Celsius temperature. If the user types an unreasonable value, one that is extremely low or extremely high, the program keeps asking for another temperature using a WHILE loop.

Listing 14.10. A temperature conversion program.

```
' Celsius to Fahrenheit conversion
'

PRINT "** Temperature Conversion **"      ' An opening title message
```

```
INPUT "What is the outside Celsius temperature"; ctemp

WHILE (ctemp > 42)                  ' Assumes that the temperature can't
   PRINT "That is too high!"        ' be as high as the user entered.
   PRINT "Try again..."
   PRINT
   INPUT "What is the outside Celsius temperature"; ctemp
WEND

ftemp = (9 / 5) * ctemp + 32        ' Perform the conversion

PRINT "The Fahrenheit equivalent is"; ftemp

END
```

Following is the output. Notice that the WHILE loop ensures that the user types a reasonable temperature.

```
** Temperature Conversion **
What is the outside Celsius temperature? 495
That is too high!
Try again...

What is the outside Celsius temperature? 17
The Fahrenheit equivalent is 62.6
```

The choice of which kind of loop to use, either a FOR or a WHILE, is up to the programmer. They are usually interchangeable. Sometimes one makes more sense depending on the problem your program is trying to solve. For example, you can write the 10-9-8... countdown program using a WHILE loop rather than a FOR loop, as in Listing 14.11.

Listing 14.11. The revised countdown program.

```
' Countdown using a WHILE loop
'
ctr = 10

WHILE (ctr >= 1)
   PRINT ctr
   ctr = ctr - 1          ' Subtract one each time the loop repeats
WEND

PRINT "Blast off!"
```

Subroutines

Programs can be quite long. In this chapter, you've seen fairly short programs. When a program gets too big, it often gets complex. To tackle the complexity, break the program into smaller pieces, or sections, of code called *subroutines.* Instead of writing one huge program, you can write several sections of one program by putting each section of code in a subroutine and allowing each section to execute individually.

If you have never programmed before, understanding the advantage of subroutines might be difficult. Subroutines enable you to compartmentalize pieces of a long program. You then can test each piece individually, making sure each section works, before putting them together into one program.

You have several ways to write subroutines depending on the version of BASIC you use. One of the most common ways, although it is not always the easiest, is using the GOSUB statement. GOSUB requires that the beginning line of each subroutine have a line number. If you've had to use line numbers for all your BASIC programs up to this point, you don't have to do anything differently. If you have been following along and all the programs in this chapter work as you see them, you have a newer version of BASIC that does not require line numbers. The newer versions of BASIC support an advanced subroutine style. To understand the lowest common denominator versions of BASIC, learn GOSUB first. All BASIC languages support GOSUB, but not all support the other methods of calling subroutines.

To see GOSUB in action, consider the payroll computation program in Listing 14.12. This version does not use GOSUB; rather, it is one long program. The program asks the user for payroll information, computes the paycheck information, and prints a payroll check. Be sure to turn on your computer's printer before running this program so the check prints properly. Because this program is longer than the others you have seen in this chapter, it is a great candidate for subroutines. After looking over this version, check out the better version that uses subroutines and GOSUB in Listing 14.13.

Listing 14.12. The payroll program without *GOSUB*.

```
' Payroll program that does not use GOSUB
' to separate sections into manageable subroutines

PRINT "** Payroll Program **"      ' Title

' Ask if user wants to see calculations and check
```

```
INPUT "Do you want to see your payroll and print a check? (Y/N)"; Ans$
IF (Ans$ = "N") THEN
    END                     ' Quit program if user responds with N
END IF                      ' Anything other than N falls through
                            ' triggering rest of the program


' Data gathering section
INPUT "What is your name"; Fullname$
INPUT "How many hours did you work"; Hours
INPUT "How much do you make per hour"; Rate

' Calculation section
TaxRate = .35
GrossPay = Hours * Rate
Taxes = TaxRate * GrossPay
NetPay = GrossPay - Taxes

' Screen display of the data
PRINT                               ' Prints a blank line
PRINT "Here is your payroll information:"
PRINT "Name: "; Fullname$
PRINT "Gross pay: $"; GrossPay
PRINT "Taxes: $"; Taxes
PRINT "Net pay: $"; NetPay

' Print the paycheck
LPRINT "Pay to the order of "; Fullname$
LPRINT
LPRINT "                        The amount of: *********$"; NetPay
LPRINT "Benson Corp."
LPRINT "1212 E. Oak"
LPRINT "Miami, FL 21233          _____ "
LPRINT "                            (Jim Gaines, Treasurer)"

END
```

Following is the output of the preceding program. The check information that would go to the printer is repeated here.

```
** Payroll Program **
Do you want to see your payroll and print a check? (Y/N)? Y
What is your name? George Smith
How many hours did you work? 42
How much do you make per hour? 4.70
```

```
Here is your payroll information:
Name: George Smith
Gross pay: $ 197.4
Taxes: $ 69.09
Net pay: $ 128.31
Pay to the order of George Smith

                       The amount of: **********$ 128.31

Benson Corp.
1212 E. Oak
Miami, FL 21233            _____
                          (Jim Gaines, Treasurer)
```

The same payroll program, this time with subroutines, is presented in Listing 14.13. At this point, you may not totally understand the advantages of subroutines. The important thing for you to do now is learn to recognize them. The more you program and the longer the programs that you write, the more that subroutines will make your programming job easier.

Notice that, instead of being one long program in Listing 14.13, the primary part of the payroll program is short. The code at the top of the program, the five GOSUB statements, controls the subroutines. Subroutines are like detours in the program. The subroutine starting at line 100 is executed first. Therefore, after GOSUB 100, find line 100 in the program; that is the next statement executed. Control continues from line 100 until the RETURN statement is reached. RETURN is the end of the detour; control returns to the statement that called the subroutine and continues to the next statement, GOSUB 200.

The logic and output of this version is exactly the same as that in Listing 14.12. Nevertheless, the program is now made up of more distinct components, like a kit of components in a model you build. The longer the program becomes, the more breaking it into subroutines aids your programming.

Listing 14.13. The payroll program with *GOSUB*.

```
' Payroll program that uses GOSUB to
' separate sections into manageable subroutines

PRINT "** Payroll Program **"      ' Title

GOSUB 100     ' See if user wants to continue
GOSUB 200     ' Get the payroll data
GOSUB 300     ' Calculate the payroll information
```

```
GOSUB 400     ' Display the information on the screen
GOSUB 500     ' Print the check
END


100 ' Ask if user wants to see calculations and check
    INPUT "Do you want to see your payroll and print a check? (Y/N)"; Ans$
    IF (Ans$ = "N") THEN
        END                     ' Quit program if user responds with N
    END IF                      ' Anything other than N falls through
    RETURN                      ' triggering rest of the program

200 ' Data gathering section
    INPUT "What is your name"; Fullname$
    INPUT "How many hours did you work"; Hours
    INPUT "How much do you make per hour"; Rate
    RETURN

300 ' Calculation section
    TaxRate = .35
    GrossPay = Hours * Rate
    Taxes = TaxRate * GrossPay
    NetPay = GrossPay - Taxes
    RETURN

400 ' Screen display of the data
    PRINT                               ' Prints a blank line
    PRINT "Here is your payroll information:"
    PRINT "Name: "; Fullname$
    PRINT "Gross pay: $"; GrossPay
    PRINT "Taxes: $"; Taxes
    PRINT "Net pay: $"; NetPay
    RETURN

500 ' Print the paycheck
    LPRINT "Pay to the order of "; Fullname$
    LPRINT
    LPRINT "                              The amount of: **********$"; NetPay
    LPRINT "Benson Corp."
    LPRINT "1212 E. Oak"
    LPRINT "Miami, FL 21233        _____ "
    LPRINT "                              (Jim Gaines, Treasurer)"
    RETURN
END
```

You can imagine another advantage to GOSUB if you look at the early part of this program. Suppose you have to rearrange sections of a program. Although you do not have to rearrange this payroll program, you might have to rearrange other programs. Maybe the program prints a report and you want the order of the report changed. Instead of rearranging your program, you only have to rearrange the order of the GOSUB calls, making the program much easier to change.

As mentioned earlier, BASIC handles subroutines several other ways. With many of the newer versions of BASIC, you can use labels rather than line numbers. With labels, the GOSUB statements in the previous program might look like the following:

```
GOSUB Prompt      ' See if user wants to continue
GOSUB GetData     ' Get the payroll data
GOSUB CalPay      ' Calculate the payroll information
GOSUB DispPay     ' Display the information on the screen
GOSUB PrntPay     ' Print the check
```

Instead of seeing line numbers before the subroutines, you see the labels Prompt:, GetData:, and so on. Using descriptive labels instead of numbers makes the program easier to understand and maintain.

This program's logic is used at the end of the next three chapters, so you can compare and contrast the same program written in four different languages.

Summary

You now have a general understanding of the BASIC programming language. BASIC is a relatively simple language, but it still has the power to handle numerous programming tasks. BASIC is a great language for beginners and can be used as a stepping stone to more complicated languages.

Some of the newer versions of BASIC contain powerful programming statements that rival those of other programming languages, such as Pascal and C. One drawback of BASIC, however, is that it is not as efficient as some other programming languages, nor is it as powerful as Pascal or C. Sometimes you must write long programs in BASIC to accomplish what a much shorter program can accomplish in Pascal or C. If you become familiar with more than one programming language, you will have a better idea which language is best for your specific application.

15

Overview of Pascal

by Greg Perry

The Pascal programming language was developed during the early days of microcomputing to meet the programmers' demand for a more powerful language than BASIC. Whereas BASIC is a good language for beginners, Pascal is an excellent general-purpose language for business and engineering. Pascal's strength lies in its highly structured language elements.

This chapter gives you an overview of Pascal, offering a history of the language and a description of its fundamental commands—including the major similarities and differences between Pascal and BASIC. Today, BASIC has become a fairly powerful language with features that imitate some of Pascal's. That is a tribute to Pascal, one of the first programming languages designed from the start as a well-structured programming language. Pascal offers significant speed improvements over BASIC because it always runs in a compiled environment.

Pascal's Background

In the early 1970s, a man named Niklaus Wirth saw the need for teaching structured programming techniques. As described in Chapter 14, "Overview of BASIC," structured programming is the process of writing orderly programs without excessive, unnecessary branching. Structured programs are easy to maintain—an important consideration, because today's data processing departments must change their computer software systems to meet the changing demands of the world.

Niklaus Wirth noticed that his students did not adapt well to structured programming techniques. He blamed the languages of the day, not the students. Mr. Wirth set out to design his own programming language that strongly supported structured programming—a language that included control constructs and made it difficult *not* to write structured programs. Mr. Wirth named his language *Pascal* after the 17th century mathematician Blaise Pascal. (Pascal was one of the first programming languages whose name was not an acronym for something else.)

Mr. Wirth designed the language as a tool for teaching proper programming methods; he was as surprised as anyone that Pascal became an enormously successful general-purpose programming language.

Pascal's Popularity

Pascal became one of the most widely used programming languages for microcomputers—second only to BASIC—during the late 1970s and 1980s. Although there were other languages that offered similar structured commands, such as Algol, none of the other programming languages was small enough to fit in the limited memory space of the early microcomputers.

Pascal enjoyed an overwhelming success. Entire programming magazines were devoted to the language, and programming departments all over the world started using Pascal exclusively. Pascal became a requirement in college curriculums—right after BASIC—so that new programmers could learn as early as possible to program the "right way."

During the 1980s, it appeared the entire world would convert almost exclusively to Pascal. There had been many programming languages created before Pascal, and many were thought to be the answer to various programming needs. However, no language before Pascal created such a furor in the programming community; Pascal generated a devoted following never before seen for a programming language. As Pascal began to be ported to larger computers, many people thought Pascal would become the language choice of businesses that had stayed with COBOL and FORTRAN throughout the previous language "fads."

Perhaps as a result of the times, Pascal's huge popularity dwindled almost faster than it grew. Although Pascal still enjoys a large following, and Pascal compilers continue to sell well, Pascal has ended up where it began—in the classroom. Today, Pascal is taught to new programmers because it uses the "proper" programming techniques that a good programmer should possess. Nevertheless, Pascal is no longer taught for its own sake. Pascal is viewed as a language that teaches the proper fundamentals that a programmer needs before moving on to another language—most commonly C (described in Chapter 16).

Pascal's use in data processing departments is limited these days. C has taken the world by storm since the mid 1980s and continues to do so (along with C's successor, C++, described in Chapter 17).

Given its decline in use, should you spend time learning Pascal? Of course. Pascal is still the cornerstone of proper programming techniques, easier to learn than C, and the skills you learn with the Pascal language stay with you no matter which language becomes your primary programming language.

Listing 15.1 shows you the structure of a simple Pascal program. Do not be concerned with understanding everything—or anything—in this program just yet. Simply skim through it to get a feel for the way Pascal programs look. Pascal's key features and programming statements are described throughout the next few sections.

Listing 15.1. A simple Pascal program.

```
PROGRAM ShowName;
USES Crt;
VAR    Row:          INTEGER;
       Col:          INTEGER;
       FirstName: STRING[10]; {use only first 10 chars of name}
BEGIN
   CLRSCR;
   WRITE('What is your first name? ');   { Get name to display}
   READLN(FirstName);

   { Show the name randomly on the screen }
   BEGIN
      GOTOXY(10, 15);
      WRITE(FirstName);
      GOTOXY(50, 20);
      WRITE(FirstName);
      GOTOXY(1, 1);
      WRITE(FirstName);
      GOTOXY(70, 5);
      WRITE(FirstName);
      GOTOXY(60, 10);
      WRITE(FirstName);
   END;
```

continues

243

Listing 15.1. Continued

```
   { Show name in columns }
   FOR Row := 1 TO 24 DO
      BEGIN
         GOTOXY(1,Row);
         FOR Col := 1 TO 5 DO WRITE(FirstName:10);
      END;  {for}
   { Show message in the middle of the screen }
   GOTOXY(30,12);
   WRITE('That''s all, ',FirstName);
   READLN;  { Wait for an ENTER keypress }
END. {ShowName}
```

The Pascal Language

Pascal is a rich programming language with lots of power. Its many control structures give you a wide assortment of commands from which to choose. The following
sections explain the key language elements of Pascal and guide you through an
overview of the language. Once you finish this chapter, you will have a good idea of
what Pascal programs look like and you will be able to read and understand simple
Pascal programs.

Program Outline

All Pascal programs begin with the keyword PROGRAM. As with any Pascal command,
PROGRAM may be in uppercase or lowercase letters—but most Pascal programmers
put commands in uppercase to distinguish them from variable names. After PROGRAM,
you must specify a name for your program. The name is not the filename—it is just a
name from 1 to 63 characters, beginning with any letter of the alphabet, which refers
to the program that follows. The PROGRAM line should look similar to this:

PROGRAM *ProgramName*;

> *ProgramName* does not have to be the actual filename; however, many
> programmers use the actual filename for easier documentation.

The PROGRAM statement line must end with a semicolon. Unlike BASIC, all statements in Pascal—with one minor exception explained later in this section—must end in a semicolon. The semicolon tells Pascal that the statement has ended and it can move on to the next statement. For beginning Pascal programmers, the semicolon is one of the easiest things to forget when writing a Pascal program. If you forget a semicolon at the end of a command, Pascal reminds you with an error when you compile the program.

Somewhere near the top of every Pascal program is a BEGIN statement. The actual body of the program begins with BEGIN.

All Pascal programs end with the END keyword followed by a period. The last line, END, is the only exception to the rule that all Pascal statements end in a semicolon (see Note that follows). Unlike BASIC's optional END statement, Pascal requires END. Therefore, here is a skeleton of a Pascal program with the proper starting and ending lines.

```
PROGRAM CalWages
BEGIN
   .
   .                        { Body of program goes here }
   .
END.
```

Semicolons always end *executable* statements. Statements such as IF-THEN, FOR, and REPEAT introduce a series of one or more statements, each ultimately ending with a semicolon. The actual IF-THEN, FOR, and REPEAT lines, however, do not end with a semicolon; they begin the statement but are not, themselves, complete statements.

There is always a matching END for every BEGIN (as you saw with record variables in Chapter 4, however, there is not always a BEGIN for every END). As you will learn later in this chapter, there can be more than one pair of BEGIN-END statements. A *block* is one or more statements between each pair of BEGIN-END statements.

Pascal Comments

Pascal comments—the lines of documentation you put into your programs to make the code more understandable to other people—reside between two curly braces. Unlike comment statements in BASIC, requiring REM on every line that is a remark, Pascal's comments can span many lines in the program. The comment begins with a left brace and ends with a right brace—even if that right brace appears many lines later.

There is another kind of Pascal comment that is rarely used today. It begins with (* and ends with *). Pascal treats all text between (* and *) as a comment. The following two examples are valid comments:

```
{ Calculate net pay }
```

and

```
(* Calculate net pay *)
```

Listing 15.2 is a small program with comments scattered throughout. The first three lines contain a multi-line comment. A single-line comment appears on a line by itself before the WRITELN() statements. A few comments are scattered to the right of some later statements as well.

Listing 15.2. A program demonstrating the use of comments.

```
{ This program puts a few values in variables
  and then displays those values to the screen.
  These three lines are comments. }

PROGRAM DEMO;
USES Crt;

VAR Age:        INTEGER;
    Salary:     REAL;

BEGIN
   CLRSCR;
   Age       := 32;          { Stores the age }
   Salary    := 25000;       { Yearly salary }

   { Display the results on the screen }

   WRITELN( Age );
   WRITELN( Salary );

END {DemoComments1}.
```

As shown in the preceding program, Pascal programmers often put the name of the program (first seen after the PROGRAM statement) in a comment directly following the final END. This signals to anyone reading the program that the entire program has come to an end (of course, so does the period after END).

Use ample comments throughout your Pascal programs to increase their readability and maintainability.

Pascal Data

Pascal's variable and data types are similar to those used in BASIC, which you learned about in Chapter 14. Because you, the Pascal programmer, are responsible for the variables your programs need, you should learn the naming rules for variables. Here are the variable naming rules for most versions of Pascal:

1. All variable names must be between 1 and 63 characters in length.

2. All variable names must begin with a letter of the alphabet or the underscore character (_).

3. All characters following the first character can be any mixture of letters, numbers, and underscores.

The following are all valid variable names:

```
SALES

Payroll93

_AcctRec

Volume_DECEM
```

These, however, are not valid variable names:

`93Payroll`	*Variable names cannot begin with a number*
`Total Amount`	*Variable names cannot contain a space*
`Dept$@#$Mktg`	*Variable names cannot contain special characters*

As with BASIC, Pascal does not distinguish between uppercase and lowercase variable names. Therefore, the following four examples represent the same variable in Pascal:

```
Sales

sALES

SALES

sales
```

Pascal variables can hold different types of data. The data can be either numeric or character. Table 15.1 describes the types of data that variables can hold and gives an explanation of each type. Pascal supports many more data types than BASIC.

Table 15.1. Pascal data types.		
Type	**Examples**	**Description**
CHAR	'A', '*'	Single characters.
STRING	'Harry'	String of zero or more characters.
SHORTINT	-19, 0, 88	Whole numbers, without decimal points, from −128 to 127.
BYTE	1, 255	Whole positive numbers, without decimal points, from 0 to 255.
INTEGER	45, -179	Whole numbers, without decimal points, from −32768 to 32767.
LONGINT	456787	Extremely large or extremely small whole numbers.
WORD	7, 60000	Whole positive numbers, without decimal points, from 0 to 65535.
REAL	0.01	Real numbers, with decimal points, from -2.9×10^{-39} to 1.7×10^{38}.
SINGLE	956.534	Real numbers, with decimal points, from -1.5×10^{-45} to 3.4×10^{38}.
DOUBLE	83544972.8	Real numbers, with decimal points, from -5.0×10^{-324} to 1.7×10^{308}.
EXTENDED	7628295237.212	Real numbers, with decimal points, from -3.4×10^{-4932} to 1.1×10^{4932}.

Unlike BASIC, Pascal requires that you explicitly *define* all variables before you use them. To define a variable in Pascal means to list—at the top of every program—each variable name and its corresponding type. You must define each variable to the program before the body of the program can do anything with that variable.

The first column in Table 15.1 shows the names you must use when you define variables in Pascal. Notice that the name of each data type is in uppercase, which is the preferred, but not required, method in Pascal.

To define one or more variables at the top of a Pascal program, begin the line with the VAR command. VAR informs Pascal that a variable definition is about to follow.

You only have to list your variable names and their respective data types following the VAR statement. The following is a variable declaration section of a Pascal program:

```
VAR Age:        SHORTINT;
    Salary:     REAL;
    Dependents: BYTE;
```

After Pascal compiles the three lines, it recognizes three variables named Age, Salary, and Dependents to be used later in the program. Because Pascal is a freeform language, the extra spaces in the variable definition code are optional. Pascal would understand the code if it looked like this:

```
VAR Age:SHORTINT; Salary:REAL; Dependents: BYTE;
```

Obviously, the first method—with spacing—is more readable. The more examples you see, and the more you program in Pascal, the quicker you establish good spacing technique in your Pascal programs.

When you define a string variable in Pascal, you must think ahead more than you have to in BASIC. To write an efficient program, you must tell Pascal—at variable definition time—the longest string value you will ever store in a string variable. In other words, if you want to define a variable to hold your company's name, you must count the number of characters in the company name and provide this information to Pascal at the time you define the variable. If your company name is 14 characters long, the following statement could be used to define a string variable to hold the name:

```
VAR CompName : STRING[14];   { No name longer than 14 will fit }
```

Actually, you can leave off the string's maximum length in brackets, but if you do, Pascal reserves 255 characters of storage for the string. If your string is much shorter than 255 characters, this can waste a lot of extra memory space.

Assigning Values

Similar to BASIC, Pascal uses an assignment operator to store values in variables, with one exception—Pascal uses a two-character operator (:=) for assignment. Pascal reserves the equal sign for testing within relational operations (BASIC used = for both assignment and testing). Here are some examples of assigning values to variables in Pascal:

```
Age := 32;

MyName := 'Sally';
```

Put single quotation marks around any data you assign to a string variable—unless you are assigning it the value of another string variable. In the following line, for example, you should not put single quotation marks around MyName because it is the name of another string variable:

```
OurName := MyName;  { Assign one string variable to another }
```

Simple Math Operators

Pascal uses math symbols that are similar to those used in BASIC. Pascal's operator hierarchy is also similar to BASIC's. Table 15.2 shows the regular Pascal math operators and their precedence.

Table 15.2. Pascal's primary math operators.			
Precedence	**Operator**	**Example**	**Description**
1	(,)	(3+2)/2	Overrides all other precedence.
2	*, /, DIV	8 DIV 2	Multiply, real divide, and integer divide.
3	+, -	2+3-2	Addition and subtraction.

When you divide an integer variable or an integer constant by another integer, you must use the DIV operator. Although DIV looks more like a command than an operator, Pascal performs integer division when it sees DIV. When you use DIV, the result Pascal returns is always an integer (whole number). For example, the following statement stores a 6 in the integer variable Result because 4 goes into 25 six times.

```
Result := 25 DIV 4;
```

If you define Result as a REAL variable and use the real number division operator (/), the following statement would store 6.25 in Result.

```
Result := 25 / 4;
```

Input and Output

The WRITE and WRITELN functions are Pascal's primary methods of writing data to the screen. These are not true Pascal commands. Pascal does not include any commands that perform input or output (neither do C and C++, as you see in Chapters 16 and 17). WRITE and WRITELN are *functions,* or built-in routines—supplied by the makers of your Pascal compiler—that perform output. The distinction between *command* and *function* is trivial for beginners of the language.

WRITELN sends data to the screen in a manner similar to PRINT in BASIC. WRITE also sends data to the screen, but does not perform an automatic carriage return; that is, the cursor stays on the same line. Look at the following two examples,

```
WRITELN('I am learning Pascal.');
WRITELN('Pascal is a well-structured language.');
```

which displays this on-screen:

```
I am learning Pascal.
Pascal is a well-structured language.
```

WRITE is not as generous. These three lines,

```
WRITE('One');
WRITE('Two');
WRITE('Three');
```

produce on-screen the following *single line*:

```
OneTwoThree
```

Therefore, if you are calculating results and printing them as you calculate, you can use a combination of WRITE and WRITELN. WRITE will display the values across one line as you calculate and print them. Then, display the last value with WRITELN so that the cursor moves down to the succeeding line for the next group of output statements.

The program in Listing 15.3 uses a combination of WRITE and WRITELN statements to print the values of some data.

Listing 15.3. A program that assigns values to variables and prints them on-screen.

```
{ This program puts a few values in variables
  and then displays those values and labels
  to the screen. }

PROGRAM DemoStringConstants;

VAR Age:        INTEGER;
    Salary:     REAL;
    Dependents: BYTE;

BEGIN
```

continues

Listing 15.3. Continued

```
   Age        := 32;          { Stores the age }
   Salary     := 25000.50;    { Yearly salary }
   Dependents := 2;           { Number of dependents }

 { Display the results }

   WRITE( 'Age: ' );
   WRITELN( Age );
   WRITE( 'Salary: ' );
   WRITELN( Salary );
   WRITE( 'Dependents: ' );
   WRITELN( Dependents );
END. {DemoStringConstants}
```

The preceding program produces the following output:

```
Age: 32
Salary: 25000.500001
Dependents: 2
```

As is obvious from this example, something odd happens when you print REAL data in Pascal. Pascal does not realize that you want only two decimal places. Because Pascal internally stores REAL data (along with all the other real data types such as SINGLE and DOUBLE) to several decimal places, it prints those extra decimal places. Sometimes, as happened here, a slight fractional error creeps in as well. You can limit the number of decimal places printed by following the variable with a width and decimal specifier as in the following statement:

```
WRITELN( Salary:8:2 );
```

The :8:2 tells Pascal to print the Salary variable within eight spaces, reserving two of those eight spaces for the fractional part of the number. If this WRITELN statement had been included in the preceding program, the following results would have been displayed on-screen:

```
Age: 32
Salary: 25000.50
Dependents: 2
```

You must do some extra work if you want to print values to your printer instead of to your screen. Anytime you want to output data to your printer, you must include the following statement after the PROGRAM line in your program:

```
USES printer;
```

When Pascal compiles this line, it loads some extra code it needs to output to your printer. Additionally, at the beginning of each WRITE and WRITELN statement in your program you must include the LST device name. LST instructs Pascal to write to the printer and not to the screen when you request WRITE or WRITELN. The program in Listing 15.4 outputs the data to the printer instead of to the screen.

Listing 15.4. This program prints the variable values to a printer.

```
{ This program puts a few values in variables
  and then prints those values and labels
  to the printer. }

PROGRAM DemoStringConstants;
USES printer;      { Sets up the printer }

VAR Age:        INTEGER;
    Salary:     REAL;
    Dependents: BYTE;

BEGIN

   Age        := 32;          { Stores the age }
   Salary     := 25000.50;    { Yearly salary }
   Dependents := 2;           { Number of dependents }

   { Print the results }

   WRITE(LST, 'Age:' );
   WRITELN(LST,  Age );
   WRITE(LST, 'Salary:' );
   WRITELN(LST, Salary:8:2 );
   WRITE(LST, 'Dependents:' );
   WRITELN(LST, Dependents );
END. {DemoStringConstants}
```

Pascal offers a READLN function that gets input from the keyboard and is similar to BASIC's INPUT command. Unlike INPUT, however, READLN does not display a question mark when it executes; if you want a question mark to appear as a prompt, you must supply your own.

The following statement waits for the user to type a number, and then stores that number in the Sales variable before proceeding to the rest of the program:

```
READLN( Sales );
```

253

The following statement reads three values from the keyboard:

```
READLN( Num1, Num2, Num3 );
```

With a multiple-input READLN, the user must separate each input number with a space. Be sure to tell the user exactly what she or he must type at the keyboard. The program in Listing 15.5 prompts each segment of input with an appropriate message.

Listing 15.5. A Pascal program that prompts the user for input.

```
{  User inputs 3 values using READLN.
   The values then print to the printer. }

PROGRAM NameEmp;
USES Printer;

VAR Name    : STRING[25];
    Years   : INTEGER;
    Balance : REAL;

BEGIN
    WRITE( 'What is your name? ' );
    READLN( Name );
    WRITE( 'How many years have you worked here? ');
    READLN( Years );
    WRITE( 'What is your investment plan balance? ');
    READLN( Balance );

    WRITELN( LST, 'You typed the following:');
    WRITELN( LST, 'Name: ', Name);
    WRITELN( LST, 'Years: ', Years);
    WRITELN( LST, 'Balance: ', Balance);

END. {NameEmp}
```

Comparing Data

When comparing data, Pascal uses the same relational operators as BASIC. Unlike BASIC, however, Pascal's equal sign is used solely for equality testing—not for assignment. Pascal has an IF-THEN command, similar to BASIC's. The format of Pascal's IF-THEN is

```
IF condition THEN
   BEGIN
      .
      .                  { One or more Pascal statements go here }
      .
   END;
```

The IF-THEN command is used to make a decision. If the condition is true, every statement between BEGIN and END executes. If the condition is not true, none of the statements between BEGIN and END execute. Whatever the condition, the rest of the program following END continues execution when IF finishes.

If you only want to perform one statement if the condition is true, you do not need to specify BEGIN and END. For example, here is a valid Pascal IF-THEN statement:

```
IF (Bonus >= 5000) THEN WRITELN('You did well!');
```

This is the same statement with a BEGIN-END block:

```
IF (Bonus >= 5000) THEN
   BEGIN
      WRITELN('You did well!');
   END;
```

This IF says that if Bonus is greater than or equal to 5000, display a message on-screen that says You did well!

Pascal also includes an ELSE option for the IF-THEN command. The format of the IF-THEN-ELSE is

```
IF condition THEN
   BEGIN
      .
      .                  { One or more Pascal statements go here }
      .
   END
ELSE
   BEGIN
      .
      .                  { One or more Pascal statements go here }
      .
   END;
```

As with the simple IF, when the body of the ELSE is only one line, you do not have to use the BEGIN-END keywords.

The program in Listing 15.6 demonstrates the IF-THEN-ELSE control statements.

Listing 15.6. A program that demonstrates the *IF-THEN-ELSE* comparison.

```
{ Improved program to display a message
  depending on years of service using
  the IF-THEN-ELSE. }
PROGRAM Service2;

VAR Yrs: INTEGER;

BEGIN
   WRITE( 'How many years of service? ' );
   READLN( Yrs );
   IF (Yrs > 20) THEN
      BEGIN
         WRITELN( 'Give a gold watch' );
      END
   ELSE IF ((Yrs > 10) AND (Yrs <= 20)) THEN
            BEGIN
               WRITELN( 'Give a paperweight' );
            END
         ELSE WRITELN( 'Give a pat on the back' );
END. {Service2}
```

Try to follow the program's logic. It uses an IF-THEN-ELSE within a simple IF statement. The program displays an appropriate company reward based on the employee's years of service. The IF lets the program work differently for different employees. Here is a sample output from the program:

```
How many years of service? 5
Give a pat on the back
```

The program makes a different decision if the number of years of service is greater, as the following output shows:

```
How many years of service? 16
Give a paperweight
```

Looping Statements

Pascal has both a FOR loop and a WHILE loop that correspond to those in BASIC. Pascal also offers another loop construct called the REPEAT loop. Depending on your program, the REPEAT might be easier to use than the WHILE. This section shows you how to loop in Pascal.

The *FOR* Loop

Here is the format of Pascal's FOR loop:

```
FOR index := start TO last DO
   BEGIN
      .
      .                   { One or more Pascal statements go here }
      .
   END;
```

The FOR loop always counts up. The loop begins by assigning to the *index* variable the value of *start*. The loop continues—with *index* incrementing by 1 each iteration of the loop—until the *index* variable becomes equal to *last*. This is exactly the same as BASIC's FOR loop, with the exception that Pascal does not allow for an increment other than 1.

Here is a simple program that prints a message five times based on the FOR loop's execution.

```
{ Program that changes the FOR loop control printing }

PROGRAM Control1;

VAR i: INTEGER;

BEGIN

   FOR i := 1 TO 5 DO
     BEGIN
       WRITELN( '*** Computers are fun! ***' );
     END;
END. {Control1}
```

If you want a FOR loop to count down, you must use a different form of FOR. The following is the format of a FOR loop that decrements the *index* variable:

```
FOR index := start DOWNTO last DO
   BEGIN
      .
      .                   { One or more Pascal statements go here }
      .
   END;
```

With DOWNTO, you must ensure that the *start* value is greater than *last* so that Pascal can decrement *index* between the two values. To illustrate the countdown FOR loop, the following program counts down from 10 to 1 and prints *** Blast off! ***:

```
{ Program that counts down using a FOR loop }

PROGRAM Control1;

VAR i: INTEGER;

BEGIN

   FOR i := 10 DOWNTO 1 DO
     BEGIN
       WRITELN( i );
     END;
   WRITELN( '*** Blast off! ***');
END. {Control1}
```

The *WHILE* Loop

Pascal's WHILE loop is similar to BASIC's WHILE loop. The Pascal WHILE loop continues looping while a relational condition is true. As soon as the relational condition is false, the WHILE loop ends and the rest of the program continues. Here is the format of WHILE:

```
WHILE condition DO
   BEGIN
     .
     .                { One or more Pascal statements go here }
     .
   END;
```

The following program demonstrates the WHILE loop and is a routine that could be used inside a larger program. This routine tests an age entered by the user to ensure that the age falls between two values. This is known as *validity checking*. When you ask the user for input, you usually check to see whether the input is valid by making sure it falls in a range between two reasonable values. For example, if the user typed 997 as an age, the number would be wrong because no one lives that long.

```
{ Program that helps ensure that age values are reasonable }
PROGRAM Age1;

VAR   Age: INTEGER;                    { age typed by user }

BEGIN
   WRITE( 'What is the age of the student? ' );
   READLN( Age );
   WHILE ((Age < 14) OR (Age > 100)) DO
     BEGIN
```

```
        WRITELN( '*** The age must be between 14 and 100 ***' );
        WRITELN( 'Try again...' );
        WRITELN;
        WRITE( 'What is the student''s age? ' );
        READLN( Age );
     END;
   WRITELN( 'You typed a valid age.' );
END. {Age1}
```

Here is the output from the preceding program. Notice that the WHILE loop keeps an incorrect age from being entered.

```
What is the age of the student? 217
*** The age must be between 14 and 100 ***
Try again...

What is the student's age? 21
You typed a valid age.
```

The *REPEAT* Loop

Pascal offers one additional loop control statement called the REPEAT statement. You can use REPEAT when the logic of the WHILE loop doesn't quite work out. Whereas WHILE continues looping as long as the relational condition is True, REPEAT continues looping as long as the relational condition is False. Here is the format of REPEAT:

```
REPEAT
   .
   .               { One or more Pascal statements go here }
   .
UNTIL condition is true;
```

REPEAT is slightly easier to program than WHILE because you don't have to worry with BEGIN-END blocks. Depending on your program's logic, REPEAT might be a better choice than either FOR or WHILE. The program in Listing 15.7 uses a REPEAT loop to get a number from the user. The program keeps repeating—and obtaining numbers—until the user types a 0.

Listing 15.7. A program that uses a *REPEAT* loop.

```
{ Program that accepts a list of numbers and
  shows the total and average. }
PROGRAM Adder;
VAR Total: INTEGER;                    { running total }
    Count: INTEGER;                    { # of numbers typed by user }
```

continues

Listing 15.7. Continued

```
   Num:    INTEGER;                        { number typed by user }

BEGIN
   Total := 0;                            { Init variables }
   Count := 0;
                                          { Get input until get 0 }
   REPEAT
      WRITE( 'What is your number (0 will end the input)? ' );
      READLN( Num );
      Total := Total + Num;   { Add 1 to the number }
      IF Num <> 0 THEN Count := Count + 1;     { Don't count 0 }
   UNTIL (Num = 0);
                                          { Control gets here }
                                          { when last number = 0 }
   WRITELN;
   WRITELN( 'The total is ', Total );
   WRITELN( 'The average is ', (Total / Count):1:2);
END. {Adder}
```

This program's logic is one of the most advanced in this chapter, and yet, it still is not too difficult to follow. The program first assigns both a Total and a Count variable to zero. As the user types numbers into the program in response to the READLN, the numbers are added to the total and the counter is incremented by 1. Because the program prints an average of the numbers, it must keep track of the total of the values as well as the number of values entered. The loop continues, thanks to the REPEAT, until the user types a 0 to end the input. A FOR loop would not work in this program because you don't know how many values the user wants to average. A WHILE would not work either because you want the program to loop as long as the number is not zero (as long as the condition is False).

Procedures

In the preceding chapter, you learned how BASIC uses GOSUB to call subroutines. By breaking your code into small pieces and executing those pieces, you can ease the programming burden for longer programs. Pascal does not contain a statement analogous to GOSUB—but that is to your advantage. Instead of having to call line-numbered statements, Pascal's subroutines are much easier to follow.

Language Spotlight

It is extremely common for you to add or subtract 1 from variables. The Adder program in Listing 15.7 used a counter variable to count the number of entries made by the user. To count, the program added 1 to a count variable with the following statement:

```
count := count + 1;
```

You can also subtract one from a variable in the same way:

```
count := count - 1;
```

Because adding and subtracting 1 is so common, the designers of Pascal included two built-in functions that make adding and subtracting 1 from variables easy. To add 1 to count, you could simply do this:

```
INC(count);        { Adds one to count. }
```

INC means *increment*. To subtract 1, or *decrement* 1 from a variable, you can do this:

```
DEC(count);        { Subtracts one from count. }
```

If you want to add or subtract more than one, you can do so with INC and DEC. The following statement adds 24 to the variable named MyNumberOfDays:

```
INC(MyNumberOfDays, 24);
```

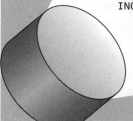

The second value, if you choose to include one, is the value Pascal adds or subtracts to or from the first variable. Using INC in this case is easier than having to write out an entire assignment expression, such as

```
MyNumberOfDays := MyNumberOfDays + 24;
```

In Pascal, a subroutine is called a *procedure*. Actually, you have seen procedures throughout this chapter. The entire Pascal program between the opening BEGIN and the final END statements is the program's *main procedure*. In other words, the entire program is one long, unnamed procedure. If you want to include several other procedures, you must name them with the PROCEDURE statement. Here is the format of the PROCEDURE statement:

```
PROCEDURE ProcName;
```

The *ProcName* can be any name that follows the same naming rules you saw earlier for variables. The following is a sample procedure definition from a program; it writes a name and address to the printer.

```
PROCEDURE NameAddr;                 { Define a new procedure }
USES printer;
BEGIN
   WRITELN(LST, "Elaine Harris");
   WRITELN(LST, "304 W. Sycamore");
   WRITELN(LST, "Burbank, CA  92332");
END;
```

This procedure might be part of a larger program that contains many procedures. Once you type this procedure into a program, you need some way to execute it.

All procedures must be placed *before* the main procedure. In other words, if you added procedures to any of the programs from this chapter, you would add the procedures before the existing BEGIN statement.

To execute a procedure in Pascal, you only have to call it by name. Pascal programs containing procedures are much easier to read than BASIC programs with lists of GOSUB statements. If you assign descriptive names to your procedures, you can then write statements such as the following

```
GetHours;
CalcPay;
PrintCheck;
```

If these three lines made up the main procedure of a Pascal program, you would be able to understand the program without even knowing Pascal! Some well-written segments of Pascal programs read just like statements written in English. This program contains the three procedures GetHours, CalcPay, and PrintCheck. Without knowing Pascal, you can assume that these three procedures ask the user for some payroll data, calculate the given payroll amounts, and, finally, print the checks.

Listing 15.8 is the payroll program from Chapter 14, "Overview of BASIC," rewritten in Pascal. The program uses readable procedure calls and reviews some of the Pascal commands you learned throughout this chapter.

Listing 15.8. The Pascal payroll program using procedures.

```
{ Payroll program that uses procedures
  to separate sections into manageable subroutines }
```

```
PROGRAM Payroll;
USES printer;
VAR Ans      : STRING[1];
    Fullname : STRING[25];
    Hours    : INTEGER;
    Rate     : REAL;
    TaxRate  : REAL;
    GrossPay : REAL;
    Taxes    : REAL;
    NetPay   : REAL;

PROCEDURE AskUser;        {Ask if user wants to see calculations and check}
   BEGIN
      WRITELN('Do you want to see your payroll and print a check? (Y/N)' );
      READLN( Ans );
      IF ((Ans = 'N') OR (Ans = 'n')) THEN
      BEGIN
         HALT;            { Quit program if user responds with N. }
      END;               { Anything other than N falls through. }
   END;

PROCEDURE GetHours;      { Data gathering section }
   BEGIN
      WRITELN( 'What is your name? ' );
      READLN( Fullname );
      WRITELN( 'How many hours did you work? ' );
      READLN( Hours );
      WRITELN( 'How much do you make per hour? ' );
      READLN( Rate );
   END;

PROCEDURE CalcPay;     { Calculation section }
   BEGIN
      TaxRate := 0.35;
      GrossPay := Hours * Rate;
      Taxes := TaxRate * GrossPay;
      NetPay := GrossPay - Taxes;
   END;

PROCEDURE DispPay;    { Screen display of the data }
   BEGIN
      WRITELN;     { Prints a blank line }
      WRITELN( 'Here is your payroll information:' );
      WRITELN( 'Name: ', Fullname );
```

continues

Listing 15.8. Continued

```
        WRITELN( 'Gross pay: $', GrossPay:8:2 );
        WRITELN( 'Taxes: $', Taxes:8:2 );
        WRITELN( 'Net pay: $', NetPay:8:2 );
    END;

PROCEDURE PrntCheck;    { Print the paycheck }
    BEGIN
        WRITELN(LST, 'Pay to the order of ',  Fullname);
        WRITELN(LST);
        WRITELN(LST, '                                    The amount of: *********$',
                NetPay:8:2);
        WRITELN(LST, 'Benson Corp.' );
        WRITELN(LST, '1212 E. Oak' );
        WRITELN(LST, 'Miami, FL 21233            _____');
        WRITELN(LST, '                              (Jim Gaines, Treasurer)' );
    END;

{Main procedure follows}

BEGIN
    WRITELN( '** Payroll Program **' );     { Title }
    AskUser;
    GetHours;
    CalcPay;
    DispPay;
    PrntCheck;
END. {Payroll}
```

When a Pascal program contains multiple procedures, keep in mind that the main procedure appears *last*. The first statement that actually executes in this program is the WRITELN statement in the last (main) procedure.

Look at the program in Listing 15.7; then refer back to the BASIC program shown in Listing 14.13. As you can see, a Pascal program is not always shorter than its equivalent BASIC program. After the Pascal compiler finishes compiling, however, the resulting Pascal program generally is smaller than a BASIC program—and usually runs faster. In other words, a shorter program listing does not always mean a better program. Although the Pascal code might be longer, the procedure names that Pascal requires make the program much easier to follow than similar BASIC code, which uses a web of cryptic line numbers.

The only statement in this program that you have not yet been introduced to is the HALT statement in the AskUser procedure. If the user types an N in response to the question, the HALT statement forces the program to end and returns the user to the operating system.

Summary

You now have a preliminary understanding of the Pascal programming language and how it compares to BASIC. Pascal's readable procedure names, rich assortment of data types, and abundant control statements—such as WHILE, FOR, and REPEAT—made it one of the first truly structured, easy-to-maintain programming languages written for microcomputers.

Although compiled programs take longer to prepare than interpreted ones (such as BASIC programs), the compiled programs run faster. Businesses prefer compiled programs because runtime speed is important. Most of today's Pascal compilers compile at tremendous speed. For shorter programs, you notice very little difference in the compilation times of Pascal programs and the startup times of interpreted code. Consequently, Pascal is a good language to use when optimization of both compilation time and runtime is important.

Despite its richness as a structured programming language, Pascal has been ousted as the preferred language among microcomputer programmers. Today, the C programming language—although often not as easy to read and understand—has gained a much wider acceptance among programmers. Nevertheless, most people find that first learning Pascal makes learning C easier.

16

Overview of C

by Greg Perry

Today, the C programming language is the most popular professional programming language for microcomputers. C is also a crossover language because several minicomputer and mainframe computer programming departments are moving to C as well. C's primary strength lies in its efficiency. A program written in C usually runs faster than a program written in any other high-level programming language.

C has been criticized as being a cryptic language. It is cryptic compared to Pascal and BASIC. Although you can add comments to a C program and write C code so it is less cryptic, C uses more special operators and symbols than almost any other programming language. C uses more than double the number of operators that Pascal and BASIC each use. C's use of these operators, instead of using commands, adds to C's difficulty.

As you will see in this chapter, a C program does not have to be much harder to understand than Pascal or BASIC, but C takes a little time to get used to. This chapter attempts to give you an overview of the C programming language and offer you advice so you can learn the language faster.

C's Background

In the 1970s, Bell Laboratories was writing an operating system for a new computer. The programmers wanted to use a highly efficient programming language to write the operating system. (This operating system eventually became *UNIX*, a popular multiuser operating system in widespread use today.)

Because no programming language at the time suited their needs, the programmers at Bell Labs set out to write their own. The result was C, a language that was highly efficient and gave the programmers access to the low-level parts of the computer, such as memory locations. The other programming languages of the time did not have this access.

Throughout the years, C has evolved into a general-purpose programming language, suitable for both business and scientific programming applications. C is currently one of the most widely used programming languages in the world. Many of the popular microcomputer spreadsheet and word processor programs are written in C. The classified job advertisements are routinely flooded with requests for C programmers. These days, it seems that if you know C, you've got a reliable profession as a programmer.

C is a highly *portable* language. That is, if you write a program in C that runs on one computer, you should be able to run that program on any computer, big or small, that has a C compiler.

Although C takes time to master, programmers seem to enjoy programming in the C language. C's philosophy is "trust the programmer." C has few rules. For example, C is a weakly typed language; you can define a character variable and then store a floating-point number in it. (With Pascal and BASIC, the data stored in a variable can only be one type, depending on the variable definition.)

C is not without its critics, however. It does offer some frustrations at times. You get a glimpse at C frustrations when you see how much work C makes you do to get input from the keyboard.

Listing 16.1 shows you a typical C program. Look it over. The remaining sections of this chapter explain some of the key features and commands of the C language.

Listing 16.1. A sample C program.

```
/* Requests a name and prints it five times */
#include <stdio.h>

main()
{
   int ctr=0;        /* Integer variable to count through loop */
   char fname[20];   /* Define character array to hold name */

   printf("What is your first name? ");   /* Prompt the user */
   scanf(" %s", fname);   /* Get name from the keyboard */
```

```
    while (ctr < 5)
    {
       printf("%s\n", fname);
       ctr++;
    }

}
```

The C Language

C offers almost as many language commands as Pascal while still offering more execution speed. The following sections explain the key language elements of C and guide you through an overview of the language. After you finish the chapter, you will have a good idea of what C programs look like, and you will be able to read and understand simple C programs.

Program Outline

All C programs include a main() function. In Pascal, a subroutine is called a *procedure,* in BASIC it is a subroutine, and C offers an additional name: *function.* If your C program contains no subroutines but contains only one single block of code (as short programs might), the entire program is called main(). A C function's name always ends in parentheses to distinguish it from a variable name, which cannot contain parentheses. (In Pascal, the primary controlling procedure—the entire program if it is made up of a single procedure—has no name.)

Besides requiring a main() function, C is also strict about the case of your commands and functions—it requires that you type all commands in lowercase. If you want to perform a while loop (C has one that is similar to Pascal's), you must call the command while—not While or WHILE. If you have used other programming languages, typing commands in lowercase is difficult to get used to.

As with Pascal, all executable statements end with a semicolon. Another similarity between C and Pascal is the concept of *blocks.* In Pascal, a block always begins with BEGIN and ends with END. In C, a block always begins with a left brace, {, and always ends with a right brace, }. Blocks are important to C; a function always begins a block, so a function definition is always followed by an opening brace. As you can see from Listing 16.1, additional blocks can be inside other blocks—just as in Pascal, additional BEGIN-END blocks can be inside others (such as when you have a multiline IF statement).

To give you a better idea of a C program's structure, consider the following skeleton of every C program:

```
#include <stdio.h>
main()
{
    .
    .                    /* Body of program goes here */
    .

}
```

Before getting into the C language specifics, this program outline probably causes you to ask several questions. Those questions are easily answered, and it is probably best to answer them before going too much further into the specifics.

The first line that begins #include appears in almost every C program ever written. The #include tells the C compiler to go to the disk and load the filename listed between the two angled brackets. The file named stdio.h comes with every C compiler. This file is called a *header file* (hence, its .h filename extension). A header file defines to the compiler certain built-in C routines your program uses later. Depending on what your program does, you must load one or more header files. Because most programs perform input and output and because stdio.h is the standard input/output header file that you need, most programs include this file. Many people program in C for several years and never know what is inside stdio.h. That's okay, you don't have to either. Just include this file so your compiler will perform the input/output needed for most general programs.

As you learn new C features and new built-in functions that come with most C compilers, you will also learn about additional header files you should include for certain situations.

This outline also shows that main() always begins a new block (see the opening brace after main()), and the C program's code goes between main()'s braces. The remainder of this chapter discusses individual commands that make up the body of a C program.

All C comments begin with /*, and all C comments end with */. For Pascal programmers converting to C, this convention causes confusion. Braces { } signal comments in Pascal, but /* and */ signal comments in C. The braces are reserved to designate beginnings and endings of blocks.

Caution:

Be extremely careful that you get all your symbols exactly correct. To C, braces ({ }), brackets ([ ]), parentheses (( )), and angled brackets (< >) all mean different things.

C Data

C's variable and data types are similar to those of the Pascal programming language, which you learned about in Chapter 15. Because you, the C programmer, are responsible for the variables your programs need, you should learn the naming rules for variables. Following are the variable naming rules for most versions of C:

1. All variable names must be from 1 to 31 characters long.

2. All variable names must begin with a letter of the alphabet or an underscore.

3. The rest of the name can be a mixture of letters, numbers, and underscores.

The following are all valid variable names:

```
SALES
Payroll93
_AcctRec
Volume_DECEM
```

These, however, are not valid variable names:

93Payroll	*Variable names cannot begin with a number.*
Total Amount	*Variable names cannot contain a space.*
Dept$@#$Mktg	*Variable names cannot contain special characters.*

Unlike both BASIC and Pascal, C distinguishes between uppercase and lowercase variable names. Therefore, the following are all different names to C:

```
Sales
sALES
SALES
sales
```

If you use a mixture of uppercase and lowercase variable names at the beginning of a C program, retain that same upper- and lowercase name throughout the program.

C requires that you define all variables at the top of a block of code before you use them. As with Pascal, if you use an integer variable named age somewhere in the program, you must define age as an integer toward the top of the program. Some of the common C data types are shown in Table 16.1.

Table 16.1. C data types.		
Type	**Examples**	**Description**
char	'A', '*'	Single characters
int	-19, 0, 88	Whole numbers, without decimal points, from -32,768 to 32,767
long int	12193432	Whole numbers, without decimal points, from -2,147,483,648 to 2,147,483,647
float	-59.545	Real numbers, called *floating-point* numbers, with decimal points, from -3.4×10^{38} to 3.4×10^{38}
double	232.34444333	Real numbers, with decimal points, from -1.7×10^{308} to 1.7×10^{308}

There are more data types in C, but the ones listed in Table 16.1 are the most common. The data type names listed in the first column are the C names for those types. To define one or more variables before you use them, you have to list only your variable data types and their names.

The following is a section of a C program that defines three variables. After C compiles these three lines, it records the location of the three variables named Age, Salary, and Initial so they can be used later in the program.

```
int    Age;
float  Salary;
char   Initial;
```

C is a free-form language, so you don't have to include as much spacing as you see here. Remember, though, that the more spacing you put in a program, the more readable it usually is.

You use the equal sign (=) to assign values to variables in C. The program in Listing 16.2 defines the Age, Salary, and Initial variables and assigns values to them. Such a program is not useful without some kind of output commands, but it gets you used to the way C handles data.

Listing 16.2. Assigning values to variables.

```
#include <stdio.h>
main()
{
    int    Age;
    float Salary;
    char   Initial;

    Age = 26;
    Salary = 3432.56;
    Initial = 'Q';
}
```

Any time you assign a value to a single character variable, you must enclose the value in single quotation marks, as shown in Listing 16.2. Without the single quotation marks around the Q, C would interpret Q as a variable name. If C cannot find a variable named Q and there are no quotations marks, C generates an error.

Working with Character Strings

Look one more time at the data types in Table 3.1. A data type that both BASIC and Pascal supported is missing. C has no string data type; there is no such thing as a string variable in C.

At first, this difference seems like a severe limitation of C, and it would be, except that C offers a way around the problem. Rather than define a character string variable, you can define an *array of characters* that act like a string variable. For the beginning C programmer, an array of characters works much like a string variable. As with Pascal's string variable, when you define a string array in C, you put the maximum length of the string into brackets after its definition. The only additional requirement is that you leave one extra space for something called a *string terminator*. C must put something at the end of the string (more accurately, at the end of the character array) so it knows when it reaches the end of the string.

Suppose, for example, you want to store your company name, which is 14 characters long, in a variable. There are no string variables in C, but you can define a character array that holds a string as follows:

```
char coname[15];    /* Reserve a string of 14 plus terminator */
```

Remember, you must reserve one extra space for the string terminator. From that point forward in the program, coname is a variable that can hold up to 14 characters.

C puts one additional burden on you if you use string data (and most programmers do). You must learn how to put data into an array such as coname. You cannot enter the following:

```
coname = "Widgets Srvcs.";    /* INVALID */
```

Because there is no such thing as a string variable, you cannot directly assign a value to a string in C. Instead, you must resort to a built-in function named strcpy(). To assign a company name to the company array, you enter the following:

```
strcpy(coname, "Widgets Srvcs.");  /* Assign a string to an array */
```

There is one more requirement before the strcpy() works. Any program that uses strcpy() must include an additional header file named string.h. Therefore, a program that defines this string and initializes it with a company name might start out looking like the following:

```
#include <stdio.h>
#include <string.h>
main()
{
   char coname[15];    /* Reserve a string of 14 plus terminator */
   strcpy(coname, "Widgets Srvcs.");  /* Assign a string to an array */
   /* Rest of program follows */
```

You can begin to see why C takes some getting used to. Some things that are simple in other languages, especially string variables, are more difficult to handle in C. The tradeoff with C is that it works with these character arrays more efficiently than other languages work with string variables. Therefore, more of the burden is on your back as the programmer, but the end result is often well worth the effort.

Simple Math Operators

C uses math symbols similar to those used in BASIC and Pascal. As mentioned earlier, C has many more operators than either Pascal or BASIC, but the regular operators work the same way they do in most programming languages. Table 16.2 shows the regular C math operators and their precedence.

Precedence	Operator	Example	Description
Table 16.2. Pascal's primary math operators.			
1	(,)	(3+2)/2	Overrides all other precedence
2	*, /	8/2	Multiply, real divide, and integer divide
3	+, –	2+3-2	Addition and subtraction

Unlike Pascal, C does not have a DIV integer divide operator, but C still supports integer division. If a divide sign, the forward slash, contains integers on either side of it, C performs integer division and discards the remainder. Therefore, the following statement stores six in Result because 4 goes into 25 six times:

```
Result = 25 / 4;   /* Integer division */
```

In the following statement, C stores 6.25 in Result because a floating-point number (called REAL in Pascal) appears on both sides of the division operator. For Result to hold a floating-point number, it should be defined as a float variable.

```
Result = 25.0 / 4.0;
```

If one side of division is of type float and the other side is of type int, floating-point division still occurs.

Increment and Decrement

C includes two operators not found in other programming languages: the *increment* (++) and the *decrement* (--) operators. Increment adds one to a variable, and the decrement subtracts one. Because adding and subtracting one are so common in programming, the designers of C decided to supply these two efficient operators. Listing 16.3 is an example of how they work.

Listing 16.3. Using the increment and decrement operators.

```
/* Shows the increment and decrement operators */
#include <stdio.h>
main()
```

continues

Listing 16.3. Continued

```
{
   int count;
   count = 10;

   count++;       /* Add 1 to count */
   printf("After the increment, count is %d \n", count);

   count--;       /* Subtract 1 from count */
   printf("After the decrement, count is %d \n", count);
}
```

When you run this program, you see the following output:

```
After the increment, count is 11
After the decrement, count is 10
```

As mentioned in the "Language Spotlight" section in Chapter 15, Pascal does include two functions that increment and decrement variables, but C's operators work much faster than Pascal's INC and DEC.

The increment and decrement operators can go before or after a variable. The following ways of adding 1 to a variable are equivalent:

```
count = cout + 1;   /* Adds 1 to count */

count++;            /* Also adds 1 to count */

++count;            /* Also adds 1 to count */
```

Here are three equivalent ways of subtracting 1 from a variable:

```
count = cout - 1;   /* Subtracts 1 from count */

count--;            /* Subtracts 1 from count */

--count;            /* Subtracts 1 from count */
```

As your programs become more complex, the difference between count++; and ++count; becomes more important. If you combine them with other calculations, as in the following line, the result becomes difficult to predict:

```
sum = count++ * 12 - ++result;
```

As long as you use only increments and decrements by themselves, without combining them with other variables, they work the same whether you put the increment before or after the variable.

Input and Output

Input/output is another area in which C seems to suffer. Actually, C handles I/O well, but to a beginner or to someone familiar with another language, C's I/O capabilities seem awkward. Nevertheless, you must perform I/O to see results of calculations or to get input from the user. This section gives you an overview of the two most important I/O functions to a new C programmer: printf() and scanf().

The printf() and scanf() functions are just that: functions. They are not true commands. Remember that a C function always has parentheses after its name. printf() and scanf() are functions that come with your C compiler; you don't have to write the functions yourself. printf() sends output to your screen, and scanf() gets input from the user at the keyboard. (There are some advanced ways to override the default devices, redirecting the I/O to devices other than the screen and keyboard.)

The simplest data to write is a string or a character array that holds a string. For example, the following statement writes I am learning C to the screen:

```
printf("I am learning C");
```

A previous example showed you how to declare a character array that held the company name. The following printf() prints the company name to the screen:

```
printf(coname);
```

The tricky aspect of printf() appears when you try to print data that is something other than a single string. If you wanted to print an integer, the following printf() would not do the job:

```
printf(42);   /* INVALID */
```

The printf() function understands only how to print string data. It has no idea how you want the 42 printed, so it either prints nothing or you see garbage characters on-screen (depending on your compiler). In C, you must *format* your output; that is, you must describe exactly how you want your output to appear.

BASIC does not need formatting characters. If you try printing 42 with BASIC's PRINT, BASIC prints the 42. Pascal is almost as generous, but remember that if you print a REAL value in Pascal, Pascal prints extra decimal places, often many more than you want. Therefore, you can add a width and decimal specifier to Pascal's WRITELN when printing REAL numbers to specify exactly how wide and how many decimal places you want printed.

C requires that you tell it whether the data is an integer, character, or floating-point value. You do so with the following *format specifiers:*

%d means decimal integer

%c means character

%f means floating-point

Suppose, for example, you have the three variables shown in Listing 16.2: Age, an integer; Initial, a character; and Salary, a floating-point variable. You cannot print the following because printf() would not know how to print the three values (they are not strings):

```
printf(Age, Initial, Salary);   /* INVALID */
```

When you want to print numbers, you must include a *format string,* which contains one or more of the format specifiers. Therefore, the proper way to print the previous three variables is as follows:

```
printf("%d  %c  %f", Age, Initial, Salary);   /* OK */
```

This printf() function prints the three values on the same line, separated by two spaces (because each of the format specifiers is separated by two spaces). If you want to print the values on three separate lines, it is a little trickier. You must use the *newline* character: \n. The backslash tells C that the next character is not an n, but it stands for newline (a fancy way of combining a carriage return and line feed, a combination of characters that puts your cursor at the beginning of the next line).

Everywhere \n appears in a format specifier, C moves down to the next line on-screen. The following printf() prints the three values on three separate lines:

```
printf("%d\n%c\n%f", Age, Initial, Salary);   /* OK */
```

Try to pick out the pieces of this strange format specifier. The %d tells C that an integer variable is first in the list (it is, Age), and the \n tells C to move down to the next line after printing that integer. The %c tells C that a character variable comes next, the \n moves the cursor down again, and then the final %f tells C to print a floating-point variable. It prints Salary because that is the next variable.

If you want the Salary limited to two decimal places, you must tell C to do so inside the printf(). The following printf() is similar to the previous one, except it prints the Salary variable with only two decimal places because of the .2 between the % and the f:

```
printf("%d\n%c\n%.2f", Age, Initial, Salary);   /* OK */
```

There is much more to printing with `printf()`. However, this book's aim is not to teach you all there is to know about C, but simply to acquaint you with the language. To make sure you understand the basics of `printf()`, try to follow the logic of the program in Listing 16.4. It is a complete version of the program you've seen pieced together in this section; it is relatively easy to understand.

Listing 16.4. Using *printf()* to print.

```
#include <stdio.h>
main()
{
   int   Age;
   float Salary;
   char  Initial;

   Age = 26;
   Salary = 3432.56;
   Initial = 'Q';

   printf("%d\n%c\n%.2f", Age, Initial, Salary);   /* OK */
}
```

Listing 16.4 produces the following output:

```
26
Q
3432.56
```

It helps to first understand `printf()` before you learn `scanf()`. `scanf()` gets input from the keyboard and uses the same format specifiers as `printf()` does. `scanf()` is, however, one of the strangest language elements in C. Here is why.

Suppose that instead of assigning Age, Initial, and Salary values as in Listing 16.4, you want the user to type the three values at the keyboard. The following `scanf()` gets the integer Age from the keyboard:

```
scanf(" %d", &Age);   /* Get the age from the user */
```

There are similarities between `scanf()` and `printf()`. Both require a format string with at least one format specifier. In this example, the `%d` informs the C compiler that it should accept an integer value. You might think that C should look at Age and realize that it is an integer, but that is not the case.

You also see two things about scanf() that do not appear in printf(). Notice that the format specifier begins with a space. The space does not imply that the user types a space before the integer; rather, the space is recommended so scanf() works more accurately when you list several concurrently in a program. Although there is a technical reason for the recommended space, it is one of those things that you, the programmer, should not have to worry about, but you must include it anyway.

Also, before the Age variable, you notice an ampersand, &. The & is called the *address of* operator. The address of operator is used frequently in advanced C programs, especially when pointers are involved. Although you don't have to understand pointers to use scanf(), you must use the & operator anyway—except in certain situations. Following are the rules for using &:

1. Always put an ampersand (&) before regular variable names inside a scanf().

2. Never put an ampersand (&) before an array name, such as a string character array.

Therefore, if you want to get a string into a character array, such as the company name explained earlier, you can do as follows:

```
scanf(" %s", coname);
```

No & is required because coname is an array. The %s is an additional format specifier that you can use to input strings; you do not need it when printing simple strings with printf() as you saw earlier.

Your program can input more than one value at the same time by getting more than one value with scanf(). The program in Listing 16.5 combines some of these concepts. In it, scanf() gets three values at once, another scanf() gets a string, and printf() prints the data to the screen.

Listing 16.5. Using *scanf()* and *printf()*.

```
/* Demonstrates scanf() and printf() */
#include <stdio.h>
main()
{
   char   Code;
   int    Depend;
   float  Balance;
   char   Name[25];

   printf("What is your name? ");
   scanf(" %s", Name);
```

```
    printf("What is your character code, dependents, and balance? ");
    scanf(" %c %d %f", &Code, &Depend, &Balance);

    printf("Here is the data your entered: \n");
    printf("Code: %c, Dependents: %d, Balance: %f\n", Code,
            Depend, Balance);
    printf("Thanks and have a nice day!");
}
```

Notice that you never put a newline specifier, \n, inside a scanf() format string. The scanf() automatically ends when the user presses the Enter key.

Language Spotlight

C works closely with a special type of variable called a *pointer*. A pointer variable does not hold a value in the same way that integer variables, floating-point variables, and all the others do. Rather, a pointer holds the location of some data inside the computer. For example, an integer pointer variable does not hold an integer, but it holds the location (called the *address*) of an integer value.

Although Pascal also supports the use of pointers, pointers do not play as big a role in Pascal as they do in advanced C programs. You learned what a character array is earlier in this chapter. Because C does not support string variables, you must make a character array hold a string. A character array name is nothing more than a pointer; the array name simply points to the start of the string somewhere in memory.

Why are pointers valuable? They play a major role in C's efficiency. Suppose you have a list of 1,000 names and addresses in strings of memory and you decide you want to alphabetize and print those names. Instead of moving thousands of strings, which takes a lot of processing time, you only have to set up 1,000 pointers that point to the start of each name and address. Then, your program rearranges the pointers and not the long strings of data, saving a tremendous amount of time.

Comparing Data

C compares data using an `if` statement that is similar to Pascal's and BASIC's `IF` statements. C, however, uses a couple different relational operators; they are listed in Table 16.3.

Operator	Example	Description
==	if (a == b)	Test for equality
>	if (a > b)	Test for greater than
<	if (a < b)	Test for less than
>=	if (a >= b)	Test for greater than or equal to
<=	if (a <= b)	Test for less than or equal to
!=	if (a != b)	Test for not equal to

Table 16.3. C relational operators.

The format of C's `if` statement is

```
if (condition)
        {
        .
        .                 /* One or more C statements go here */
        .
        }
```

You must put parentheses around the relational condition test in the C `if` statement. Also, if the body of the `if` contains only one statement, the braces are optional.

Notice that C does not use the equal sign for equality, rather it uses a double equal sign, ==. C uses the equal only for assignment of values to variables and nothing else. If you program in other languages that use an equal sign and then move to C, you might be tempted to do something like the following:

```
if (Salary = Top)
{
   printf("You made the highest salary! \n");
}
```

The problem with such an `if` is that C does not compare `Salary` to `Top`; it instead assigns the value of `Top` to `Salary` no matter what was in `Salary` to begin with. Therefore, the `if` wipes out any value that was previously in `Salary`; an `if` test should not do this under most conditions.

C offers a shortcut to testing some conditions. Zero always means a False condition. If you test to see whether something is not zero, therefore, you only have to specify the test like this:

```
if (Bonus)
{
   printf("You worked hard! \n"); /* Prints only if Bonus not zero */
}
```

instead of the following:

```
if (Bonus!=0)
{
   printf("You worked hard! \n"); /* Prints only if Bonus not zero */
}
```

This shortcut is one way C attempts to be more efficient than other programming languages. Knowing about such internals enables you to write quicker code. The test for 0 takes longer than the first `if` that didn't test for 0 explicitly.

C also includes an `else` option for the `if`. The format of the `if-else` is

```
if (condition)
        {
          .
          .                 /* One or more C statements go here */
          .
        }
    else
        {
          .
          .                 /* One or more C statements go here */
          .
        }
```

The parentheses after `if` are required and you should never put a semicolon after the closing parenthesis (but semicolons do go after each statement in the body of the `if` loop). As with the simple `if`, if the body of the `else` is only one line, you do not have to use the braces. Listing 16.6 demonstrates the C `if-else` control statements.

Listing 16.6. Using the *if-else* control statements.

```
/* Prints a message depending on years of service */
#include <stdio.h>
main()
```

continues

Listing 16.6. Continued

```
{
    int yrs;
    printf("How many years of service? ");
    scanf(" %d", &yrs);    /* Get the years they have worked */

    if (yrs > 20)
        { printf("Give a gold watch\n"); }
    else
        { if (yrs > 10)
            { printf("Give a paper weight\n"); }
          else
              { printf("Give a pat on the back\n"); }
        }
    return;
}
```

The Conditional Operator

One additional way C attempts to offer more efficiency is the conditional operator: ?:. The conditional operator has no comparable equivalent in other programming languages (except for C++). With it, C accomplishes in one statement what takes other programming languages several statements to accomplish.

The format of the conditional operator is

conditional expression ? expression1 : expression2;

The conditional operator replaces simple if-else statements. Here is how it works: If the *conditional expression* is True, *expression1* executes; if the *conditional expression* is False, *expression2* executes.

Suppose you have an if-else conditional test that looks like the following:

```
if (a > b)
    { ans = 10; }
else
    { ans = 25; }
```

You can easily rewrite this if-else by using a single, more efficient conditional operator, as follows:

```
a > b ? (ans = 10) : (ans = 25);
```

Looping Statements

C contains both a for loop and a while loop, which correspond to Pascal's and BASIC's versions. C also offers another loop construct called the do-while loop. Depending on your program, using do-while might be easier than using while. This section shows you how to loop in C.

The *for* Loop

C's for loop is more cryptic than Pascal's, but it works the same way. Here is the format of C's for loop:

```
for (start expression; relational expression; count)
      {
        .
        .                  /* One or more C statements go here */
        .
      }
```

The parentheses after for are required, and you should never put a semicolon after the closing parenthesis (but semicolons do go after each statement in the body of the for loop). If the body of the for loop contains only one statement, you don't have to use the braces.

Consider the following for loop:

```
for (ctr=1; ctr<=10; ctr++)
{
   printf("%d \n", ctr);
}
```

When the for loop begins, C assigns the variable named ctr the value of 1. The body of the loop continues to execute as long as ctr is less than or equal to 10. The increment (the *count* expression) operator after ctr means that ctr increments each time through the loop.

The following is an equivalent BASIC FOR loop. Notice how C's loop is similar:

```
FOR CTR = 1 TO 10
   PRINT CTR
NEXT CTR
```

With BASIC (and Pascal), the increment is automatic. In C, if you don't want to increment by one, you don't have to. The following C for loop adds 5 to ctr each time through the loop:

```
for (ctr=1; ctr<=25; ctr=ctr+5)
{
    printf("%d \n", ctr);
}
```

The *while* Loop

The while loop is similar in both C and Pascal. The format for C's while loop is

```
while (relational expression)
        {
         .
         .              /* One or more C statements go here */
         .
        }
```

The body of while repeats continuously until the *relational expression* becomes False. Following is an example while loop:

```
while (a > b)
{
    a = a + 2;
    b = b * 3;
}
```

The two assignments that make up the body of the while loop continue executing as long as a is greater than b.

The *do-while* Loop

C supplies another form of the while loop called the do-while. The format of the do-while loop is

```
do
  {
   .
   .              /* One or more C statements go here */
   .
  } while ( relational test )
```

Unlike the regular while, the do-while loop always executes at least one time. The regular while statement might never execute. Notice that the relational test occurs at the top of the while loop, but does not occur until the end of the do-while. This placement ensures that the body of do-while executes at least once.

Listing 16.7 demonstrates the use of the do-while. The program gets sales amounts from the user and calculates extended totals. It then prints the quantity sold, part number, and the *extended total* (quantity times the price per unit).

Listing 16.7. Using the *do-while* loop.

```c
/* Gets inventory information from user and prints
   an inventory detail listing with extended totals */
#include <stdio.h>
main()
{
   int part_no, quantity;
   float cost, ext_cost;

   printf("*** Inventory Computation ***\n\n");    /* Title */

   /* Get inventory information */
   do
    { printf("What is the next part number (-999 to end)? ");
      scanf(" %d", &part_no);
      if (part_no != -999)
         { printf("How many were bought? ");
           scanf(" %d", &quantity);
           printf("What is the unit price of this item? ");
           scanf(" %f", &cost);
           ext_cost = cost * quantity;
           printf("\n%d of # %d will cost $%.2f",
                  quantity, part_no, ext_cost);
           printf("\n\n\n");       /* Print two blank lines */
         }
    } while (part_no != -999);        /* Loop only if part
                                         number is not -999 */

   printf("End of inventory computation\n");
   return;
}
```

Following is the output from this program:

```
*** Inventory Computation ***

What is the next part number (-999 to end)? 123
How many were bought? 4
What is the unit price of this item? 5.43

4 of # 123 will cost $21.72



What is the next part number (-999 to end)? 523
How many were bought? 26
```

```
What is the unit price of this item? 1.25

26 of # 523 will cost $32.50


What is the next part number (-999 to end)? -999
End of inventory computation
```

Functions

C functions are to C what procedures are to Pascal. A C function is a routine, some-times called a subroutine, that enables you to divide your code into small pieces and execute those pieces. You can lift the programming burden for longer programs by using functions. As you first learned in this chapter, C requires that every program have at least one defined function named main(). You can also have other functions that main() calls. Most C programmers list main() as the first function in a program because it controls all the other functions.

(The main() function is always the first function C executes, no matter where it falls in the code.)

Just as in Pascal, you call C functions by listing their names (versus calling statements such as the BASIC GOSUB). The program in Listing 16.8 contains two functions; see if you can find them.

Listing 16.8. A program using two functions.

```
/* Program that demonstrates the nature of C functions */
#include <stdio.h>

int gallons;    /* A global variable */

main()
{
   printf("Richard's Paint Service \n");
   printf("How many gallons of paint did you buy? ");
```

```
    scanf(" %d", &gallons);        /* Get gallons in main() */

    computesale();           /* Compute total in a function */
}

computesale()
{
    float priceper, totalsale;   /* Local to computesale */
    priceper = 12.45;
    totalsale = priceper * gallons;
    printf("The total is $%.2f \n", totalsale );
}   /* Returns to main() */
```

This program has two functions—main() and computesale(). The main() function asks the user for the number of gallons of paint, and the computesale() function calculates the amount of the sale based on a price per gallon. In the true spirit of functions, main() does one thing and computesale() does something else. Each function is distinct in its task and each function is almost a stand-alone miniature program in its own right.

There is one thing to consider about this program that you have yet to see in C. The variable definition for gallons appears before main(). Anytime you define a variable before main() (or between any two functions), it is known as a *global* variable. All the variables defined inside a function are known as *local* variables. A local variable is known only to the function in which you define it. Therefore, if you define gallons in main(), the computesale() function cannot use it; gallons is known only to main(). A global variable, however, is known in every function that follows its definition. Therefore, because gallons is global, both main() and computesale() can use it.

One function, through a mechanism known as *passing parameters,* can share a local variable with another. (Pascal also includes this capability.) Actually, the procedure of passing parameters is the primary reason that function names always contain parentheses. This is because variables that you pass, or share, between functions are placed inside the parentheses.

As you program more in C, the concept of local and global variables becomes much more important. For the next program, Listing 16.9, all variables are global to ease you into a C program that contains several functions. This program is the C version of the program you saw at the end of the BASIC and Pascal chapters (Chapters 14 and 15), so you can compare the similarities. Remember that the C program should run faster than the other two, even though the code is similar, thanks to C's efficiency.

Listing 16.9. The payroll program.

```
/* Payroll program that uses functions
   to separate sections into manageable functions */
#include <stdio.h>
/* Global variables follow */
    char Ans;
    char Fullname[25];
    int Hours;
    float Rate, TaxRate, GrossPay, Taxes, NetPay;

/* main controlling function code follows */
main()
{
   printf("\n** Payroll Program **\n" );     /* Title */
   AskUser();
   GetHours();
   CalcPay();
   DispPay();
   PrntCheck();
}

AskUser()      /* Ask if user wants to see calculations and check */
{
   printf("Do you want to see your payroll and print a check? (Y/N)");
   scanf(" %c", &Ans );
   if (Ans == 'N')
      {
         exit();              /* Quit program if user responds with N */
      }                       /* Anything other than N falls through */
}

GetHours()      /* Data gathering section */
{
   printf("What is your last name? ");
   scanf(" %s", Fullname );
   printf("How many hours did you work? ");
   scanf(" %d", &Hours );
   printf("How much do you make per hour? ");
   scanf(" %f", &Rate );
}

CalcPay()       /* Calculation section */
{
   TaxRate = 0.35;
   GrossPay = Hours * Rate;
```

```
   Taxes = TaxRate * GrossPay;
   NetPay = GrossPay - Taxes;
}

DispPay()      /* Screen display of the data */
{
   printf("\n\n");   /* Prints a blank line */
   printf("Here is your payroll information:\n" );
   printf("Name: %s\n", Fullname );
   printf("Gross pay: $%.2f\n", GrossPay );
   printf("Taxes: $%.2f\n", Taxes );
   printf("Net pay: $%.2f\n", NetPay );
}

PrntCheck()      /* Print the paycheck */
{
   printf("Pay to the order of %s\n",  Fullname);
   printf("\n");
   printf("                            The amount of: **********$%.2f\n",
            NetPay);
   printf("Benson Corp.\n" );
   printf("1212 E. Oak\n" );
   printf("Miami, FL 21233                  _____\n");
   printf("                              (Jim Gaines, Treasurer)\n" );
}
```

The exit() function halts the program if the user changes her or his mind about running it in the AskUser() function. Other than the exit() function, you should be able to understand everything about this program.

One more item important to C programs, although not required, is recommended to speed up the program even further and to prepare you for writing more extensive programs. You should include *function prototypes* at the top of each program (after the #include statement). A function prototype is a function definition that informs the C compiler that a function appears later in the program and that the compiler should expect it.

To prototype a function, you have to copy only the function's first line to the top of the program and end it with a semicolon. This step is easy to do with most C compiler editors. For example, the first few lines of Listing 16.9, with prototypes at the top of the program where they should be, look like the following:

```
/* Payroll program that uses procedures
    to separate sections into manageable functions */
#include <stdio.h>
/* Prototypes follow */
AskUser();
GetHours();
CalcPay();
DispPay();
PrntCheck();

/* Global variables follow */
    char Ans;
    char Fullname[25];
    int Hours;
    float Rate, TaxRate, GrossPay, Taxes, NetPay;

/* main controlling function code follows */
main()
{
    printf("\n** Payroll Program **\n" );    /* Title */
    AskUser();
/* Rest of program follows as you saw earlier */
```

Notice that you don't have to prototype `main()` because it is the first function that appears in the program (although it does no harm if you do).

With simple programs, prototypes can be difficult to understand because they seem redundant. Think of them the same way you think of variable definitions. You must define all variables in a C program before you use them. You should also prototype all functions at the top of a C program before you use them later in the program.

Summary

You now have been exposed to the C programming language. C is often touted as being difficult to understand due to its rich use of operators instead of its reliance on commands as much as other programming languages. As you saw in this chapter, C is no different than other programming languages—it has variables, loop-controlling statements, and subroutine-like functions.

C includes some additional operators that substitute for code and that improve efficiency. The conditional operator (?:) and the increment and decrement operators (++ and --) all perform succinctly and efficiently.

Despite C's widespread use and popularity, it has its drawbacks. C allows some freedoms that other languages do not, which is not always good. For example, you can define a character variable and then store a floating-point number in it. Although you probably should not do that, C does allow it. Being able to mismatch variables and their values can get you in trouble. The danger lies in being able to do this at times when you don't know you are (such as using the wrong format specifier in a `printf()` and having your output be mangled).

In the 1980s, programmers at the AT&T laboratories decided to improve the way C works. The result was C++—a new language that is a superset of C. C++ is stricter than C and also goes much farther than C or any other procedural programming language, such as Pascal or BASIC. As you see in the next chapter, C++ offers another way to view your programming problems and improves on some of C's flaws (such as the `scanf()` function).

Overview of C++

by Greg Perry

If C is the language of choice for today's programmers, C++ appears to be the language of choice for tomorrow's. Industry watchers say that C++ will become the dominant programming language by the mid-1990s. If computer conferences, seminars, and magazine articles are any indication of trends, C++ is certainly headed toward the role of most-used language by data processing departments across the country.

This chapter gives you an overview of C++. As its name implies, C++ is an incremental improvement over C. You might recall from the preceding chapter that C's ++ operator is called the *increment* operator. In C, when you want to increment or add 1 to a variable, you use the increment operator. AT&T (part of the group who invented C a few years earlier) created the first C++ language. They originally began improving the way C works. They wanted to create a better C, an incrementally better language; hence, the name C++.

The designers of C++ went much further than simply improving a few C commands. Advantages of C++ over C fall into two categories:

- Improved C commands
- Object-oriented programming (OOP)

The first part of this chapter shows you how the C++ language improves several C commands and functions. Because of the problems associated with it, C++ programmers flee from the vague scanf() input method you read about in the last chapter. C++ really is a better C. C++ offers many new and better ways of programming.

The last part of this chapter is unlike any of the previous three chapters because none of the languages covered in those chapters were *object-oriented languages (OOP);* they were *procedural languages*—the opposite of object-oriented languages. An OOP language offers a unique way of programming and also offers many advantages over procedural languages. (There is an object-oriented version of Pascal, but OOP Pascal is sold by only a couple of vendors and is no longer considered a major player in the world of OOP.) You learned much about the background and philosophy of OOP in Chapter 11.

The C++ Language

There is a strong debate in the programming world over the prerequisites to learning C++. Many people believe that you must know C to learn C++. Others believe that C++ offers many advantages over C, and that by learning C, you slow yourself down. The proponents of the latter philosophy say that you must "unlearn" some things before learning C++.

The majority of C++ teachers and writers lean towards C as a prerequisite for C++. After all, that was the historical progression of the language; C++ was designed to improve what programmers already did in C. When you begin using OOP concepts, you do have to change the way you view programming. The concepts you know from C, however, save you a great deal of time when learning C++. After all, if you learn C++ without learning C, you have all the new language commands and C-like operators to learn, as well as OOP—a separate topic in itself.

As you see by looking at many C++ programs, they look very similar to C programs. C++ uses many of the same operators as C, as well as statements such as `for`, `while`, and `if`. Although the preceding chapter gave you only a brief exposure to C, you can see in the next few sections that C++ really does improve on C, while at the same time respecting the C language and utilizing as many commands from it as possible.

To give you an idea of the similarities, Listing 17.1 contains a C++ program. This program contains a few OOP concepts that are not discussed until later in this chapter, but by skimming through the program, you can recognize many C language elements.

Listing 17.1. A sample C++ program.

```
/* A date class program */
#include <iostream.h>
```

```
class Date {
    int day;        // Private data members
    int month;
    int year;
    int test_day(const int d)      // Private member functions
        { return (d>31) ? 0 : 1; }
    int test_month(const int m)
        { return (m>12) ? 0 : 1; }
    int test_year(const int y)
        { return (y<1990) ? 0 : 1; }
public:
    int bonus_flag;         // Public bonus date flag
    int get_day(void)       // Public member functions
        { return (day); }   // inline functions
    int get_month(void)
        { return (month); }  // No inline keyword needed
    int get_year(void)
        { return (year);   }
    int set(const int d, const int m, const int y)
        { if (test_day(d) && test_month(m) && test_year(y))
            { day=d;         // Assign each of the data members
              month=m;       // the passed arguments
              year=y;
              return (1);
            }
          else return(0); } // Bad date
};  // End classes with semicolons

void main()
{
    Date today;       // Define a class variable
    int m, d, y;      // Holds user's input values

    cout << "What is today's day, month, and year (i.e., 18 3 1993)? ";
    cin >> d >> m >> y;

    // Set the date class values, printing them if correct
    if (today.set(d, m, y)) {  // returns 1 if date okay
        cout << "The date is set to " << today.get_month();
        cout << "/" << today.get_day() << "/" ;
        cout << today.get_year() << "\n";
    }
    else {
        cout << "You did not enter a correct date."; }
}
```

The Similarities of C and C++

C++ supports the same data types, operators, control statements, and built-in functions as C. Like C, for example, C++ has no character string variables; you must define a character array to hold a string and use the strcpy() function if you want to assign that string a value. Such similarities make the transition to C++ relatively smooth for C programmers.

> Most C programs will also run in C++ because C is virtually the same as C++. C++ takes the language one step further, but retains the primary C language elements.

There is no reason to repeat all that coverage here. This chapter shows you the differences between C and C++. After looking at the program in Listing 17.1, the first difference that you probably noticed is the way C++ handles comments.

C++ Comments

In C++, comments begin with two forward slashes (//). The comments end only when the end of line is reached. Here is a single-line comment:

```
// This is a comment in C++
```

This is a multiline comment:

```
// Although some comments span several
// lines of your program, in C++, you
// must begin all comments with two slashes
```

In C, a comment could span several lines without requiring you to type /* before each line. Of course, you had to remember to end a C comment with */; otherwise, the comment would not end properly. In C++, you don't have to remember to end each comment because each comment takes a maximum of a single line.

C++ still recognizes the C-style comments. If you program with C++, though, you should use the language as it was designed to be used—so stay with the double slash.

Input and Output

You will be thankful that C++ improves upon C's input/output capabilities. Rarely does a C++ programmer use printf() and scanf(). In C++ you use the *inserter* operator (<<) and the *extractor* operator (>>). Use the inserter operator with an object called cout and the extractor operator with an object called cin. Don't let the word *object* frighten you; although it is related to object-oriented programming, you don't have to know anything about OOP to use cout and cin.

Think of cout as your screen and cin as your keyboard. If you can picture this, the rest is easy—as the following line shows:

```
cout << "I am learning C++";
```

The string I am learning C++ is being routed to the screen (the cout object). This line does exactly the same thing as the following C statement:

```
printf("I am learning C++");
```

If you want a newline printed after the string, just insert the newline character at the end of the string, as follows:

```
cout << "I am learning C++\n";
```

You can display variables much easier with cout than with printf(). You don't have to use any of the format specifiers that C requires. The program in Listing 17.2 uses cout to display several values on-screen. You must include iostream.h instead of stdio.h when using the C++ cout and cin operators.

The stdio.h header file describes how printf() and scanf() work in C programs. Because most C++ programs do not use these I/O functions, you do not need to include stdio.h.

Listing 17.2. Using *cout* to display values on-screen.

```
// Demonstrates C++ output with cout
#include <iostream.h>
void main()
{
    int i;
    float x;
    char c;

    i = 25;
    x = 12.345678;
    c ='X';

    cout<< "i is " << i << "\n";
    cout<< "x is " << x << "\n";
    cout<< "c is " << c << "\n";

}
```

Listing 17.2 produces the following output:

```
i is 25
x is 12.345678
c is X
```

It might look as though the `main()` function has a new name, but it does not. The `main()` function is still named `main()`, but the `void` command in front of `main()` is required in C++ although it was optional in C. In advanced C++ programs, you can return a value from one function called by another function. The `main()` function is called from the operating system because it is the first function always executed in a C program. Because the `main()` function has no need to return a value back to the operating system, you must tell the C++ compiler that the `main()` function is return-ing `void` or no value at all. (Likewise, you see `int` before a function's name if it returns an integer, `float` for a floating-point value, and so on.)

Input with `cin` is just as easy as output with `cout`, so you might wonder what the designers of C were thinking when they came up with `scanf()`. Although beyond the scope of this book, there actually were good reasons why some of the seemingly strange functions were included in C. When you are learning the language, however, it seems as though the developers intentionally made things difficult.

The following statement gets a value for `Sales`—assuming that `Sales` is defined earlier in the program—whether `Sales` is a floating-point, integer, or character variable:

```
cin >> Sales;    // Get a Sales value from the keyboard
```

Now look at the same statement written in C.

```
scanf(" %f", &Sales);    /* Type a Sales value into a float variable */
```

As you can see, the C++ version (using `cin`) makes more sense than the C version (using `scanf()`).

The program in Listing 17.3 gets three values from the keyboard with `cin` and displays them on-screen with `cout`.

Listing 17.3. Using *cin* to get values from the keyboard.

```
// Demonstrates C++ input and output with cin and cout.
#include <iostream.h>

void main()
{
    int i;
```

```
    float x;
    char c;

    cout << "What is the value of i? ";
    cin >> i;
    cout << "What is the value of x? ";
    cin >> x;
    cout << "What is the value of c? ";
    cin >> c;

    cout<< "i is " << i << "\n";
    cout<< "x is " << x << "\n";
    cout<< "c is " << c << "\n";

}
```

The operators >> and << are reversed for input and output. As long as you think of cin being the keyboard, you can picture

```
cin >> x;
```

as saying, "Input keyboard values to the variable x." If you think of cout being your screen, you can picture

```
cout << x;
```

as saying, "Output the variable x to the screen."

Defining Data

C++ gives you more freedom as to where you define your variables. In C, you have to define all local variables after the opening brace of a block, even if you do not use those variables until many lines later. In C++, you can define a variable right before you use it.

Consider the program in Listing 17.4. The variable i is defined after the opening brace of the main() block, the same place C requires that it be defined. The variable j is defined two lines later, after two executable statements have been performed. In C, you cannot put an executable statement before any variable definition. The variable ctr is defined inside the for loop. Because only the for loop uses the loop counter, C++ allows you to define the counter variable right before the for statement, instead of defining it many lines earlier as C requires.

Listing 17.4. Defining variables in C++.

```
#include <iostream.h>
void main()
{
    int i=5;
    cout << "\nVariable definition program.\n";
    cout << "i is " << i << "\n";

    int j;  // New variable
    j = 25;
    cout << "j is " << j << "\n";

    for (int ctr=0; ctr<5; ctr++)
    {
        cout << "A for loop that keeps looping...\n";
        cout << "  ctr is " << ctr << "\n";
    }
}   // End of main()
```

The advantage of late variable definition is that it helps you keep better track of your data. You can never have two variables with the same name defined within the same block. It is common for you to forget, in a large program, that you have already defined a variable, so you might be tempted to define another in an inside block when the outer block already uses that variable.

Dynamically Allocating Data

C++ provides a way to dynamically allocate memory. If you take a class or read a book on standard C, you will learn how to dynamically allocate memory late in the course. It is considered an advanced topic in C because it is so difficult to do. C++, however, makes it a breeze. Although there is much more about dynamic memory allocation than this chapter can get into, the following overview gives you a glimpse into the power of C++.

Dynamic memory allocation simply means that you decide when a variable takes memory and when it does not. As mentioned earlier in this chapter, you can define variables almost anywhere in a C++ program (in C, you define variables at the top of the block right after the opening brace). Listing 17.5 is a short program that defines a variable in the middle of the program.

Listing 17.5. Defining a variable in the middle of the program.

```
// Defines a variable right before it is used
#include <iostream.h>
void main()
{
    cout << "In just a couple of lines, ";
    cout << "this program will define a ";
    cout << "variable. \nIt would have ";
    cout << "to be done before the first cout ";

    cout << "if this were regular C.\n";

    int i = 25;
    cout << "The value of i is " << i;
}
```

This program is not an example of dynamic memory allocation, but it gets close to the issue. In Listing 17.5, you do not define i until right before you use it. A previous section explained how this was an improvement over having to lump all your variable definitions together at the top of the program and then not use some of them until many lines later. By putting the variable definition close to its use, you help improve the readability of the program.

Despite the fact that defining variables later in the program offers a coding improvement, it does not represent dynamic memory allocation. In the previous program, the compiler knew you needed an integer variable because it scanned ahead and found the definition. Even though the compiler did not actually create the variable until you defined it, the compiler did reserve space for the variable from the beginning.

The goal of dynamic memory allocation is to let you tell the compiler exactly when you want it to reserve space for a variable and exactly when you want the variable defined. You do not always know exactly how many variables you will need. Suppose you were writing a word processor program. You cannot make assumptions about how much available memory a user's computer has because every computer could be different. Therefore, you must use dynamic memory allocation to allocate memory as the user types. When all available memory has been used, you can tell the user that the memory limit has been reached and that no additional text can be typed into the word processor. This limit would vary for different users, depending on the memory limits of their computers.

The opposite of memory allocation is memory *deallocation*. After your program finishes with allocated memory, you should give that memory back to the system rather than keeping it reserved after you are done with it. With regular C and C++ programs, all variable space remains reserved until the program ends. If, however, you dynamically deallocate the memory, you tell the computer to release it back to the system.

The concept of dynamic memory allocation and deallocation is advanced, but not too advanced for you to get a general understanding of it here. One of its biggest advantages is on multiuser systems. Most PCs today are *single-user* computer systems. That is, there is one single user at any one time. You probably are aware that you can hook several PCs together to form a *network* of computers. The larger computers used by businesses and universities, called *mainframes*, let several hundred and sometimes several thousand people use the same computer at the same time (these mainframes are really fast!). PCs are getting faster every day. The point will come in the not-too-distant future when you will be able to plug several screens and keyboards into your PC and access that PC from anywhere in your house—and let others in your family use it at the same time. Actually, the networking hardware to do that is already available, but its use will grow in the future as computers get even faster.

When many people are on the same computer at the same time and are all wanting as much memory space as they can get, your program cannot afford to reserve space it doesn't need, taking precious memory away from other people. You cannot afford to keep memory reserved throughout the life of your program if you don't need it that entire time. By dynamically allocating and deallocating your variables, you ensure that your program uses only the memory resources it needs at the time—no more and no less.

C++ uses two operators named `new` and `delete` to allocate memory. Although they act like commands, these are not really C++ commands. As you begin to learn the language, though, it does not hurt anything to think of them as such. (They are really operators.) Following is the format of `new`:

```
datatype ptrvar = new datatype;
```

The format for `new` is not as tricky as it looks. Suppose you want to create a new integer variable dynamically (right before you use it). You can do so as follows:

```
int ip = new int;     // Allocates a new integer
```

The only thing unique about the variable `ip` is that it is not really an integer, but it contains the address of one. In C++, programmers say that "`ip` points to an integer."

Therefore, you cannot treat `ip` as though it were a regular integer by assigning it an integer value such as the following:

```
ip = 6;   // You should not treat ip as if it were an integer
```

You must dereference the pointer before you can use it as a regular variable. *Dereference* means that you want the value pointed to by the pointer variable. To dereference a variable, you must add the `*` prefix; C++ does not confuse the dereferencing prefix (`*`) with the multiplication operator (`*`) because of the different contexts in which you use the two operators. For dereferencing, the `*` goes immediately before a single pointer variable, and when you multiply, the `*` goes between two values. Therefore, to assign a 6 to the newly allocated integer in memory, you could write the following:

```
*ip = 6;   // Puts a 6 where ip points
```

You can do a lot of advanced computing with pointers. For the time being, however, even though their dereferencing syntax (`*`) is strange-looking, pointers give you a way to dynamically allocate memory.

When you want to deallocate memory, use the `delete` operator. The format for `delete` looks like the following:

```
delete [ ] ptrvar;
```

For simple variables, such as integers and floating-point variables, leave the brackets empty. Later in this section, you see what the brackets are for when character arrays are allocated.

Listing 17.6 is equivalent to the program in Listing 17.5. This program uses `new` and `delete` to allocate and deallocate the integer.

Listing 17.6. Using *new* and *delete* to allocate and deallocate integers.

```
// Allocates and deallocates a variable
#include <iostream.h>
void main()
{
   cout << "In just a couple of lines, ";
   cout << "this program will define a ";
   cout << "variable. \nIt would have ";
   cout << "to be done before the first cout ";
   cout << "if this were standard C.\n";

   int *i = new int;  // Allocates i
   *i = 25;
```

continues

Listing 17.6. Continued

```
    cout << "The value of i is " << *i;
    delete [] i;        // Deallocates i
}
```

The output of Listing 17.6 follows. After you allocate i, referring to it as *i is just like referring to regular integers in programs that don't use memory allocation.

```
In just a couple of lines, this program will define a variable.
It would have to be done before the first cout if this were standard C.
The value of i is 25
```

> Never refer to i without the asterisk, or C++ will not use the value stored in i. Instead, C++ will use the address in memory where i is stored.

For such a simple program, dynamically allocating variables might not make as much sense as it does for extremely large programs that use several variables throughout. Nevertheless, if you always allocate and deallocate variables, you can use memory as efficiently as possible. There are two side effects to memory allocation, however. Even though new and delete are easy to use, they are not as easy as the simple definition of variables. Also, you lose some program speed if you allocate and deallocate every variable. Therefore, only the programmer can determine if the trade-off of memory and speed are worth the benefits. For large, multiple-user systems, allocating is almost always the wisest choice.

Arrays are also easy to allocate. Suppose you need a character array to hold your full name. You could dynamically allocate a character array of 10 characters like this:

```
char * name = new char[10];     // Allocate a 10-character array
```

One of the nice things about C++ arrays is that they perform automatic dereferencing. Therefore, you don't have to use the * before an array that you allocated. To get a name into the name array from the keyboard, you only have to do the following:

```
cin >> name;
```

To print the name, you would do this:

```
cout << name;
```

To deallocate an array, you should put the array subscript inside the `delete` brackets. For instance, the following deallocates the `name` array:

```
delete [ ] name;    // Sends the name memory back to the free memory
```

You can have arrays of other data types as well. If you need lists of integers, floating-points, or any other data types, you can allocate them just as easily as the character array shown here. Although beginning C++ programmers probably only need character arrays, when it comes time for you to use other types of arrays, consider allocating them as we allocated character arrays.

A Little about C++ and OOP

Chapter 11 introduced the concepts of object-oriented programming. Rather than repeating much of that chapter here, the rest of this chapter shows only a few key OOP C++ concepts that you should understand to begin C++ programming.

The most important feature of C++ is a class. A *class* is a new data type you define that includes data and code to manipulate that data. A class is like a little program within your C++ program. A C++ program can have one or many classes, depending on the needs of your application.

 C++ lets you use *structs* as does C. A struct is the record variable type you read about in Chapter 4, "Sophisticated Data Structures." Because classes offer more data protection than do structs, however, most C++ programmers use classes to define their record variable data.

Classes enable you to define your own data types. Sometimes, there are not enough built-in data types, or the built-in data types are not advanced enough for your needs. Your own data types can hold any data you want them to hold; once you define them, you can work with them almost as easily as if they were built-in.

Before you can use a class, you must define it. Here is the format of a class definition:

```
class classname
    {
.
.          // One or more built-in data types go here.
.
    };
```

Suppose you want to keep track of an employee's last name, salary, and number of years of service. You could keep these values in three separate variables, but a class would be a better alternative if you were using C++. Here is a possible class definition for the employee:

```
class Employee {
    char  lname[15];    // The employee's last name
    float salary;       // Monthly salary
    int   years;        // Years of service
};
```

After you define the Employee class, you can treat it just as you treat an int or a float. There are some differences between a built-in data type and a class; for instance, you cannot add two classes because C++ would not know how to add two Employee classes together. With some advanced C++ programming, however, you can describe to C++ how to add them.

For example, if you want to define an integer variable called i and an Employee variable called person, you can do so with these two lines:

```
int i;             // Define a built-in typed variable
Employee person;   // Define a class variable
```

The variable named person now looks like the Employee class. In other words, it is a single variable that is made up of a character array, a floating-point value, and an integer. In C++ terminology, person is an object. An object is any variable in the program, even variables defined from built-in types, although the term object is usually associated with class variables.

This class contains only data members, but you can also put functions in the class. By default, all members of a C++ class are private. C++ does not let the rest of the program access the *private* members of a class. For instance, you cannot print the value of an Employee's salary from inside the function main(). This may seem limited, but it is not. You can access the data in a C++ function from anywhere in the program—like you did in C—by declaring the class members *public*. The rest of a C++ program can access public members of a class. A *member function* is any function within a class; the member function is known as a member of the class just as the data members are members of the class. Generally, all member functions should be public, and you declare them to be public with the public command as follows:

```
class Employee {
    char  lname[15];    // The employee's last name
    float salary;       // Monthly salary
    int   years;        // Years of service
public:
```

```
displname()  {
   cout << lname; }
dispsalary()  {
   cout << salary; }
dispyears()   {
   cout << years;  }
};
```

Always follow the public keyword with a colon (:), as shown in the preceding code example. Later in the program, main(), and all the other functions, can see the private members by calling these three public functions: displname(), dispsalary(), and dispyears().

class definitions almost always appear in a program before all other functions—including main().

Before looking at a complete program that uses this class, consider one more thing. The class contains functions that print their own class's members. Only the public section of a class can access the private data members. So far, there is no way for any program using this class to initialize the three data members. Therefore, you must add three more functions to initialize the values.

The following is the expanded class listing with the initialization member functions:

```
class Employee {
   char  lname[15];    // The employee's last name
   float salary;       // Monthly salary
   int   years;        // Years of service
public:
   getname()  {
      cout << "What is this employee's last name? ";
      cin >> lname; }
   getsalary()  {
      cout << "What is the employee's monthly salary? ";
      cin >> salary; }
   getyears()  {
      cout << "How many years has the employee worked here? ":
      cin >> years; }
   displname()  {
      cout << lname; }
   dispsalary()  {
      cout << salary; }
   dispyears()   {
      cout << years;  }
};
```

Classes can become extremely long. When you first learn about classes, they might seem like a lot of trouble. However, the more work your classes do, the less work the rest of the program has to do. What you are really doing is shifting the burden of the program to your data. You still have to write the code, but instead of your program having extraneous data for which you must write a bunch of code, your data becomes intelligent. Your data now knows how to get its own values and how to print those values. The data becomes active instead of passive.

After you create classes for your data, the rest of the program has to deal less with the petty details of getting and displaying variables. When the program wants a variable to be printed, the program only has to tell the variable to print its own values. For large-scale programming projects, working with class objects moves the petty details from the rest of the code into its own compartment. After you get the class details worked out, you've got the details out of the way and can concentrate on the rest of the program.

Listing 17.7 is a full program that uses three class Employee objects.

Listing 17.7. Using three class *Employee* objects.

```
#include <iostream.h>
class Employee {
   char  lname[15];    // The employee's last name
   float salary;       // Monthly salary
   int   years;        // Years of service
public:
   getname()  {
      cout << "What is this employee's last name? ";
      cin >> lname; }
   getsalary()  {
      cout << "What is the employee's monthly salary? ";
      cin >> salary; }
   getyears()  {
      cout << "How many years has the employee worked here? ";
      cin >> years; }
   dispname()  {
      cout << lname << "\n"; }
   dispsalary()  {
      cout << salary << "\n"; }
   dispyears()   {
      cout << years << "\n";  }
};
void main()
{
```

```
Employee person1, person2, person3;   // 3 Employee variables
person1.getname();    // Call the member functions for person1
person1.getsalary();
person1.getyears();
person2.getname();    // Call the member functions for person2
person2.getsalary();
person2.getyears();
person3.getname();    // Call the member functions for person3
person3.getsalary();
person3.getyears();

person1.dispname();   // Call the display member functions
person1.dispsalary();
person1.dispyears();
person2.dispname();
person2.dispsalary();
person2.dispyears();
person3.dispname();
person3.dispsalary();
person3.dispyears();
}
```

As you do more programming in C++, you will learn several ways to improve this program—but this is a good start. The dot operator (.) is an important operator in C++ programs because it goes between the object and the function you want performed on that object. In other words, the first half of the main() function tells the person1, person2, and person3 objects to call their own data-entry statements (located in the get...() functions: getname(), getsalary(), getyears()[]). The last half tells the three objects to display themselves. In OOP terminology, therefore, you don't call member functions, but you pass messages to objects and let them do the work.

You could add a fourth member function, display(), to call the other three display functions, and a fifth member function, get(), to call the other three input member functions. If you do, you could shorten the main() function to resemble the following:

```
void main()
{
   Employee person1, person2, person3;   // 3 Employee variables
   person1.get();    // Call the member functions for person1
   person2.get();    // Call the member functions for person2
   person3.get();    // Call the member functions for person3
```

```
  person1.disp();   // Call the display member functions
  person2.disp();
  person3.disp();
}
```

Advanced C++ programming using constructors, destructors, and polymorphism (subjects explained in Chapter 11) can improve this program even further.

Summary

Because there is no way to teach you all the object-oriented aspects of C++ in one short chapter, this chapter explained the advantages of C++ over other programming languages and also showed you how C++ is a better version of C.

With your introduction to OOP in Chapter 11 and your exposure to C++ in this chapter, you should begin to see how OOP differs from the procedural programming methods used by other languages. The variables (objects) begin to do all the work, taking a load off the rest of your program.

This chapter concludes the overviews of BASIC, Pascal, C, and C++. At this point, you may be asking, "Which language is best?" Good question. It would not be a cop-out to answer that question with "All of them, and none of them." The best language depends on you and your application. If you are a true beginner, BASIC is the language you should first tackle, whether or not it ends up being your final programming language. Pascal then teaches you new structured programming techniques, C offers efficiency, and C++ introduces you to the new object-oriented methods of programming.

All four languages offer something new. The more programming languages you learn, the easier the next one is to learn. Therefore, learning as much as you can—in as many programming languages as you feel necessary—offers a synergy that increases your overall computer skills and, maybe more important, your marketability in the programming community.

III

Programming
Products

Database Products

by David Veale

PC databases have come a long way in the past 15 years. They have grown from programs in which a hacker would store his wife's recipes to powerful multiuser systems running mission-critical, line-of-business applications on large corporate networks.

Databases and PCs grew up together. As PCs became more powerful, databases added functionality to take advantage of the hardware's capabilities. When networks were introduced, databases added multiuser features. When PCs were connected to host computers (mini- and mainframes), databases added the capability to access host data and emulate mainframe database language dialects, especially SQL.

The dBASE World

Much of the acceptance PCs have achieved as powerful database tools has stemmed from one product line—dBASE. dBASE was born in the late 1970s when a young engineer at the Jet Propulsion Laboratory named C. Wayne Ratliff wanted to find a way to keep track of a company football pool on his personal computer. He was familiar with a mainframe database system called JPLDIS. Using JPLDIS as a model, he created a database management program for his PC. He called his program *Vulcan*. Ratliff eventually met a man named George Tate, who renamed Ratliff's product dBASE II (there never was a dBASE I). Tate founded a company called Ashton-Tate to market the new command-line-driven database management system. (In case you're wondering, Ashton was George Tate's parrot.)

dBASE was a huge success and became the de facto standard for PC database management. It had a simple-to-use programming language and had the capability to have two data files open simultaneously. Soon the product was upgraded to dBASE III, then dBASE III PLUS. dBASE III PLUS added several extensions to the language, a screen designer, a report and label generator, decent multiuser support, an optional menued interface, and the capability to have up to 10 data files open at once. dBASE III PLUS was also a monstrous success for Ashton-Tate. In fact, even though dBASE III PLUS is more than six years old, it is still being sold and supported. dBASE III PLUS compatibility is still a marketing requirement for most PC database products marketed today—it is still the standard.

In 1988, Ashton-Tate brought out the successor to dBASE III PLUS, dBASE IV, which is discussed in detail next. In 1991, Ashton-Tate was purchased by Borland International. dBASE IV currently is in its third major release, called dBASE IV 1.5.

dBASE IV 1.5

The first thing a programmer notices about dBASE IV is how much can be accomplished without programming. Tools are included to create, edit, and index database structures; design screens; perform complex multifile queries; design labels and reports; and even create complete simple applications—all without writing a line of code.

What gives the user all this capability is the dBASE IV Control Center, a menu-driven interface to a collection of powerful tools (see Figure 18.1).

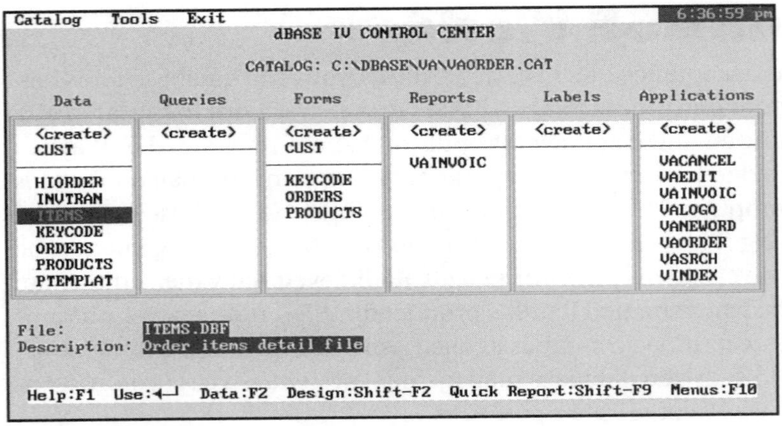

Figure 18.1. The dBASE IV Control Center.

Most of the Control Center tools provide access to design screens and code generators. For example, to create a data entry screen, you go into the Create Form tool and literally draw the form on-screen using the keyboard, menus, and mouse (see Figure 18.2).

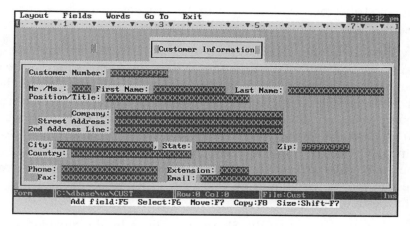

Figure 18.2. The dBASE IV forms designer screen.

The forms designer also includes extensive data validation capabilities (see Figure 18.3), which help ensure valid input. All the tools have the capability to call built-in dBASE functions and functions written by the programmer to add such features as additional validation, pick lists, multifile editing, and the creation of calculated fields.

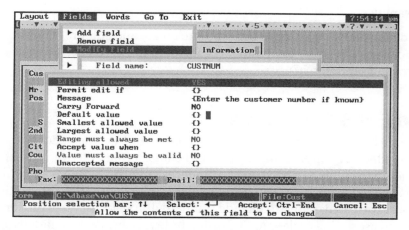

Figure 18.3. Data validation features in the forms designer help ensure valid input.

317

When all your fields, labels, boxes, and lines are just as you want them, you hit a key and the code generator literally writes a dBASE language program for you to create the form you designed. When you want to enter or edit data using that form, dBASE simply runs the program it wrote.

The Report and Label tools work similarly to the form designer—draw what you want on-screen, and the tool writes a program for you.

The Query tool uses a concept called *Query by Example*. When you enter the Query tool, it shows you skeletons of the structures of the various tables that will be included in the query. You select the fields you want included in the query with the keyboard or mouse. You can then enter expressions into fields to limit the records that the query will return. For example, to limit the query to returning sales order records in which the sale was greater than $5,000, you would enter the expression "> 5000" in the field representing the sales amount. When the query is processed, a dBASE routine Borland calls IQ (for Intelligent Query) decides on the fastest way to return the data you want from the files you want. It then writes a dBASE program to produce the desired result.

The Applications tool also writes dBASE programs but adds the capability to pull in the code from the forms, reports, labels, and queries you've designed using the other tools. It combines them with menus, windows, and pop-ups that you create in the Applications tool to create complete menu- and mouse-driven applications.

How the code generator writes these programs is also under the control of the programmer. Code generation is controlled by special user-modifiable files called *templates*. How templates work is beyond the scope of this text, but you should know that they exist and that you can modify them to force dBASE to write code the way you want it.

Also included in dBASE is a simple text editor to create and edit program source code. You can use the editor to modify the code dBASE tools create, or you can write your own code from scratch.

The dBASE Engine

The backbone of a dBASE program is the database engine (see specifications in Table 18.1). dBASE IV supports having up to 40 database files, often called tables, open at once. Each table can have up to 47 indexes opened automatically whenever the table is opened. Each index can be defined on an individual field or multiple fields. Index expressions can also include standard dBASE or user-written functions and may be in ascending or descending order. Indexes can also be defined to include only the first record with a given value in the indexed field (called a *unique* index) or can include only records meeting a condition defined by the user.

Table 18.1. dBASE IV 1.5 specifications.	
Database Files	
Maximum number of bytes per table	2,000,000,000
Maximum number of records per table	1,000,000,000
Maximum number of bytes per record	4,000
Maximum number of fields per record	255
Maximum number of tables open at once	40
Index Files	
Maximum number of indexes per index file	47
Field Sizes	
Maximum length of character field	254
Maximum length of date field	8
Maximum length of logical field	1
Maximum length of numeric field	20
Maximum length of floating-point field	20
Maximum length of memo field	unlimited*

64K limit using dBASE internal editor

In a network environment, in which databases are shared among users, dBASE IV automatically handles file and record locking to ensure data integrity. In certain circumstances, if one user changes a record that is being viewed by other users, the screens of the other users automatically update with the new information.

dBASE also includes network *transaction processing*. Transaction processing ensures that when multiple files need to be updated, they all must be successfully updated or none is updated. For example, in a simple order entry system, there may be a customer table, an orders table, and an inventory table to be updated each time a new order is entered. If there were a network or computer failure when, say, the customer table had been updated but the orders and inventory tables had not yet been updated, the transaction processing system would *rollback* (that is, cancel) the update to the customer table to ensure that the tables remained in sync.

Language Features

dBASE IV includes a rich programming language suitable for many types of applications. The dBASE IV language implementation is virtually 100 percent compatible with dBASE III PLUS, so dBASE III PLUS programs can run under dBASE IV with no change.

There is a rich set of built-in data types for memory variables ("memvars" in dBASE lingo) corresponding to database field types. These data types include *character* for single characters or strings, *numeric* for binary-coded decimal numbers, *float* for floating-point numbers, *date* for dates, and *logical* for Boolean values. dBASE supports one- and two-dimensional arrays of any data type. Memvars of different data types can be used in the same array; that is, x[1] can be of type character while x[2] is of type numeric. For manipulating memvars, dBASE supports a full set of standard operators, including raising to a power and date arithmetic.

dBASE has extensive support for structured programming. Such control structures as IF-ELSE-ENDIF, DO WHILE-ENDDO, SCAN-ENDSCAN, and DO CASE-ENDCASE are included. Code can be easily arranged into modules as separate source code files and further divided into individual procedures and functions.

A *procedure* is a formal language construct that performs a single unit of functionality. For example, you can write a procedure to draw a message window, process a menu selection, or get input from the user. Parameters can be passed to procedures either by reference or by value, meaning you can pass an actual memvar to the procedure or just the value contained in it.

A *function* is virtually identical to a procedure, except that it returns a value. For example, you can write a function to calculate the yield of a bond called YIELD(). Then, call the function and assign the result to a memvar, for example, mYield = YIELD(bond, term, intrstRate). Collections of these user-written, or *user-defined*, functions (UDFs) can be stored together in a library that is accessible from anywhere within dBASE. These UDFs thus essentially become extensions to the dBASE language. The addition of UDFs was probably the most important change to the dBASE language in the dBASE III PLUS to dBASE IV upgrade.

dBASE contains commands and functions to support the development of sophisticated user interfaces. Bar, pop-up, and pull-down menus are supported, as well as pop-up windows. These elements can be combined to produce slick dialog boxes and pick lists. Mouse support is automatically built into the interface without any additional programming.

In all, the dBASE language contains nearly 175 commands and nearly 160 functions, enough to cover most situations. But if you need to do something not covered by the extensive language, it is possible to write routines in assembly language or C and call the compiled routine from within dBASE. Because there are limitations on dBASE's capability to run external code, it should be used only when necessary, and the routines should be kept small and single purpose. A good example would be a small routine to perform a low-level DOS function not supported by dBASE.

SQL

In addition to the standard dBASE language, dBASE supports writing programs using Structured Query Language (SQL). SQL is a query language traditionally used in mini- and mainframe computer database products. It is becoming increasingly popular for PC databases, especially database products designed for large networks. dBASE's implementation of SQL is a subset of the language used in IBM's DB2, a very popular mainframe relational database. SQL enables you to easily produce queries that utilize data from several tables at once. It also provides facilities to ensure that all the tables which make up a complete database stay in sync, capabilities beyond dBASE's native transaction processing system.

The dBASE native language and dBASE SQL are largely mutually exclusive. You cannot access SQL tables using dBASE commands, and you cannot access dBASE tables using SQL commands. Many programmers still haven't used dBASE's SQL capabilities in earnest, choosing instead to concentrate on the more familiar dBASE language. But as SQL grows in popularity, it is comforting to know that it is already implemented as part of the dBASE product.

Compiling and Debugging

All dBASE source code files are automatically compiled before they are run. The dBASE compiler does not compile programs to .OBJ or .EXE files like a C or Pascal compiler. Instead, it compiles them to a *pseudocode* file. A pseudocode file is simply an optimized version of your source code file. The comments and spaces are stripped out, dBASE-reserved words are tokenized (that is, converted to numbers that can be more quickly evaluated), and code is slightly rearranged to allow for faster execution. The pseudocode file is then interpreted by dBASE as the program is run.

Besides the improved execution speed these "pseudocompiled" program files provide, they also result in better security for a developer. If you are distributing an application, you need only provide the compiled versions of your program files—which are not readable by people, only by dBASE.

Debugger

dBASE includes an excellent full-screen source code debugger that enables you to step through your code, watch memvars, and set breakpoints on code lines or on expressions.

Import and Export Features

dBASE is able to import and export data files in other formats such as ASCII, Lotus 1-2-3, and Framework formats. In addition, the language contains C-like functions for low-level file access, enabling a knowledgeable programmer to read from, or write to, virtually any type of file.

Security

dBASE provides extensive multilevel password protection for the entire dBASE system, or file by file. Data files can be encrypted so they cannot be viewed or changed by unauthorized users.

Because only the compiled versions of program files are needed to run a program, source code security can be maintained. Because report formats, screen designs, queries, and labels are also ultimately dBASE programs, they can be distributed as only their compiled program files as well.

System Requirements

The DOS version of dBASE IV runs entirely within the 640K DOS conventional memory space. dBASE does not use expanded or extended memory except for an optional disk cache. This means that all the power of dBASE IV can still be used on 8086/8088-based XT-class computers (although for performance reasons, at least an 80286 processor is recommended). A hard disk is required. dBASE supports all the major NetBIOS-compatible network operating systems, including Artisoft's LANtastic, Banyon Vines, the IBM PC-LAN Program and LAN Server, Microsoft LAN Manager, and Novell NetWare. Keep in mind that with DOS, the network software, and any other memory-resident programs loaded on the computer, at least 450K of DOS conventional memory must be available for dBASE to run reliably.

Distribution

Borland provides a selection of distribution methods for your dBASE programs. Obviously, everyone using your program could have a copy of dBASE IV. This solution makes sense if your users are running on stand-alone PCs and need to use dBASE for purposes other than running dBASE programs (creating ad hoc queries or custom reports, for example).

If you are installing your program in a LAN environment, you can install a single copy of dBASE IV on the server and purchase a dBASE LAN Pack for each user. The LAN Pack is essentially just a license for additional users to use the same copy of dBASE IV over a network. It is less expensive to buy LAN Packs than additional copies of dBASE. Again, the assumption of a LAN pack is that the user needs to do more with dBASE IV than just run programs.

If you are distributing your program to users who do not need to use dBASE beyond running your application, you should get a copy of the dBASE IV RunTime. RunTime is a program that does nothing but run dBASE applications without having the actual dBASE system installed. If you, as a developer, purchase one copy of RunTime, you are free to distribute as many copies of RunTime as you need to support your applications. Your application can be installed on a network with one copy of RunTime, and as many users can run it simultaneously as are desired. RunTime is a very economical way to distribute your programs.

Portability

Versions of dBASE IV, or at least the RunTime system, have been produced for the Apple Macintosh, the Sun workstation, several versions of the UNIX operating system, Microsoft/Sybase's SQL Server database server, and Digital Equipment's VAX/VMS operating system. Each of these will run DOS dBASE IV code unmodified. In many cases, you do not even need to recompile your source code files to run them in these other environments. dBASE is supported on more platforms than any of its competitors. So your dBASE programs have the widest market available.

As of this writing, only dBASE IV for DOS was shipping at the 1.5 release level. All other platforms were still at the previous 1.1 release level. Therefore, a few features of the dBASE IV for DOS 1.5 product are not portable to other environments at this time. Borland has not yet announced when upgrades for non-DOS environments will be available.

Documentation

The dBASE IV 1.5 program comes with about 1,800 pages of documentation. The documentation includes tutorial information, information on the database system, instructions on using the Control Center and the tools, a programming tutorial, and a detailed language reference. In addition to the printed information, dBASE IV includes an online help system that summarizes the use of each command and function and explains procedures to follow when using the Control Center tools.

Support Policies

Borland offers various free and fee-based support programs to dBASE users. Users can pose general questions about dBASE installation and use on a free (except for long-distance charges) support phone line. In addition, Borland maintains an active dBASE forum on CompuServe in which users can ask questions and download files related to dBASE. Borland technicians monitor the CompuServe forum and respond to questions. Borland also maintains a computer bulletin board that users can call to download dBASE-related files and patches.

Users can ask specific questions about programming issues or especially complicated dBASE problems by calling a Borland 900 number. The caller is charged a per-minute fee but can get more detailed help and explanations than are available on the free support line.

Borland publishes a monthly newsletter called *TechNotes* that contains dBASE tips, techniques, and ways to overcome known bugs (workarounds). A subscription to *TechNotes* can be purchased from Borland.

Professional dBASE developers who expect to call for support often can purchase an annual support subscription. The subscription includes a toll-free support number, a subscription to *TechNotes,* automatic shipment of maintenance releases of dBASE, and a special section on the CompuServe dBASE forum for subscribers only with a guaranteed four-hour response to questions from a Borland technician.

Vendor Information

Borland is proving that the dBASE standard still has a long, happy life ahead. dBASE IV is a complete applications development environment that provides excellent programmer productivity and creates powerful, robust applications.

The listing prices for Borland's dBASE products at the time of writing were

dBASE IV 1.5	$795.00
dBASE IV 1.5 RunTime	$250.00
dBASE IV 1.5 LAN Pack	$395.00

For more information on dBASE products, call or write Borland at

Borland International
1800 Green Hills Road
P.O. Box 660001
Scotts Valley, CA 95067-0001
(800) 331-0877

FoxPro 2.0

FoxPro 2.0 is Microsoft's DOS database product. FoxPro was originally developed by Fox Software, which was purchased by Microsoft in 1992.

FoxPro is one of several products on the market that is based on dBASE, but FoxPro adds new features to attempt to improve on the dBASE model. Of these dBASE-compatible products, or "xBASE" products as they are commonly called, FoxPro is the most popular, especially with developers.

User Interface

FoxPro features a modern mouse- and menu-driven user interface (see Figure 18.4). It has a CUA-style menu bar with pull-down menus. Users can open, view, and edit data files easily by making menu selections. To browse a database, a user selects Open from the File menu and selects the file to open, then selects Browse from the Database menu. The browse screen comes up in a window, as do most of the objects FoxPro puts on-screen. The windows are all resizeable, zoomable, moveable, and closeable using the keyboard or a mouse. You can have as many windows as you want on-screen. So it is often not necessary to exit one operation before starting another.

If a command line, or "dot prompt," is more to your liking, you can use a command window to type in FoxPro's dBASE-like commands. One great feature is that all menu selections which translate into FoxPro commands are placed in the command window as you work. So when you select File, Open, and a file name from the menus, the command USE filename appears in the command window. This is a terrific learning tool for users trying to learn FoxPro's language. It is also convenient because a user can easily reexecute a previously entered command by placing the cursor on it in the command window and pressing Enter, rather than going through a long series of menu selections again.

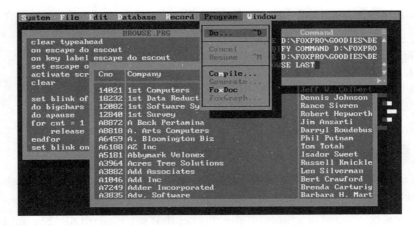

Figure 18.4. The FoxPro environment.

Like dBASE, FoxPro has screen, label, report, query, and applications generators, although there are some major differences in implementation. For example, the screen generator has the capability to generate input windows as well as screens. Whereas dBASE generates a dBASE language program from its screen generator, FoxPro generates a proprietary file. The file can be modified only by returning to the screen generator and making changes there. The label and report generators work similarly.

Queries are done in an interesting way. Rather than generating a FoxPro language program to query tables in a database, FoxPro generates an SQL program. The SQL statements are highly optimized and efficient. FoxPro does not need to be put into "SQL mode" to run the SQL. You are free to use these SQL statements from the command line or embed them in your programs.

One of FoxPro's claims to fame is the speed of its queries. Using its patented *Rushmore* technology (a very intelligent indexing system), query results come back in speeds that rival mainframe database systems.

Database Engine

The database engine uses the same .DBF file format used by dBASE, except that a proprietary format is used for memo fields. FoxPro has its own indexing scheme that permits up to 254 index tags to be opened automatically with the database file. The algorithms used by FoxPro's indexes (part of Rushmore) are generally considered to be the fastest available in an xBASE database product. Further specifications on the engine are provided in Table 18.2.

Table 18.2. FoxPro 2.0 specifications.	
Database Files	
Maximum number of bytes per table	2,000,000,000
Maximum number of records per table	1,000,000,000
Maximum number of bytes per record	4,000
Maximum number of fields per record	255
Maximum number of tables open at once	25
Index Files	
Maximum number of indexes per index file	254
Field Sizes	
Maximum length of character field	64K
Maximum length of date field	8
Maximum length of logical field	1
Maximum length of numeric field	20
Maximum length of floating-point field	20
Maximum length of memo field	unlimited

To run FoxPro on a network, a network version of the program, called FoxPro/LAN, is required. FoxPro/LAN supports automatic file and record locking but does not support transaction processing and rollback.

Language Features

The FoxPro programming language is based on dBASE but has many extensions. You can set the language to a "compatibility mode" so that FoxPro can run dBASE III PLUS and some dBASE IV programs. The native FoxPro language will not run many dBASE programs without using a compatibility mode.

FoxPro includes the basic set of data type (character, numeric, date) but has some extensions. For instance, character string variables can be up to 64,000 characters in length. dBASE limits such variables to 254 characters.

FoxPro supports one- and two-dimensional arrays. The language contains several functions for populating, manipulating, and sorting arrays.

Structured programming is supported through support for all the major control structures, including a FOR-ENDFOR structure which simplifies loops that run a fixed number of times. FoxPro supports programs built from multiple source files and includes a project manager to help the programmer keep track of which modules go together and to ensure that all modules are properly compiled.

FoxPro fully supports user-defined procedures and functions. User-defined functions are extremely important in FoxPro programming.

The FoxPro language supports the FoxPro-style interface. A programmer can easily define windows to hold screen elements. Windows are automatically moveable, resizeable, and closeable via the keyboard or a mouse. The language has full support for bar, pop-up, and pull-down menus, dialog boxes, and pick lists. FoxPro is about the closest one can get to graphical user interface programming in a character-based system.

Like dBASE, FoxPro supports the calling of small external routines written in assembly language or C. FoxPro also supports the creation of libraries of routines, usually written in C, that can be called by a FoxPro program as if these routines were part of the built-in language. FoxPro uses an applications programming interface (API) to pass information back and forth between these routines and FoxPro. Building these API libraries requires the purchase of the FoxPro Library Construction Kit.

Import and Export Functions

FoxPro has the capability to import and export data in a variety of formats, including ASCII, Lotus 1-2-3 (both .WK1 and .WK3 formats), Microsoft Excel, and Borland's Framework and Paradox formats.

Security

FoxPro programs can be distributed solely in their compiled form, providing source code security for the developer. FoxPro provides no security system to prevent someone from running the program or accessing data files. Security issues of this type must be dealt with in another fashion.

Memory Management and System Requirements

Although FoxPro is a DOS program, and can run within as little as 512K of conventional memory, it is not limited by DOS's 640K memory limit. On 8086/80286 (XT/AT class) computers, FoxPro not only uses conventional memory, but also takes full advantage of expanded memory if present. This is one of the reasons FoxPro is so fast. It does not need to constantly load overlays from disk as your programs execute. It is also possible to write very large FoxPro programs because they have a larger memory space to run in.

If you have an 80386-based computer, or better, and at least 1.5M of RAM, FoxPro can run in "extended mode," meaning that it can use all of conventional memory plus any extended memory as one memory pool. Not only can programs be huge in this scenario, but so can data elements. For example, standard FoxPro limits the number of elements in an array to 3,600. In extended mode, that limit is bumped up to 65,000. Programs running in this mode will also achieve the maximum possible speed.

FoxPro supports most networks that support an IBM-compatible NetBIOS protocol. This includes all the networks previously listed as supporting dBASE IV. Keep in mind that you must have the network version of the software to run on a network.

FoxPro requires a hard disk on all versions.

Compiling and Debugging

All FoxPro code is compiled before it is run. Like dBASE, the compiler in FoxPro creates psuedocode files that are interpreted by the FoxPro system.

FoxPro includes a source-level debugger that enables users to step though code, set breakpoints, and watch variables. The debugger runs in a window, so you can run the debugger side by side with your code for easier debugging.

FoxPro also includes a source code documenter. This utility produces a complete chart of your program showing which routines call which, what modules are in your program, what order they are run in, and what files your program uses, among other useful information. Not only is this tool useful for debugging, but it is a great way to document your program so that you, or someone else, can maintain it easily.

Distribution

Microsoft provides several means of distributing FoxPro applications. Of course, each user could have a full copy of FoxPro. If your user is running on a stand-alone PC and needs to use FoxPro for purposes other than running your application, having a full copy of FoxPro makes the most sense.

If the users of your program are on a network and need to use FoxPro for more than just running programs, a copy of FoxPro/LAN can be installed on the network server. One copy of FoxPro/LAN enables up to six simultaneous users to access FoxPro.

If your user needs only to run your program, you can purchase a copy of the FoxPro Distribution Kit. This kit includes a runtime system that allows your program to run without FoxPro. You are free to distribute as many copies of the FoxPro runtime as are necessary to support your application. The Distribution Kit also includes an .EXE compiler. This compiler binds your compiled FoxPro code with the runtime system to produce a stand-alone .EXE file. These .EXE files tend to be quite large—2M or more.

Portability

FoxPro is also available for the Apple Macintosh and for some versions of UNIX. It will soon (probably by the time you read this) be available for Windows. The Windows interface is a natural for FoxPro. FoxPro looks and acts like a "character-based Windows" now.

Documentation and Support

FoxPro includes about 2,000 pages of printed documentation plus an online hypertext help system. The documentation includes tutorials on the tools and language, and extensive reference material.

Microsoft maintains an extensive support network for developers. Microsoft has a forum on CompuServe for FoxPro, as well as forums dealing with DOS and other programming tools. These forums are staffed by Microsoft technicians. Also on CompuServe is the Microsoft Knowledge Base, a searchable database of common questions and answers, known bugs, and tips and techniques.

Microsoft has free (except for the cost of the phone call) support for questions regarding the setup and use of FoxPro's commands, interface, and tools. Limited assistance for programming problems is also available.

For developers who need help with the actual FoxPro programming, Microsoft offers a multi-tier fee-based support system ranging from a 900 phone line for questions on DOS to on-site consulting services for development problems.

Microsoft also offers training courses through Microsoft University. It also publishes the *Microsoft Systems Journal,* a paid-subscription, bimonthly technical journal dealing with development issues. Microsoft Press publishes books and manuals dealing with Microsoft products.

Vendor Information

FoxPro is the fastest xBASE database on the market today. It includes a robust programming language and a very slick interface.

Now that FoxPro is owned by software giant Microsoft, we can expect that what was already a successful product will become much more so. The coming Windows version and Microsoft's ongoing development of the DOS version show that Microsoft is serious about making an impact in this market.

The listing prices for Microsoft's FoxPro products at the time of writing were

FoxPro 2.0	$795.00
FoxPro/LAN 2.0 (6 users)	$895.00
FoxPro Distribution Kit 2.0	$500.00
FoxPro Library Construction Kit 2.0	$500.00

For more information on FoxPro products, call or write Microsoft at

Microsoft Corporation
One Microsoft Way
Redmond, WA 98052-6399
(800) 426-9400

Clipper 5.01

Clipper is an xBASE language compiler originally developed by Nantucket Corporation, and purchased in 1992 by Computer Associates. The first thing you need to know about Clipper is that it is a product for the serious developer only. Clipper is a compiler and only a compiler. There are no menus, dot prompt, or "environment" of any kind—just a small collection of DOS command-line programs. But in the hands of a competent developer, Clipper is also the most versatile and powerful of all the products reviewed in this chapter.

Clipper can be used to create almost any type of program short of an operating system. In fact, Computer Associates markets a dBASE IV code compiler written entirely in Clipper.

When a dBASE or FoxPro programmer first tries to work with Clipper, she's in for a culture shock. A C programmer would be more at home here than a dBASE programmer. Clipper cannot be used interactively. All commands must be compiled and linked into .EXE files to be run. Clipper works on the classic edit, compile, link, run, debug, edit cycle that is the hallmark of traditional programming.

Database Engine

By default, Clipper uses standard dBASE-type .DBF data files and .DBT memo files. Clipper uses a proprietary index file format, although the dBASE III+ format is supported as well. Each index must be defined in its own index file, and each index must be explicitly opened by the programmer when the database file is opened; otherwise, the unopened index will not be updated as database files are changed. Table 18.3 shows some more database specifications.

Table 18.3. Clipper 5.01 specifications.	
Database Files	
Maximum number of bytes per table	2,000,000,000
Maximum number of records per table	1,000,000,000
Maximum number of fields per record	1,024
Maximum number of tables open at once	254
Index Files	
Maximum number of indexes per index file	1
Maximum number of index files per database	15
Field Sizes	
Maximum length of character field	64K
Maximum length of date field	8
Maximum length of logical field	1
Maximum length of numeric field	30
Maximum length of floating-point field	30
Maximum length of memo field	unlimited

The database engine can determine the presence of a network, but all file and record locking must be performed by the programmer through calls to file and record locking and unlocking functions. There is no built-in support for transaction processing. There is also no security system. You need to write your own or rely on your network operating system.

Note that it was stated earlier that Clipper uses dBASE file formats *by default*. One of the features of Clipper is that it has a replaceable database engine. Hence, if you wanted Clipper to use Paradox database and index files rather than the dBASE format, you could theoretically purchase or write a Paradox engine library for Clipper and begin using that file format.

Language Features

The best way to describe the Clipper language is as a 50-50 combination of the dBASE language and C. Clipper uses many of the same commands as dBASE (USE, REPLACE, SET, and so on), but Clipper programs tend to be structured like C programs.

Most nontrivial Clipper programs use C-style header files. The header files define constants and user-defined commands. A user-defined command is similar to a C macro, in which a name is given to a short piece of code. Wherever the name is encountered in the source code file, the code is substituted. This feature gives a programmer the power to extend the Clipper language, adding whatever commands he feels are appropriate to support his application.

Indeed, the bulk of the standard Clipper commands is declared in supplied header files. This feature leaves the programmer free to change or extend the meaning of the standard Clipper commands. This feature should be used only with great care.

You can write Clipper programs using dBASE-style syntax. But a real Clipper program is written more like a C program. It is a series of functions calling functions. The way functions are defined is reminiscent of C. Instead of passing parameters using the dBASE PARAMETERS keyword, such as

```
FUNCTION FOO
PARAMETERS x, y, z
```

parameters are passed in the parentheses following the function name:

```
FUNCTION FOO(x, y, z)
```

Even comments now use the C /* */ and C++ // style rather than the old dBASE * and &&. (The dBASE style of parameters and comments is still supported but is discouraged.)

Classes

Clipper has some very limited support for the concept of object-oriented programming. Clipper ships with a few predefined *classes*. A class in Clipper, as in C++, is a new data type that encapsulates all the data and code necessary to perform some specific function. For example, Clipper has no BROWSE command, but it does have a class called TBrowse. By declaring a memvar of type TBrowse, you are creating a memvar that has all the code and data available to it to put a browse window on-screen. The programmer still has quite a bit of work to do to create a dBASE-style Browse. For instance, each column of the Browse table must be individually defined, and the capability to get and save changes to data must be added. Clipper comes with a sample program that uses TBrowse to create a minimal browse window with data editing capability. That program is still about 500 lines of code. But without the TBrowse class to use as a base, such a program could easily be a couple thousand lines of code.

Clipper also includes an Errors class and a Gets class. These classes provide functionality to react to and recover from errors, and handle user input, respectively.

The class concept, new in the latest release of Clipper, is not yet fully developed. There is no facility for the programmer to define her own classes, and classes cannot be derived from the existing classes, as in real object-oriented languages. But what's here is a start and is likely to be expanded on in future releases.

Other Features

Clipper includes functions to create on-screen windows, pop-ups, and pick lists. Mouse support is not built into the language but can be added using third-party libraries. Although Clipper is no FoxPro in terms of ease of building a slick user interface, the power is there to produce almost any look the programmer desires.

Clipper exploits arrays of memvars to the fullest. Several functions are included to support arrays, including functions to create a multidimensional array from a database structure and copy the contents of the file to the array (and vice versa). An array can be nested inside another array.

The Compiler

The centerpiece of the Clipper system is the compiler. The entire compiler is included in the CLIPPER.EXE file, which is run from the DOS command line. The compiler reads an ASCII text source code file and produces an object (.OBJ) file.

Each source code file produces an .OBJ file. The .OBJs are then linked with the Clipper libraries by a utility called a linker to produce an .EXE file. Clipper includes a customized version of Pocket Soft's RTLink for this purpose.

In addition to producing the .EXE, Clipper can produce special runtime libraries called *pre-linked libraries* (.PLLs). The .PLL files contain code that may be needed by several Clipper applications installed on a computer. Rather than including the same routines in each .EXE, the programmer can place these common routines in a .PLL. Each Clipper application can then access the code in the PLL as it is running, and execute the code contained therein as if it were included in the .EXE. If you are familiar with Microsoft Windows or OS/2 dynamic link libraries (.DLLs), this is the same principle. The advantage is that the programs take less memory, and .EXE size is kept down.

In addition to pre-linked libraries, standard overlays can be created for large programs that cannot fit all their code in memory at once. Intelligent use of pre-linked libraries and overlays should permit programmers to produce extremely large and complex programs and still run them successfully under DOS.

Is Clipper a "Real" Compiler?

A debate has long raged among Clipper developers as to whether Clipper is a true compiler in the traditional sense. A traditional compiler compiles source code into machine code, the binary code that the computer understands, and the linker links that machine code with other machine code contained in libraries to produce a machine-executable program. A true compiled program should not need any supporting software, except for the operating system, to run.

In that traditional sense, Clipper is not a true compiler. When a Clipper program is compiled, the .OBJ file contains highly optimized pseudocode. This pseudocode is then combined with the Clipper libraries. The libraries contain the code for all the commands and functions, which is composed of both more pseudocode and machine code. Also in the libraries is a runtime system or "engine" that actually executes your programs. This is why the one-line program `? "Hello World"`, which simply prints `Hello World` on-screen, produces a 145K executable file! Don't worry; 145K is about the minimum size for an .EXE, but executable files grow pretty slowly beyond that. A 500-line program produces an .EXE of only about 200K.

Clipper is different from traditional compilers. However, Clipper still produces stand-alone .EXE files, and its code is extremely optimized and efficient. The fact that the compiler may not produce true machine code should not be a mark against the program. The development process is the same as with a C or Pascal compiler.

And a user running a Clipper program would not have any reason to doubt the robustness of the code produced.

Utilities

Clipper includes an excellent source code debugger. The debugger supports multiple breakpoints on both individual lines and logical expressions, and watching memvars values during execution.

You will need your own editor to write Clipper programs. A very simple editor, written in Clipper, is included in the package. But this editor is intended primarily as a demonstration program and is not particularly useful. You should use a good programming editor such as Brief with dBrief or Multi-Edit.

Also included is a simple file editor, also written in Clipper, to permit the programmer to create or edit .DBF file structures and index files without having to write Clipper programs. It also has a simple Browse function, primarily intended to be used for debugging.

One other utility is a simple report and label builder. This program is useful for producing a simple list-type report of data in a file or simple mailing labels. This program is also written in Clipper.

Source code is provided for all the previously mentioned programs except the debugger.

Portability

Clipper is strictly a DOS programming system. The compiler and programs work on any IBM-compatible system with 640K of memory and a hard disk.

Computer Associates is continuing development, started by Nantucket, on a Windows language product based on Clipper. Code-named Aspen, this new product is expected to be an object-oriented version of the Clipper language with full support for the Windows environment. As of this writing, no release date has been announced.

Documentation and Support Policies

Clipper comes with about 1,100 pages of documentation covering the language and the use of all the tools. Also included is the Norton Guide, a memory-resident hypertext help system, with help files containing reference material on Clipper commands, functions, classes, and programming rules.

As of this writing, Computer Associates is continuing Nantucket's support policies. Telephone support is available free for a limited time after the product is registered. After that, a fee is charged for each incident requiring telephone support. A support subscription can also be purchased by those who tend to need to call for support often.

Computer Associates also maintains a Clipper forum on CompuServe and publishes a paid-subscription Clipper newsletter.

Vendor Information

If you are a dBASE programmer coming into Clipper, you should be prepared to learn a new style of programming and to write a lot of code to accomplish tasks that took only a few lines in dBASE. But you gain a whole new level of power. If you need a new language feature, you can add it. If you don't like the way a feature is implemented, you can change it. If you don't want the dBASE-style database engine, you can replace it. Then compile your custom application into an .EXE, use lots of memory, and experience the speed and efficiency that only a compiler can provide.

If you are a C programmer coming into Clipper, be prepared to write a lot less code and have far fewer issues to concern yourself with, such as file handling and memory allocation. But your style of programming need not change dramatically. You still write functions that call functions, still pass parameters by value or by reference (without all the pointer issues), and still maintain a high level of code efficiency, relatively speaking.

If you are a new programmer, Clipper provides you with the simplicity of the dBASE language with a lot of the power of C or Pascal. You can write complex, mission-critical applications with a powerful database engine, learn a little about object-oriented programming, and give your clients stand-alone, compiled programs.

The listing price for Computer Associates' Clipper at the time of writing was

    Clipper 5.01 $795.00

For more information on Clipper, call or write Computer Associates at

    Computer Associates International, Inc.
    One Computer Associates Plaza
    Islandia, NY 11788-7000
    (516) 312-5224

Paradox 4.0

Some of you may remember seeing the television show "Sesame Street" when you were young, or perhaps you saw it with your own children. On "Sesame Street," one of the popular games to play was to show a collection of related objects and have people (or muppets) guess which one was "not like the others." If they were to use this chapter for that game, Borland's Paradox would be the program that "doesn't belong."

Paradox takes a different approach to database management than the other products discussed in this chapter. Whereas many other PC database programs followed after dBASE's lead, Paradox was beating its own path.

Paradox is the most "end-user friendly" of the programs discussed here. In fact, many Paradox users use the program daily for all sorts of tasks and have never written a line of code. Paradox is also the fastest PC database product out there now. Queries and searches are completed with lightning speed.

Interacting with Paradox

In Paradox, there is no command line. Users interact with data through a Windows-like character-based user interface. All functionality is provided by a mouse- or keyboard-driven menu system.

Paradox draws heavily on the relational model of database management by having users work with logical views of their data, viewing data from five tables as easily as viewing data from one table.

Paradox was the first PC database product to use query by example (QBE). In Paradox's QBE implementation, users can see the fields from one or more tables available to them on-screen. The user selects the fields he needs to see, and the order to show them in, and defines the records he wants to see by entering conditions (for instance, the date field of the record must be within a given range of dates). When the user presses the Paradox "Do it!" key (a function key), Paradox creates a new table containing the records and fields the user requested. The user has the option of saving this new table if the data is required for further reference.

Screen Designer

To help get the data into the system in the first place, Paradox includes a sophisticated multi-table screen designer. You lay out screens by dragging fields to positions on-screen, then filling in labels and drawing lines and boxes to design a form.

338

Because the screen designer supports multi-table editing, you could, for example, have a data entry form for an order-entry system contain information from a customer table, an inventory table, and an invoice table. Paradox makes it very easy to allow information from up to nine tables to be included in one form. Most other PC database products require some programming to build multi-table forms.

Paradox takes the form design process to a new level of intelligence by allowing relationships to be defined between tables. This intelligence enables Paradox to stop a user from deleting from the customer table a customer who still has orders in the invoice table, for example.

Output

Paradox includes a sophisticated multi-table report writer. Reports support groups, sorting, summary data, and calculated fields. Predefined mailing-label formats are also included, or you can design your own.

Paradox stores forms and reports as part of the database file, not as a separate file. You are limited to 15 form and 15 report designs per table.

Paradox also supports creating colorful business graphics based on data. Line, bar, 3D-bar, and pie charts are supported. Unfortunately, printing of these graphs is not supported by Paradox. There are, however, third parties that sell Paradox add-ons to support graph printing.

Applications Generator

The Paradox Application Workshop (PAW) is an application generator written in the Paradox language. Fully integrated into the overall Paradox product, PAW enables developers and end-users to create fairly sophisticated multiuser applications with menus, dialogs, and mouse support. End-users can use PAW to create their own interfaces and streamline their work. Developers can use it as a prototyping tool and as a way to save a lot of hand coding of interfaces.

Security

Paradox has optional password protection for files. Access levels can be set for each field within a table based on the password. File encryption is not supported.

Database Engine

The Paradox database engine, described in Table 18.4, has features not found in the xBASE world. There are two unusual numeric data types: integer, for relatively small numbers, and currency, for numbers with up to two decimal places for which absolute accuracy is a must.

Table 18.4. Paradox 4.0 specifications.	
Database Files	
Maximum number of bytes per table	262,000,000
Maximum bytes per indexed record	1,350
Maximum bytes per unindexed record	4,000
Maximum number of fields per record	255
Maximum number of tables open at once	24
Index Files	
Maximum number of primary indexes	1
Maximum number of secondary indexes	unlimited
Field Sizes	
Maximum length of character field	255
Maximum length of date field	8
Maximum length of logical field	1
Maximum length of numeric field	15
Maximum length of currency field	15
Maximum length of integer field	5
Maximum length of memo/BLOb field	256M

The most interesting type of field is the binary large object, or BLOb, field. BLObs are used for storing virtually any type of binary data. That data could be anything from a word processing file to a graphics to a scanned photograph. Imagine the convenience for a real estate broker to have not only the specs on a property in a database, but a photo as well!

Indexing is handled in a two-tiered system in Paradox. Each table can have one primary key. The primary key is the method by which the database would intuitively be ordered. A customer table would use the customer number as its primary key, for example. The primary index, which is automatically maintained by Paradox, is the default order in which records will be presented when a user is running queries and reports.

A secondary key is an index, often built on the fly, for use in a query or report for which the primary key is not the desired order. Usually these indexes are used for the task at hand, then discarded. Indexes may be built on a single field or a combination of fields.

Paradox supports automatic file and record locking when run on a network. The program includes a quick-lock algorithm to speed record locking and unlocking.

Paradox Programming

It is possible to "write" Paradox programs without writing a single command. All the tasks Paradox can perform are accessible from its menus. Paradox includes a scripting capability (similar to macros in spreadsheets) that enables the user to program all the menu steps required to complete a task. Using a script, the user can completely automate a complicated task and reduce it to one keystroke. Paradox even includes a "record" feature, which permits Paradox to store all the keystrokes and menu selections to perform a task to a script file as they are done.

But to write a truly professional and bulletproof system, you need to write code. Paradox includes a programming language all its own, called the *Paradox Application Language,* or PAL. Paradox also includes a reasonably good text editor for writing programs. But you can use any ASCII text editor. After the programs are written, you can use the built-in debugger to step through code, set breakpoints, and watch variables. The debugger runs in a window, so the debugger and your application can be on-screen at the same time.

PAL

PAL looks a little like a combination of the dBASE language, Pascal, and a spreadsheet macro language. In dBASE, many programs are written so that the user would have a hard time knowing that his program is running on top of dBASE. In Paradox, this is not so true. PAL is closely tied to the Paradox system and interface. Many of the PAL "commands" simply mimic the pressing of keys in the Paradox system. This approach has some advantages. Why reinvent keystrokes and procedures to get to the query design screen? Just have your PAL program "press the keys" to make Paradox move there for you.

But PAL still has all the tools to make it a real structured language. It supports variables and arrays. Programmers can create their own procedures and libraries of procedures. The major control structures, such as IF-THEN-ELSE, WHILE, and CASE, are supported.

The major difference is that PAL programs tend to control the order of execution of standard Paradox tasks rather than do the actual work of database management. Hence, PAL programs tend to be smaller than programs written in other database languages. It is necessary to have a thorough understanding of Paradox to be able to effectively write programs in PAL.

PAL programs are not compiled. Because these programs work primarily by running already-compiled Paradox tasks, compiling the PAL source code was not considered necessary. Unfortunately, this means that your users cannot be kept from seeing and modifying your PAL code (at least not by Paradox).

Event-Driven Programming

Paradox has an event-driven interface. A Paradox user can click the mouse in any open menu, dialog, or window at any time to make something happen. Therefore, PAL programs must work in the same way. Those used to straight procedural programming may have trouble with this at first. Many programmers are used to controlling when the user is allowed to do certain tasks. But in Paradox, most things are accessible most of the time. Your programs must reflect this new reality.

PAL makes event-driven programming easy because it has the capability to trap events as they happen and act on them. So you can tell your program to jump to a given routine when a user clicks the mouse on a certain area of the screen or presses a certain key. You can even tell Paradox what to do when the user isn't doing anything!

Interface Support

Paradox may be a character-based program, but it looks and acts as though it has a graphical user interface. PAL exploits this capability by providing commands to create menus, windows, and sophisticated dialog boxes. Windows are automatically resizeable, movable, and closable via the keyboard or the mouse.

System Requirements

The minimum system required is an 80286-based computer with 2M of memory. Paradox uses a DPMI-compliant DOS extender, so it can be run as a DOS application under Microsoft Windows and OS/2 2.0. A hard disk is required. A graphics-capable display is required to use the presentation graphics features.

Paradox is supported on all the major NetBIOS-compatible networks.

Distribution

Borland's choices for distributing Paradox applications are identical to its choices on dBASE. The user must have a full copy of Paradox if he is on a stand-alone PC and needs to use Paradox for tasks beyond running your program. Network users may install one copy of Paradox on their server and install a LAN Pack for each concurrent user. To support users who need Paradox solely to run your application, Borland sells a Paradox RunTime package. The developer needs to purchase only one copy of RunTime, and then she can distribute as many copies of RunTime as are needed to support her application.

The Paradox Engine

Borland markets a library called the *Paradox Engine* for C, C++, and Turbo Pascal programmers. The engine literally is the database engine for Paradox 4.0, allowing access and use of Paradox tables and indexes using traditional programming languages.

In a network environment, the locking mechanism in Paradox and in the Paradox Engine are compatible. So a C program accessing a table via the engine can lock a record or table so that it cannot be corrupted by a Paradox user on the same network.

Borland used the Paradox Engine in development of its *Quattro Pro* spreadsheet, which can dynamically exchange data with Paradox tables, and in its *ObjectVision* database access tool for Windows and OS/2.

Portability

Paradox is uniquely a Borland product. No "Paradox compatible" programs have as yet appeared on the market. Paradox 4.0 is available just for DOS.

Borland sells a version of Paradox 2.0 for OS/2 1.x, but this product is long out-of-date and is incompatible with Paradox 4.0.

Borland is working on a version of Paradox for Microsoft Windows (which may be out by the time you read this). This version should have a look and feel similar to Paradox 4.0. But the level of compatibility between the DOS and Windows versions is yet to be determined as of this writing. Borland has announced that the Windows version of Paradox will have a new object-oriented version of PAL called Object PAL. There may be significant differences between PAL in Paradox 4.0 and Object PAL in Paradox for Windows.

Paradox can import/export data in formats compatible with Lotus 1-2-3, Quattro Pro, dBASE III PLUS, dBASE IV, and ASCII.

SQL Link

Borland sells an add-on for Paradox called SQL Link, which allows the use of Paradox as an access tool, or *front-end*, to several popular SQL database servers. With SQL Link, users and programmers can query SQL tables on remote servers as easily as they query standard Paradox tables. Developers can embed SQL statements in PAL programs to access remote data.

SQL Link works with several database products, including Microsoft/Sybase SQL Server, IBM OS/2 Database Manager, and IBM's DB2.

Documentation and Support

Paradox 4.0 comes with about 2,200 pages of printed documentation and an extensive hypertext help system. The documentation is divided between information for users and information for developers. Remember that you need to be a Paradox user before you can be a developer.

As with dBASE, Borland offers free telephone support for general usage questions regarding Paradox. Detailed programming questions can be answered on a 900 support line for a per-minute fee. Support subscriptions are available for developers.

Borland also maintains a very active Paradox forum on CompuServe.

Vendor Information

Borland's Paradox has an easy-to-use end-user interface and a language which exploits that interface to its fullest.

Even though Paradox is different from people's preconceived notions of what a PC database is supposed to look like, it continues to grow in popularity and in the loyalty of its users.

The listing prices for Borland's Paradox products at the time of writing were

Paradox 4.0	$795.00
Paradox 4.0 RunTime	$250.00
Paradox 4.0 LAN Pack	$395.00

For more information on dBASE products, call or write Borland at

> Borland International
> 1800 Green Hills Road
> P.O. Box 660001
> Scotts Valley, CA 95067-0001
> (800) 331-0877

Summary

The performance of PC databases has matured dramatically in the last few years. These products are the market leaders because they represent some of the finest PC database technology.

All the products mentioned in this chapter were originally developed by smaller software companies, and later acquired by the industry giants. Borland, Microsoft, and Computer Associates are all committed to upgrading these products dramatically in the future. Considering the high level of competition and technical expertise among these companies, it's clear that in the end, the overall winner in the database wars will be the user.

BASIC Products

by David Veale

BASIC has been tightly integrated with the personal computer since Microsoft's founders, Bill Gates and Paul Allen, wrote the first microcomputer BASIC interpreter for the MITS Altair computer in 1975. Since then, virtually all personal computers have included some flavor of the BASIC language. Hence, BASIC is the first language of many PC programmers, and it is the most widely known language in computing.

For many years, BASIC was implemented as a simple interpreter. Programmers had to number every line of a program manually and programs could not be larger than 64K. Without much support for structured programming, many programs became an unintelligible maze of GOTOs and GOSUBS. BASIC was simply considered a language that new programmers used to learn programming. After they gained proficiency, they would move to "real" languages like C, COBOL, or Pascal.

Microsoft and others have tried to change the negative perception of BASIC by introducing BASIC compilers and extending the language to support structured programming. These efforts have paid off, and—thanks to some high-quality products—BASIC is still one of the most popular languages in use for PC programming.

Many products on BASIC are available from various companies, yet Microsoft dominates the market and provides the most complete product line available; hence, Microsoft's product is the only one discussed in this chapter.

There is a famous quote attributed to Microsoft chairman Bill Gates in which he states that he could take any PC software product on the market and rewrite it in BASIC in one weekend. Knowing the technical prowess of Mr. Gates, this statement might indeed be true, but the quote more significantly shows the special relationship that Microsoft has with BASIC. BASIC was its first product. Microsoft has expanded that product so that BASIC is not only one of its major product lines, but also is becoming the standard macro language in its applications.

Microsoft now markets six BASIC products: Microsoft QuickBASIC, Microsoft BASIC Professional Development System, Visual Basic for Windows, Microsoft Visual Basic for Windows with Professional Toolkit, Microsoft Visual Basic for MS-DOS, Standard version, and Microsoft Visual Basic for MS-DOS, Professional version. Microsoft also produces QBasic—a limited version of QuickBASIC that is packaged with MS-DOS Version 5.0. The following sections review these products.

QBasic

From 1981 to 1991, most PC users that used Microsoft BASIC were using the *BASICA* and *GW-BASIC* interpreters packaged with IBM DOS and MS-DOS, respectively. These interpreters contained a simple line-oriented editor that required programs to have line numbers and limited program size to 64K. These interpreters became all but obsolete with the release of MS-DOS Version 5.0, which includes *QBasic,* a more modern and robust BASIC interpreter.

Quick Environment

QBasic is based on the "Quick" environment included in some other Microsoft language products, such as QuickBASIC and QuickC.

This DOS-only product includes an easy-to-use text editor and all the other tools you need to edit, run, and debug BASIC programs. All the major editor functions are available, from pull-down menus to dialog boxes. You can type BASIC commands in a window on-screen to be executed immediately. This Immediate window is useful for checking the syntax of a command, testing the result of a command before putting it in a program, or checking the values of variables. Figure 19.1 shows the QBasic programming environment.

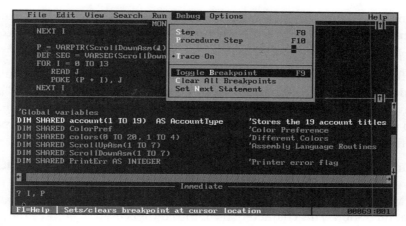

Figure 19.1. The Microsoft QBasic environment.

To help keep you out of trouble, the editor has an automatic syntax checker. As you type your program, the editor warns you about lines containing obvious syntax errors. In some cases, it corrects them for you automatically, such as if you forget to put a closing quotation mark at the end of a string. Otherwise, it gives you a suggestion as to what is wrong.

The environment also features a simple debugger that enables you to set breakpoints, trace through program execution, and change which line of the program will be the next to be executed. There is no variable watcher, but you can use the Immediate window for this purpose.

The Quick environment also features a comprehensive hypertext help system and online reference. The syntax of all BASIC commands and functions is covered with examples. DOS 5.0 does not include printed documentation for QBasic, but the online information should be adequate for most users.

QBasic Language

QBasic is a radical departure from GW-BASIC. Line numbers are no longer needed, although you can use them if you want. All the GW-BASIC data types are supported: integer, long integer, single-precision floating-point, double-precision floating-point, and string.

The infamous GOTO is rarely, if ever, required because QBasic supports structured programming. All the major control structures are supported including DO-LOOP, FOR-NEXT, IF-THEN-ELSE, and SELECT CASE.

One of QBasic's most powerful features is its support for procedures and functions. You can now write BASIC programs in a C or Pascal programming style and have higher-level procedures calling lower-level procedures. You also can use functions to extend the language. Both procedures and functions support parameter passing, and functions can return values of any type.

To encourage the use of functions and procedures, the Quick editor (QBASIC's text editor) is customized to show only the current procedure or function in the editing window. You can switch between procedures and functions in the editing window using a menu option. This characteristic of the editor is used to enforce the modularity of QBasic programs. Each procedure or function should be self-contained.

Procedures and functions can have local variables that are visible only in the procedure or function and that are destroyed, by default, when the procedure or function exits. The concept of local variables is vastly different from earlier BASICs, in which all data was global.

BASIC has hundreds of commands and functions. The language gives you a great deal of control over how input and output are handled and how data is manipulated in memory. There is full support for working with both sequential and random access disk files. There is also support for text and graphics mode display programming with support for all major graphics modes including VGA. QBasic is a complete programming language.

Quick Interpreter

QBasic might be much improved over GW-BASIC, but it is still only an interpreter. Source code is decoded and executed on a line-by-line basis. The interpreter has certain advantages over a compiler. For example, you can stop your program during execution, change some of the code, and resume execution from where you left off without starting the program over. An interpreter makes debugging a breeze compared to a compiler.

Interpreters, however, have much slower execution speeds than compiled code. Interpreters also have limits on program size. QBasic limits the total amount of code and data in your programs to 160K. The biggest limitation is that you can only distribute your QBasic programs to others if they have their own copy of QBasic. You also must distribute the program as source code; you therefore have no way to keep others from seeing, and stealing, your code.

Conclusions

QBasic is a great tool for writing short, personal programs. Because it is included with DOS, your only investment is time. If you have to write programs that are going to be used by other people, larger programs, or programs in which speed is an issue, look to one of the products in the following sections for a solution.

QuickBASIC 4.5

At first glance, there does not seem to be a great deal of difference between Microsoft QuickBASIC and Microsoft QBasic. Except for a few menu options, the environments are virtually identical. But as similar in appearance as they might be, QuickBASIC is in a class well beyond its interpreted sibling.

QuickBASIC is a BASIC compiler, not an interpreter. It generates DOS .EXE files, which can be executed directly from DOS without installing QuickBASIC. QuickBASIC's Quick environment adds menus and options for controlling the compilation of code.

QuickBASIC originally was aimed at the home or small business user who was not a programmer by profession. The simplicity of the language enabled these users to create applications with a minimum amount of effort and knowledge.

Soon, professional developers began using QuickBASIC as well. They found that they were able to create true stand-alone DOS applications in less time than with C or Pascal. QuickBASIC is also used to create working mock-ups or *prototypes* of applications to be developed in other languages. With prototypes, the developer can receive customer reaction and feedback on an application before developing the actual program.

To make the product more appealing to developers, Microsoft added sophisticated enhancements to the language such as the capability to write interrupt service routines and to link compiled BASIC code with code compiled in other languages.

Compiling Programs

QuickBASIC offers three ways to compile and run programs. The first is in the same interpreted mode used by QBasic. This mode is great for development and debugging. The built-in debugger adds a variable watch window so you can check the values of variables without entering BASIC commands in the Immediate window. Because the code is running in interpreted mode, you are free to interrupt and change the code of a running program.

The second method is to compile your program to an object (.OBJ) file, then link it with the supplied runtime library to produce an executable (.EXE) file. The runtime library is a collection of precompiled code stored in *library* files. These libraries contain the actual machine code needed to perform such commands as PRINT, INPUT, and PAINT. When you compile a program containing a PRINT command, for example, the object code produced contains only a call to the PRINT function in the runtime library. This is why you need to link the runtime library with your code to produce an .EXE. This traditional method of compiling is the way most smaller programs are compiled and run.

The third method is to compile the program but not link it with the runtime library until you actually run the program. In addition to the library files, QuickBASIC supplies the runtime library as a memory-resident .EXE file called BRUN45.EXE. When you run your program, the BRUN45.EXE program automatically executes and loads itself into memory. As your program executes, it calls on routines in BRUN45 to support its functionality.

Naturally, there are advantages and disadvantages to both methods of handling the runtime library. Linking the library into your program's .EXE can make the .EXE quite large. However, your program often runs faster because all the code it needs is "right there" in one file. This method is preferred for applications that consist of only one or two .EXE files.

Many complete applications have more than two .EXEs, however. In these cases, you might have various .EXE files that access the same runtime library functions. Linking the same functions into every executable wastes both disk space and memory. Because only one copy of BRUN45 exists in memory no matter how many .EXEs access it, you will have only one copy of each library function in memory for all the programs. Having only one copy reduces the size of the individual .EXEs and saves memory. However, with this method, the entire runtime library must be loaded into memory, even if some of the functions are never called. Your program also can run slower because it must access code in an external source.

Quick Libraries

In addition to standard .EXE files, you can use QuickBASIC to create *Quick Libraries*, which are essentially your own extensions to the runtime library. If you find yourself using functions or procedures over and over in your source code, you can compile them and store them in a Quick Library file. The next time you compile a program that requires the routines, you simply tell the compiler to link into your Quick Library. Using a Quick Library saves compile time because the routines don't have to be recompiled each time they are used.

Several third-party companies have released Quick Libraries for QuickBASIC to add functionality to the language. Libraries are available for such tasks as building user interfaces, database management, network functions, and so on.

QuickBASIC Limitations

QuickBASIC is a great development tool for many types of programs, but it does have its limitations. Code and data cannot exceed the DOS 640K memory limit. You can use chained .EXEs to run large programs, but there are still limits.

The QuickBASIC compiler was designed to compile code quickly. The trade-off for the fast compiler speed is that there is little attention paid to producing the fastest, most efficient programs possible from your source code. Microsoft wanted the product to be easy and convenient to use, which means that users should not have to wait long to receive an .EXE file from a source file. Hence, the compiled code contains few optimizations in either runtime speed or code size.

More of the runtime library is linked to the .EXE files than is necessary to run the program. Again, Microsoft felt it would take too much time for the *linker* to go through the library carefully and sort code to be linked. A *linker* is a software utility that binds the object code files and the runtime library to produce an .EXE file.

These limitations might not matter to most QuickBASIC users. Some professional developers, though, find these limitations too restrictive—especially for large corporate applications that need fast execution speed and plenty of memory.

Conclusions

For many users, QuickBASIC strikes a good balance between the simplicity of an interpreted environment and the power and efficiency of a professional-level compiler product.

By combining a fast compiler with their modern, structured implementation of BASIC—and selling it for a low price—Microsoft made QuickBASIC one of the best-selling language products ever.

Unfortunately, QuickBASIC seems to have reached the end of its life cycle. Microsoft released Visual Basic for MS-DOS (discussed later in this chapter) in the fall of 1992 and announced that there will be no further development on QuickBASIC. However, QuickBASIC remains on the market and continues to be supported.

BASIC Professional Development System 7.1

If reliability, speed, code size, and overall efficiency are important to you, you might want to try Microsoft's BASIC Professional Development System (PDS). The syntax of the PDS is compatible with QuickBASIC. However, the code is smaller, faster, and more efficient.

As a programmer, you have a great deal of control over the code produced by the compiler. You can specify several types of optimizations favoring either speed or code size. Programs can automatically use expanded memory, thus enabling you to write much larger programs without resorting to overlays and chained .EXEs. The runtime library code is more *granular,* meaning that fewer unused routines from the runtime library are linked into your program.

The trade-off for better code is a slower compiler and a higher degree of understanding by the programmer of how computers, BASIC, and DOS work. The compiler enables you to select options so as to make the most efficient program possible.

Language Features

The BASIC PDS can compile virtually all QuickBASIC programs. It also has several important language extensions that QuickBASIC lacks. One notable feature is that the PDS can produce OS/2 1.x programs as well as DOS programs. Unfortunately, OS/2 Presentation Manager programming is not supported; only character mode is supported. Microsoft Windows programming also is not supported.

In PDS, the standard string data type is enhanced. Strings can be declared *far,* meaning that a very large string can exist in its own 64K memory segment. Normally, all strings are stored in one 64K segment.

PDS added a new *currency* data type for monetary calculations that cannot have rounding errors. To accompany the currency type, a library of financial functions were added. Other added libraries include functions for time and date arithmetic and manipulation, functions to convert numbers into formatted strings, and matrix math functions.

A welcome addition to PDS is the user interface library. Functions are provided to build menus, windows, and dialog boxes, to use fonts, and to add mouse support to programs. A presentation graphics library is also included.

Database Management

PDS extends BASIC's file-handling capabilities by adding a full-blown database management system. The standard file Input/Output commands were extended to support an Indexed Sequential Access Method (ISAM) database. ISAM databases are popular in mainframe programming because of their speed and reliability. Using PDS' ISAM system, you don't have to write your own search and indexing routines for data files or purchase third-party database managers.

ISAM supports the major database features, including table creation and editing and multifile queries. Transaction processing and rollback is also supported; you therefore can undo an update to the database tables if, for whatever reason, the entire update cannot be completed successfully.

The ISAM system is powerful and can save the programmer time and effort. The only major disappointment is that it doesn't support multiuser file access on a network. Unless this feature is added in a future release, the ISAM database is limited to single users.

Development Environment

The BASIC PDS includes a customized version of the QuickBASIC environment (with extra menu options that support the additional features of the compiler). The Quick environment uses the PDS compiler, so you still reap the advantages of the advanced compiler with the Quick environment.

Also included is Microsoft's Programmer's WorkBench (PWB), which is the Quick environment on steroids (see Figure 19.2). PWB begins with the basic functionality of the Quick environment (editor, menus, and so on) but adds several important capabilities. Some of these additions are the ability to program extensions to the editor in C so you can create your own editor commands, the ability to edit multiple files similtaneously, a project manager to help manage programs that are made up of several source code files, and the ability to use one copy of PWB to edit and compile programs using any Microsoft language compiler. PWB is now included with all of Microsoft's professional-level language products. It is intended to be a complete development environment no matter what Microsoft language you are using.

PWB has a multifile editor, so you can view and edit several source files at one time. The source files need not all be in that same language; PWB is a language-independent platform. Each Microsoft language comes with "extension" files for PWB. These extension files provide PWB with the information it needs in order to compile programs written in the particular language. In the case of BASIC, PWB determines the options you can set for the BASIC compiler and provides menus and dialog boxes for you to set those options. PWB can then call the BASIC compiler to compile your program.

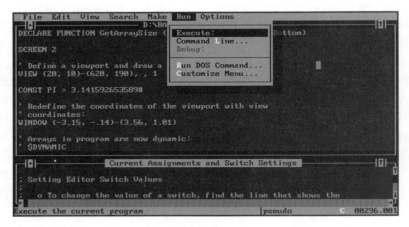

Figure 19.2. The Microsoft Programmer's WorkBench.

With PWB, you are free to mix source files from different languages in a single program. PWB calls the appropriate compilers to compile each of the source files, then links them into a single .EXE.

The PWB does not have a built-in debugger, but the BASIC PDS comes with Microsoft's CodeView debugger. CodeView is an advanced debugger that supports multiple breakpoints and watches. It also enables you to debug code on either the source-code or machine-code level.

Conclusions

The Microsoft BASIC Professional Development System is intended for the professional BASIC programmer. It includes a wealth of tools and language extensions to enable you to design powerful programs. The optimizing compiler ensures that the code is the smallest and fastest possible from a BASIC compiler.

Visual Basic 1.0

Microsoft's Visual Basic for Windows (VB/Win) is radically different from all the products that have been discussed so far in this chapter. VB/Win can develop programs only in Microsoft Windows 3.0 or later environments. All VB/Win applications use the Windows graphical user interface (GUI) and can take advantage of the Windows environment.

If you have programmed in another BASIC implementation before, QuickBASIC, for example, Visual Basic for Windows will be quite a culture shock. VB/Win programs use a BASIC-like syntax for their code but are organized differently from standard, structured BASIC programs. The main reason for this is that Windows is an event-driven environment. A user can perform any number of tasks, in any order, at any time. A Windows program must be able to perform a wide range of functions at any time. Most DOS programs impose rules on the user as to when he or she can perform certain tasks and in what order they are to be performed. Windows does not impose such rules.

How Visual Basic for Windows Works

You build Visual Basic for Windows programs by creating Windows *resources* and tying functionality to them. All Windows programs function in a similar fashion. The user selects, or "clicks," items on-screen using the keyboard or mouse. Selections include menu items, buttons or fields in a dialog box, or the border of a window, among other things. When the user clicks a screen object, a message is sent to Windows that essentially says, "Hey, Windows! This user wants me to do whatever it is I'm supposed to do when he or she clicks me." The Windows program then determines the appropriate action and carries out the task.

Using Visual Basic for Windows, you spend as much time being a graphic artist and designer as you do being a BASIC programmer. VB/Win includes tools to design graphical menus, dialog boxes, buttons, icons, and whatever other resources you need for your program. You must use these graphical tools to design all the visual objects that your program is to use. After you design a resource, you then use BASIC to attach functionality to it.

For example, most Windows programs have the word *File* (for the File menu) as the first item on the menu bar at the top of a window. You must use the tools to put File on the menu bar. This word is a Windows resource. When the user clicks File, Windows receives notice that File was clicked. Windows then executes the BASIC code that you specified to run whenever File is selected. Most likely, your BASIC code instructs Windows to display the pull-down menu associated with File.

When an option from the pull-down menu is selected, Open, for example, the BASIC code associated with Open is executed. This BASIC code probably tells Windows to display a dialog box that prompts the user for the name of the file to open. This cycle continues throughout the execution of the program. The user selects a resource, causing the resource to run some code that, among other things, displays another resource for the user to select.

The actual BASIC code that you write looks similar to QuickBASIC in the way the syntax is structured. Continuing with the preceding example, after the user selects the file he or she wants to open, the BASIC program code used to open and read the file is similar to standard Microsoft BASIC code.

Writing Visual Basic for Windows Programs

You create Visual Basic for Windows programs in two steps. You first lay out all your resources on surfaces called *forms* (see Figure 19.3). Forms are often synonymous with a Windows' window. You drag one of the various objects (also called *controls*) available from a Toolbox window to the form, then customize the control to fit the task at hand. For example, if you were constructing a dialog box, you would drag a text field control onto the form and then size it to fit the application. You would then write, in a text editor window, the BASIC code that accompanies that text field.

After you finish designing and coding the application, you can run it in interpreted mode or compile it to an .EXE, just as you do in QuickBASIC. If something doesn't work, VB/Win includes a debugger that supports breakpoints and watches.

Visual Basic and Windows

Visual Basic provides excellent support for the Windows environment. VB/Win applications can access the Windows Clipboard and support dynamic data exchange with other Windows applications. VB/Win applications also can run code located in Dynamic Link Library files (.DLL). You can add additional controls to the Toolbox window and to VB/Win applications by simply adding the desired .DLL to the Visual Basic environment. Microsoft offers an add-on called *Professional Toolkit* for VB/Win that adds controls to support Windows 3.1 features such as multimedia, pen computing, and Object Linking and Embedding.

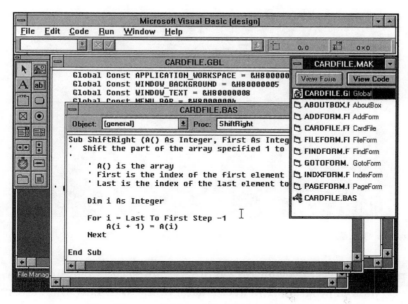

Figure 19.3.   The Microsoft Visual Basic for Windows environment.

Conclusions

Visual Basic for Windows provides one of the easiest ways available to create Windows .EXE files. Often, you spend more than half your time drawing and dragging, rather than coding. DOS BASIC programmers will be surprised by how much code they do *not* have to write. Windows and VB/Win's graphical tools actually "write" the code related to the user interface part of the program.

Visual Basic for MS-DOS 1.0

Microsoft's Visual Basic for MS-DOS (VB/DOS) is the newest member of Microsoft's family of BASIC products. It is one of the first DOS language products to be based on a Windows product (rather than the other way around).

VB/DOS comes with a mouse-driven development environment, which is a combination of the QuickBASIC environment and the Visual Basic for Windows environment. The environment runs in character-mode DOS. Figure 19.4 shows the VB/DOS environment.

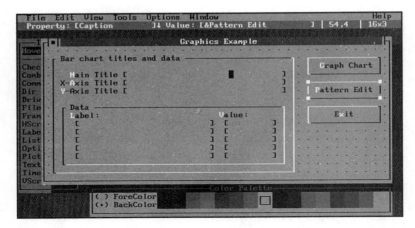

Figure 19.4. The Visual Basic for MS-DOS environment.

VB/DOS provides the same event-driven programming system as its Windows sibling. Even though programs run in character mode, they have the same mouse-driven graphical look and feel as the Windows programs.

Just as in the Windows version, you build VB/DOS programs by defining menus, dialogs, and forms, and by attaching BASIC code to these objects. DOS programming using VB/DOS is even easier than Windows programming because you don't have to worry about fonts, screen resolution, or graphics.

Like its Windows counterpart, VB/DOS includes a debugger and an .EXE compiler to produce stand-alone programs.

Visual Basic for MS-DOS Versions

Visual Basic for MS-DOS ships in two versions, a Standard version and a Professional version. The Professional version adds extra controls, a charting library, an overlay manager, ISAM database capabilities from the BASIC Professional Development System, and the option of generating 80386 real-mode code.

The Professional version also includes a toolkit for creating your own custom controls in VB/DOS. Custom controls can also be created in C, C++, or Assembler. You can easily add third-party custom controls to either version.

Compatibility

There is a reasonable level of compatibility between the DOS and Windows versions of Visual Basic. All the standard Windows controls that are needed in DOS are included in the DOS version. For example, controls for a check box and file list are in the DOS and Windows versions, whereas the control to select fonts is only in the Windows version—DOS does not support fonts. For this reason, moving code from DOS to Windows is generally easier than moving from Windows to DOS.

An important feature included in VB/DOS (and not VB/Win) is virtual 100 percent compatibility with QuickBASIC (QB) and BASIC Professional Development System (PDS) code. Existing QB and PDS programs can therefore be recompiled under VB/DOS and run without change. The only caveats are that VB/DOS has many new reserved words that can conflict with user variable names in existing QB/PDS programs. Also, QB/PDS libraries must be recompiled to be used with VB/DOS.

The VB/DOS interface tools are only available in character mode. The system supports graphics-mode programming, but only in standard procedural BASIC.

The VB/DOS Standard version is viewed as a replacement for Microsoft's QuickBASIC product. The VB/DOS Professional version replaces Microsoft's BASIC Professional Development System in most circumstances, although PDS programs tend to be smaller and faster than VB/DOS programs. In cases where speed or size is a major issue, PDS is still appropriate.

Conclusions

Visual Basic for MS-DOS brings many dimensions of the Windows interface to DOS. It also provides one of the simplest and fastest ways to develop true stand-alone DOS applications with all the modern interface features that users expect. Add to that the relative ease of moving Visual Basic code between the DOS and Windows environments, and you have an extraordinary amount of power from a system built for simplicity.

Obviously, BASIC has come a long way since Gates and Allen made the first interpreter more than a decade ago. Rather than quietly fading away, as some "experts" predicted, BASIC is still going strong—and getting stronger.

Vendor Information

The listing prices for Microsoft's BASIC products at the time of publication were

Microsoft QuickBASIC 4.5	$99.00
Microsoft BASIC Professional Development System 7.1	$495.00
Microsoft Visual Basic for Windows 1.0	$199.00
Microsoft Visual Basic with Professional Toolkit 1.0	$495.00
Microsoft Visual Basic for MS-DOS Standard 1.0	$199.00
Microsoft Visual Basic for MS-DOS Professional 1.0	$495.00

For more information on these BASIC products, call or write Microsoft at:

Microsoft Corporation
One Microsoft Way
Redmond, WA 98052-6399
(800) 426-9400

Summary

When you consider its humble beginnings, it's incredible how far this language, long considered a "toy," has come. BASIC has not only been an important part of the personal computer revolution, but also has been a leader in bringing professional programming capabilities to the masses.

With BASIC's continuing evolution into the world of graphical user interfaces and object orientation, there is no doubt that this simple language will be with us for a long time to come.

Pascal Products

by David Veale

Pascal, named for the mathematician Blaise Pascal, has come a long way in the past decade. The language was designed in the early 1970s by European mathematician Niklaus Wirth to be a teaching tool for structured programming techniques. For a decade Pascal was used and well respected in academia, but it did not achieve much commercial success.

Then, in 1983, one of Wirth's former students, Philippe Kahn, founded a company called Borland International. Borland's first product was a simple-to-use, fast, and cheap PC Pascal compiler called Turbo Pascal. Turbo was a huge success and has become the best-selling language compiler in history. It was so successful that Pascal is second only to BASIC in popularity as a "personal" programming language for PCs. Turbo Pascal dominates the PC Pascal market so completely that it is the only product examined in this chapter.

Turbo Pascal 6.0

Turbo Pascal 6.0 is the latest incarnation of the best-selling Pascal compiler for DOS. The compiler, environment, and language implementation have evolved considerably over the past decade, making Turbo Pascal a mature and feature-packed product.

Borland markets Turbo Pascal 6.0 in two versions, Turbo Pascal and Turbo Pascal Professional. Turbo Pascal has very modest hardware requirements by modern standards. The software is distributed on only two double-density 3.5-inch diskettes. It will run on almost any PC with 640K of memory. If you have expanded memory, the software will use it so you can compile larger programs.

It uses only about 3M of hard drive space when fully installed. For those who are masochistic, Turbo Pascal could be run off diskettes, but this practice is strongly discouraged.

Turbo Pascal Professional adds the "Turbo Drive" version of the Pascal compiler. This compiler version runs in extended memory and requires that you have at least 1M of extended memory (above the 640K) and at least an 80286 processor. The advantage of the Turbo Drive compiler is the capability to compile much larger programs than the standard version. Turbo Pascal Professional requires an additional 3M of hard drive space over the standard version and cannot be used on diskettes. It also has additional tools, which will be discussed later.

The Integrated Development Environment

The centerpiece of Turbo Pascal is the integrated development environment (IDE). The IDE contains a multifile editor and menus enabling the user to edit, compile, run, and debug programs from within the environment (see Figure 20.1).

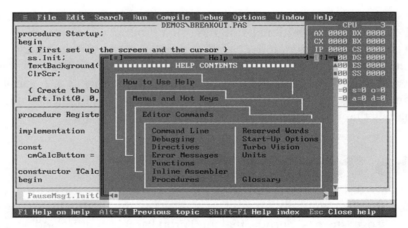

Figure 20.1. The Turbo Pascal 6.0 Integrated Development Environment.

The IDE also contains an extensive hypertext help system. The help covers Pascal language syntax, the use of the IDE and all its tools, error messages, and all Borland-supplied procedures and functions. The help on most procedures and functions includes short example programs that can be copied to the editor and compiled.

The help system eliminates the necessity of printed documentation. To help you get started using the help system and IDE, a computer-based training program is included.

The built-in debugger enables you to set breakpoints anywhere in your code, watch variables, trace through code line by line or function/procedure call by function/procedure call, and watch the registers in the CPU. The debugger is adequate for many applications.

Turbo Pascal Professional also includes the stand-alone *Turbo Debugger*. Turbo Debugger is more powerful than the integrated debugger in Turbo Pascal. You can do things such as view, and step through, the assembly language code for your program and run the program backward to find out how you got to where you are! Turbo Debugger also supports dual display debugging (that is, your program runs on one display while you watch the debugger on another screen) and remote debugging (that is, you run your program on one computer and debug it on another computer connected to the first computer via the serial ports and cable). Turbo Pascal Professional also includes *Turbo Profiler*. Turbo Profiler is a tool that enables you to time the execution speed of every section of your code. This way you can find out where your programs are spending most of their time and optimize those sections as desired.

The Compiler

Turbo Pascal got its name from the speed of the compiler. The name is well deserved. A 300-line, single-source file program compiles in less than 2 seconds. A 7,000-line multisource file program can compile in less than 10 seconds on a moderately fast 80386-based computer.

If you are sure that the target systems for your program will have at least an 80286 processor, you can tell the compiler to generate 80286 instructions. Although this feature produces faster code, it does not provide the capability to run your programs in protected mode. The .EXEs produced by Turbo Pascal are still real-mode DOS .EXEs. However, Turbo Pascal provides a very easy-to-use and transparent overlay manager. By compiling the units of your program with the overlay option, Turbo Pascal will allow your program to automatically swap parts of itself in and out of memory at runtime, thereby enabling you to create programs that appear to use more than 640K.

If you use floating-point math in your program, Turbo Pascal will automatically use an 80x87 math coprocessor if installed. Otherwise, the math coprocessor functions are emulated in software. If the target systems for your program will always have a math coprocessor installed, you can tell Turbo Pascal to always use the math coprocessor. The advantage here is that the emulator unit functions are not linked into your program, making it smaller.

The compiler contains a built-in mini assembler. So you can embed assembly language code right in your Pascal code. You can also link assembly .OBJ files into your code. Turbo Pascal Professional also includes the stand-alone *Turbo Assembler* (TASM). TASM is a Microsoft Macro Assembler–compatible assembler, with several extensions. TASM can be used to create modules for your Turbo Pascal programs, or complete programs written entirely in assembly language.

The language itself is based on standard Pascal but has so many extensions that it is likely Wirth would not recognize a lot of Turbo source code as being based on his work. Whereas Pascal was designed as a *structured* programming language, Turbo Pascal is an *object-oriented* language. Turbo supports all the major components of an object-oriented language, including encapsulation, data hiding, inheritance, and polymorphism. To accomplish this, Borland added keywords and new constructs to the language. The result is an extremely powerful system, but one that retains Pascal's capability to help the programmer keep from shooting himself in the foot.

After a decade of development as a DOS-only, PC-only system, Turbo Pascal has become one of the most efficient PC compilers around. Many Turbo Pascal .EXEs are smaller and faster than C or C++ equivalents, even though C and C++ are lower-level languages. This is because C and C++ compiler makers must be concerned with following the standards for the languages, which apply across all hardware and operating system environments. These standards limit their capability to produce machine- or operating-system-specific extensions or optimizations. But Turbo Pascal does not have those restrictions; hence, Borland could do whatever it felt necessary to produce a very efficient PC and DOS language.

Units

Many larger Turbo Pascal programs are built by creating a main module in a Pascal source file, then creating supporting code in other source files known as units. A *unit* is the Turbo Pascal equivalent to a library file in BASIC or C. But a unit is more flexible and supports data hiding. Units have an *interface* section, which contains procedures and functions that are callable from other modules, and an *implementation* section, which contains procedures and functions that support the procedures and functions in the interface section but are not directly callable by other modules.

Although units support the object-oriented concept of encapsulation and data hiding, they were added to the language long before the true object-oriented language extensions were added.

Other Extensions

In addition to object orientation and units, Borland added other extensions to Pascal to make it easier to use. For example, to create a string variable in standard Pascal, you need to create a "packed array of characters" or a collection of enough of the basic data type "character" to hold the string. In Turbo Pascal, you can simply declare a variable of type "string" with a size.

Borland also supplies a wealth of functions and procedures to support the DOS and PC hardware environments, including a sophisticated graphics unit.

Also included is an object-oriented application framework called Turbo Vision. Turbo Vision is a set of units you can use to create an interface for your programs with multiple resizable windows, pull-down menus, dialog boxes, and mouse support. Your program "inherits" the Turbo Vision interface, and then you add functionality (see Listing 20.1). If you would like to see an example of a Turbo Vision application, simply look at the Turbo Pascal IDE! It was written in Turbo Pascal with Turbo Vision.

Listing 20.1. A program written using the Turbo Vision framework.

```
program HelloApp;

program TVSample;

uses Objects, Drivers, Views, Menus, App;

const
  wCount: Integer =   0;
  cmFileOpen      = 200;
  cmNewWin        = 201;

type
  THelloApp = object(TApplication)
    procedure HandleEvent(var Event: TEvent); virtual;
    procedure InitMenuBar; virtual;
```

continues

Listing 20.1. Continued

```
    procedure InitStatusLine; virtual;
    procedure NewWindow;
  end;

  PHelloWindow = ^THelloWindow;
  THelloWindow = object(TWindow)
    constructor Init(Bounds: TRect; WinTitle: String; WindowNo: Word);
  end;

  PInterior = ^TInterior;
  TInterior = object(TView)
    constructor Init(var Bounds: TRect);
    procedure Draw; virtual;
  end;

{ TInterior }
constructor TInterior.Init(var Bounds: TRect);
begin
  TView.Init(Bounds);
  GrowMode := gfGrowHiX + gfGrowHiY;
  Options := Options or ofFramed;
end;

procedure TInterior.Draw;
const
  Message: string = 'Hello, World!';
begin
  TView.Draw;
  WriteStr(4, 2, Message,$01);
end;

{ THelloWindow }
constructor THelloWindow.Init(Bounds: TRect; WinTitle: String; WindowNo: Word);
var
  S: string[3];
  Interior: PInterior;
begin
  Str(WindowNo, S);
  TWindow.Init(Bounds, WinTitle + ' ' + S, wnNoNumber);
  GetClipRect(Bounds);
  Bounds.Grow(-1,-1);
  Interior := New(PInterior, Init(Bounds));
```

```
  Insert(Interior);
end;

{ THelloApp }
procedure THelloApp.HandleEvent(var Event: TEvent);
begin
  TApplication.HandleEvent(Event);
  if Event.What = evCommand then
  begin
    case Event.Command of
      cmNewWin: NewWindow;
    else
      Exit;
    end;
    ClearEvent(Event);
  end;
end;

procedure THelloApp.InitMenuBar;
var R: TRect;
begin
  GetExtent(R);
  R.B.Y := R.A.Y + 1;
  MenuBar := New(PMenuBar, Init(R, NewMenu(
    NewSubMenu('~F~ile', hcNoContext, NewMenu(
      NewItem('~O~pen', 'F3', kbF3, cmFileOpen, hcNoContext,
      NewItem('~N~ew', 'F4', kbF4, cmNewWin, hcNoContext,
      NewLine(
      NewItem('E~x~it', 'Alt-X', kbAltX, cmQuit, hcNoContext,
      nil))))),
    NewSubMenu('~W~indow', hcNoContext, NewMenu(
      NewItem('~N~ext', 'F6', kbF6, cmNext, hcNoContext,
      NewItem('~Z~oom', 'F5', kbF5, cmZoom, hcNoContext,
      nil))),
    nil))
  )));
end;

procedure THelloApp.InitStatusLine;
var R: TRect;
begin
  GetExtent(R);
  R.A.Y := R.B.Y - 1;
```

continues

369

Listing 20.1. Continued

```pascal
  StatusLine := New(PStatusLine, Init(R,
    NewStatusDef(0, $FFFF,
      NewStatusKey('', kbF10, cmMenu,
      NewStatusKey('~Alt-X~ Exit', kbAltX, cmQuit,
      NewStatusKey('~F4~ New', kbF4, cmNewWin,
      NewStatusKey('~Alt-F3~ Close', kbAltF3, cmClose,
      nil)))),
    nil)
  ));
end;

procedure THelloApp.NewWindow;
var
  Window: PHelloWindow;
  R: TRect;
begin
  Inc(wCount);
  R.Assign(0, 0, 24, 7);
  R.Move(Random(55), Random(16));
  Window := New(PHelloWindow, Init(R, 'Hello Window', wCount));
  DeskTop^.Insert(Window);
end;

var
  HelloApp: THelloApp;

begin
  HelloApp.Init;
  HelloApp.Run;
  HelloApp.Done;
end.
```

Portability

Because of all the extensions Borland added to Turbo, it should not be your first choice for cross-platform programming. If you have visions of porting your Pascal code to UNIX or OS/2, your object-oriented Turbo Pascal code will not make the trip with you. In fairness, it is certainly possible to ignore all the language extensions in Turbo Pascal and write standard Pascal programs, but only true Pascal purists would probably want to attempt it.

It is also not easy to use Turbo Pascal with other languages. The compiler does not produce .OBJ object code files; it just produces the .EXE. Therefore, you cannot "link" Turbo Pascal code into a C program, for example. You do have the capability to link assembler and C .OBJ files into a Turbo Pascal .EXE, but this capability is far more restricted than with other compilers.

But Turbo Pascal 6.0 is a complete PC development system with a powerful language, a great development environment, and a wealth of tools to make the job of the programmer easier. It is sufficient to meet the needs of most DOS programmers.

Turbo Pascal for Windows 1.5

Turbo Pascal for Windows (TPW) brings the simplicity and elegance of the Pascal language to what has traditionally been only a C programmer's domain: the Microsoft Windows environment.

TPW can be used only to create programs for the Microsoft Windows 3.x environment. You can create Windows .EXEs and dynamic link libraries (DLLs). The Microsoft Windows Software Development Kit is not needed. The hardware requirements are the same as those for Windows: at least an 80286 processor, at least 2M of memory (the more memory the better), and a graphics-capable display. TPW, distributed on 10 double-density 3.5-inch diskettes, uses about 11.5M of hard drive space when fully installed (hard drive installation is required).

A Windows-based version of the integrated development environment (IDE) is included. This environment is almost functionally identical to the DOS version but is completely Windows based (see Figure 20.2). The IDE takes great advantage of the Windows environment. You can easily change the size and font of the text in the editor. In addition, the editor features color syntax highlighting, so comments, keywords, constants, and variables all automatically show up in the editor in different colors so that you can easily follow your code. Several commonly used menu options are available as selectable icons on a speedbar in the editor.

The debugger, called Turbo Debugger for Windows (TDW), is not part of the Windows IDE but is a separate program. Although the debugger is technically a Windows application, it runs only in full-screen character mode. With few exceptions, the debugger will not work if you are running Windows in a video mode with greater resolution than standard VGA 640 X 480 (actually, the debugger runs but is invisible, making Windows appear to have locked up). The capabilities of TDW are the same as those for Turbo Debugger for DOS, but it adds some Windows-specific features such as the capability to trace Windows messages and debug DLLs.

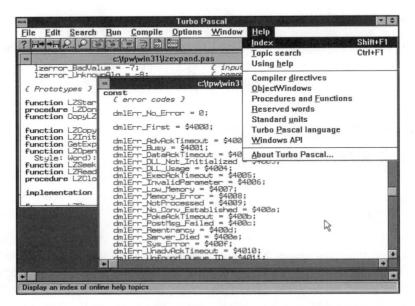

Figure 20.2. The Turbo Pascal for Windows integrated development environment.

The bulk of the menus and dialog boxes in the Windows IDE mimic the DOS version, so moving between the two platforms is relatively painless. The Windows IDE features the same extensive help system as the DOS version but is totally Windows based. The help system documents the entire Windows 3.x API, including structures, type, constants, variables, and functions—making printed documentation a convenience, not a necessity.

The compiler can create both Windows .EXEs and .DLLs. There is support for the new features of Windows 3.1, such as Object Linking and Embedding (OLE), multimedia, and the PenWindows API. Like the DOS version, you can optionally have the compiler generate 80286 instructions. Because TPW does not support the creation of Windows 3.0 real-mode applications, you should always use the 80286 instruction set. As with the DOS version, the compiler does not produce .OBJ files and does not have extensive support for mixed-language programming.

The language itself is very similar to its DOS counterpart. The standard Pascal is there, along with a host of extensions to support object-oriented programming, DOS, Windows, and PC hardware.

Besides the standard Pascal functions and procedures, TPW includes additional units designed to make Windows programming easier. The first, called *WinCrt,* allows many DOS applications to be converted into Windows applications without changing the DOS source code. By simply including this unit in your code, your DOS application will come up in a window, in graphics mode, use a Windows font, and function "normally" using TTY-style input and output. There are substantial limitations on the types of programs that can be made into Windows applications this way. But many applications that use standard I/O functions and don't use many DOS or machine-specific tricks can be converted.

The second library is called *ObjectWindows.* ObjectWindows is Borland's application framework for Windows. It encapsulates substantial portions of the Windows API into TPW objects. You can create Windows "objects" simply by creating instances of these objects. For example, to create an application's window with a title and a default menu, you declare an object of the ObjectWindows application class, and the window and supporting functionality are created (see Listing 20.2). This is opposed to making several calls to the Windows API via function calls. ObjectWindows can cut down considerably on the amount of code a Windows program requires. It does, however, require a thorough understanding of object-oriented programming.

Listing 20.2. A "Hello World" program written using the ObjectWindows framework.

```
program Hello;

uses WinProcs, WinTypes, WObjects;

type

  THelloApp = object(TApplication)
    procedure InitMainWindow; virtual;
  end;

procedure THelloApp.InitMainWindow;
begin
  MainWindow := New(PWindow, Init(nil, 'Hello World'));
end;
```

continues

Listing 20.1. Continued

```
var
  MyHelloApp: THelloApp;

begin
  MyHelloApp.Init('HelloApp');
  MyHelloApp.Run;
  MyHelloApp.Done;
end.
```

Resource Workshop

Windows programs contain many visual objects, such as menus, dialog boxes, bitmaps, and icons. Collectively, these objects are called *resources*. Creating these resources is a large part of Windows programming. To aid you in creating these resources, Borland includes a very powerful tool in TPW called Resource Workshop (Figure 20.3). Resource Workshop contains various graphical tools that enable you to create all the resources for your program by clicking and dragging. Resource Workshop also links the resources into your application. It even enables you to extract resources from one application and include them in another application.

Resource Workshop also comes with a special Borland .DLL called the Borland Windows Custom Controls (BWCC). BWCC is a set of icons, buttons, and dialogs that, in Borland's opinion, are more aesthetically pleasing than the Windows defaults. They are also designed so that your user can more easily determine a button's function at a glance. For example, instead of having a Windows cancel button that is just an oval with the word "Cancel" in it, BWCC adds a large red "X" to "Cancel," giving the user a visual clue as to the function of the button. Resource Workshop is a very powerful tool that greatly simplifies one of the more confusing aspects of Windows programming.

Although TPW can certainly be used by professional Windows programmers, the documentation makes it easy for beginners to get started in the Windows environment. There are more than 2,100 pages of printed documentation, including a 350-page tutorial on Windows programming and a 90-page "Tips and Techniques" booklet that would be valuable no matter what language you do your Windows programming in. Because most books and articles on Windows programming are geared toward C/C++ programmers, these books are a big help for Pascal users.

There are also .5M of documentation files that can be read online or printed. Most of the reference documentation is duplicated in the hypertext help system. Borland also has extra-cost video courses available on Turbo Pascal programming and ObjectWindows.

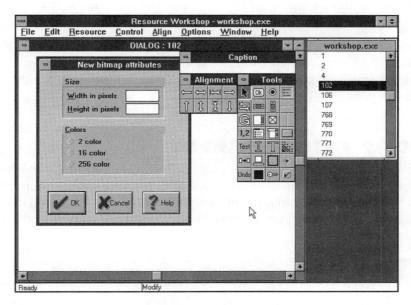

Figure 20.3.   The Borland Resource Workshop.

Support

Borland offers extensive technical support for developers using its products. Borland sponsors forums on CompuServe, including a forum focusing on Turbo Pascal and Turbo Pascal for Windows. Questions posed on the forums are usually answered by a Borland representative within 24 hours. Questions are often answered by other users as well. Borland maintains a free (except for the cost of the call) technical support hotline you can call to get general questions answered. Borland also has a TechFax line. You can call this line from your FAX telephone and request that technical documentation be faxed to you. Borland also publishes a free quarterly newsletter, called *Borland Language Express,* which contains product information and tips and techniques regarding Borland's language products.

For those who need more extensive and detailed support, Borland offers a fee-based support system. For an annual subscription fee, you get a toll-free technical support number, and you are always connected to a senior support engineer. You also get access to a special section on the Borland CompuServe forums reserved for support plan members in which a senior support engineer will respond to your questions within two hours.

If you think a support subscription is overkill but you encounter a problem that requires detailed assistance, you can call a Borland 900 number. For a per-minute fee, a senior Borland support engineer will work through the problem with you, going through your code line by line if necessary.

Vendor Information

Borland's Turbo Pascal products enjoy a large following among both professional and casual programmers. There is a good deal of third-party support for both products, so if you want to find prewritten units for interfaces, advanced math, file handling, and so on, they can probably be had. Even after 10 years, Turbo Pascal has a long life ahead of it.

The listing prices for Borland's Turbo Pascal products at the time of writing were

Turbo Pascal 6.0	$149.95
Turbo Pascal Professional 6.0	$299.95
Turbo Pascal for Windows 1.5	$149.95

For more information on Turbo Pascal products, call or write Borland at

Borland International
1800 Green Hills Road
P.O. Box 660001
Scotts Valley, CA 95067-0001
(800) 331-0877

Summary

Pascal provides a happy medium for the programmer who wants a language more powerful and efficient than BASIC but wants to avoid the complexity of C or C++.

Turbo Pascal, in particular, gives the PC programmer a tool that produces extremely efficient code, heavily optimized for PC hardware, in either the DOS or Windows environment. The powerful compiler and strong support from third-party vendors make the Turbo Pascal line a good choice for the aspiring PC programmer.

C and C++ Products

by David Veale

In the last few years, C and C++ have become the "industry standard" languages for PC development. Whatever commercial PC application programs you use, there is a good chance that many of them were written in C or C++.

Standardization

Much of the success of C is attributable to the standardization of the C language, the availability of several high-quality compilers and libraries, and the portability of C source code among different computer platforms.

Although both C and C++ were created at AT&T's Bell Laboratories, the standards for both languages have been turned over to the American National Standards Institute (ANSI). ANSI finalized a standard for the C language in 1989. Most DOS C compilers have embraced all or most of the ANSI C standard. As a programmer, you should avoid compilers that do not follow the ANSI standard. Otherwise, you forsake portability in your code and access to the wide array of commercial and public-domain libraries available.

ANSI has only recently begun creating a standard for C++, an effort that is expected to take up to five years. The base document for the creation of the C++ standard and the document that serves as the currently accepted standard for C++ is *The Annotated C++ Reference Manual* by Margaret A. Ellis and Bjarne Stroustrup (Addison-Wesley, 1990). Both authors are with AT&T, and Mr. Stroustrup is the original designer of the C++ language. The latest C++ standard is commonly referred to as AT&T C++ 3.0.

Most of the compilers discussed in this chapter are both C and C++ compilers. This is possible because C++ is a *superset* of C. In fact, the name C++ came from the syntax of C. You use the "++" operator in C to add 1 to a variable. Therefore, C++ is C plus some extra features. One of the goals of both the ANSI C standardization and the ongoing evolution of C++ is to eliminate as many of the incompatibilities between the languages as possible. As a result, much of the C source code that follows the ANSI standard compiles and runs correctly with a C++ compiler.

Although C++ contains support for object-oriented programming, many programmers who program in C are now using C++ because it offers non-object-oriented improvements to C—improvements such as better type checking, the introduction of inline functions, and the capability to declare variables when they are first used.

Borland International

Borland International is the current king of the PC language market. Since the release of its first product in 1983, Turbo Pascal, Borland has been known for producing fast, easy-to-use, and inexpensive language products. Borland's current set of C/C++ compilers is no exception. Borland basically makes two C/C++ compilers: one for standard DOS and the other for the Microsoft Windows 3.x environment. Borland packages the products in several different ways to appeal to developers of all levels.

Turbo C++

Turbo C++ 3.0 is Borland's entry-level product for the DOS programming market. Turbo C++ supports ANSI C as well as the latest implementation of C++; it is aimed at the beginner. It features an extensive tutorial of C and C++. Also included is an integrated development environment that Borland calls the *Programmer's Platform*. The Programmer's Platform consists of a multifile editor, an extensive help system, and menus that enable you to edit, compile, run, and debug programs—all from within one environment (see Figure 21.1).

The built-in editor features *color-syntax highlighting*. This means that comments, keywords, constants, and variables all automatically appear in the editor in different colors so that you can easily follow your code.

The built-in debugger enables you to set breakpoints anywhere in your code, watch variables, trace through your code line by line or function by function, and watch the registers in the CPU.

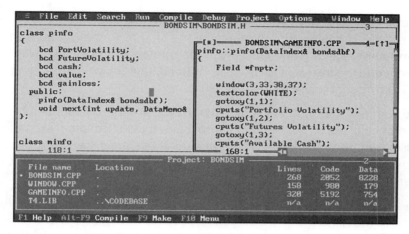

Figure 21.1. The Turbo C++/Borland C++ DOS Programmer's Platform.

The Programmer's Platform features a smart project manager. By simply adding the names of the source files and libraries that make up your program to a special window, the project manager ensures that all the proper files are compiled and linked when you build your program. The project manager does not recompile source files that have not changed since the last compile.

One more notable feature of the Programmer's Platform is the comprehensive help system. Every keyword, option, and function is covered in detail in the help system. The help for most Borland-supplied functions includes short example programs that you can easily copy from the help system to a file in the editor, where they can be compiled and run. After Turbo C++ is installed, the help system can completely take the place of the printed documentation.

The compiler also lives up to its "Turbo" name. It compiles and links code very quickly, and it produces .EXEs that are reasonably small and fast.

The compiler can use *precompiled* headers, meaning that the header files you include with the "#include" directive are compiled to a separate file the first time you compile your program. This way, you don't have to recompile the headers on subsequent compiles of the program. This feature saves significant compile time on large, multisource file projects.

If you're sure that the target systems for your program will have at least an 80286 processor, you can make the compiler generate 80286 instructions. Although this feature produces faster code, it does not provide the capability to run your programs in protected mode—the .EXEs produced by Turbo C++ are still real-mode DOS

.EXEs. Turbo C++ does, however, provide an easy-to-use and transparent overlay manager called VROOMM. By compiling the modules of your program with the overlay option on, Turbo C++ enables your program to automatically swap parts of its program code in and out of memory at runtime, thereby enabling you to create programs that appear to use more than 640K.

If you use floating-point math in your program, the programs generated by Turbo C++ automatically use an 80x87 math coprocessor if installed; otherwise, the math coprocessor functions are emulated in software. If the target systems for your program will always have a math coprocessor installed, you can tell Turbo C++ to always use the math coprocessor.

The advantage to using the math coprocessor is that the emulator library functions are not linked into your program, making the program smaller. For C++ programs only, Turbo C++ supports complex math and binary-coded decimal (BCD) numbers. BCD numbers do not suffer from the rounding errors that standard binary floating-point numbers are prone to suffer from, making BCD a better choice for financial applications.

The compiler also contains a built-in mini-assembler. You can embed assembly language code right in your C/C++ code.

You have the ability to tell the compiler to optimize code for size or speed. Other than this general optimization, Turbo C++ does not support the code optimizations usually associated with professional-level compiler products.

In Turbo C++, the compilation speed is partially achieved by compiling all source code to memory. Because of this feature, Turbo C++ requires that you have a computer with at least an 80286 processor and at least 1M of extended memory (above the usual 640K). Turbo C++ uses a DOS Protected Mode Interface (DPMI) compliant DOS extender to access up to 16M of memory. A *DOS extender* permits DOS programs to run in the computer's "protected mode," thereby allowing access to more memory. DPMI is a DOS extender standard developed primarily by Microsoft. If you're still hanging on to your old reliable IBM PC/XT, it's time for an upgrade!

If you prefer to work from the DOS command line, Turbo C++ comes with a host of command-line utilities, including a command-line version of the compiler and linker. Also included in Turbo C++ is a DOS version of the UNIX utility GREP (a text search program), a MAKE utility, a utility to convert project files from the Programmer's Platform to MAKE files, a source code preprocessor, and an object file cross-reference utility. If you prefer the command-line utilities to the Programmer's Platform, Borland provides a memory-resident utility that allows access to all the help files from DOS or a non-Borland editor.

The runtime library contains over 450 functions, including the complete ANSI C library, several UNIX extensions, DOS- and PC-specific functions, and a graphics library. The source code for the runtime library is available separately. Also, a class library contains the C++ iostreams class, various container classes, and complex- and binary-coded decimal math classes.

Not included in Turbo C++, but available from Borland, is a DOS application framework called Turbo Vision. Turbo Vision is a set of C++ classes you can use to create windowed, mouse-driven, menu-controlled DOS applications with a minimum of coding. Turbo Vision applications look and feel much like the Programmer's Platform. In fact, the Programmer's Platform in Borland's Turbo Pascal product was written using the Pascal version of Turbo Vision.

Turbo C++ is a complete product for a user getting started in DOS C/C++ development.

Turbo C++ for Windows 3.1

Turbo C++ for Windows is Borland's entry-level C and C++ compiler for the Microsoft Windows environment. Like its DOS sibling, it supports ANSI C and the latest AT&T release of C++.

You can use Turbo C++ for Windows to create programs only for the Microsoft Windows 3.x environment. You can create Windows .EXEs and Dynamic Link Libraries files (.DLL). The Microsoft Windows Software Development Kit is not needed.

A Windows-based version of the Programmer's Platform, called the Windows *Integrated Development Environment* (IDE), is included. This environment is almost functionally identical to the DOS version, but is completely Windows-based (see Figure 21.2). The IDE takes great advantage of the Windows environment: several commonly used menu options are available as icons on a speedbar in the editor, and you can easily change the size and font of the text in the editor.

The debugger, called the Turbo Debugger for Windows, is not part of the Windows IDE, but is a separate program. Despite the fact that the debugger is technically a Windows application, it runs only in full-screen character mode. With few exceptions, the debugger does not work if you are running Windows in a video mode with greater resolution than standard VGA 640x480 (actually, the debugger runs, but is invisible—making Windows appear to have locked up).

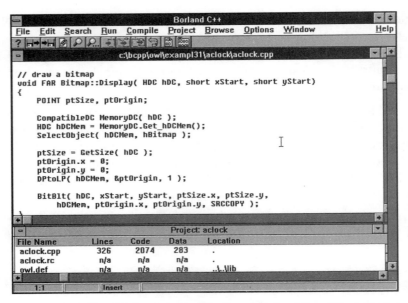

Figure 21.2. The Turbo C++ for Windows/Borland C++ Windows Integrated Development Environment.

Turbo Debugger is more powerful than the integrated debugger in Turbo C++ for DOS. You are able to view and step through the assembly language code for your program, for example, and run the program backwards to find out how you got to where you are. You can trace window messages and debug .DLLs. Turbo Debugger also supports dual-display debugging (your program runs on one display while you watch the debugger on another screen) and remote debugging (you run your program on one computer and debug it on another computer connected via the serial ports and cable).

Also included is a Windows-based object browser. The browser enables you to graphically display C++ class hierarchies so you can understand the relationship between base and derived classes.

The bulk of the menus and dialog boxes in the Windows IDE mimic the DOS version, so moving between the two platforms is relatively painless. The Windows IDE features the same extensive help system as the DOS version, but is totally Windows-based. The help system documents the entire Windows 3.x applications programming interface (API) including structures, type, constants, variables, and functions—making printed documentation a convenience, but not a necessity.

The compiler can create both Windows .EXEs and .DLLs. There is support for the new features of Windows 3.1, such as Object Linking and Embedding (OLE), multimedia, and the PenWindows API. Like the DOS version, you can optimize for size or speed and optionally have the compiler generate 80286 instructions. Turbo C++ does not support the creation of Windows 3.0 real-mode applications, so you should always use the 80286 instruction set.

Besides the standard C libraries and standard C++ class libraries, Turbo C++ for Windows includes two additional libraries designed to make windows programming easier. With the first, called *EasyWin*, you can convert many DOS applications into Windows applications without changing the DOS source code. By simply setting a compiler option that links an extra library to your code, your DOS application comes up in a window in graphics mode, uses a Windows font, and functions "normally" using TTY-style (standard text) input and output. There are, however, substantial limitations on the types of programs that you can convert into Windows applications this way. But you can convert many applications that use standard I/O functions and do not use many DOS- or machine-specific tricks.

The second library is called *ObjectWindows*. ObjectWindows is Borland's application framework for Windows. It encapsulates substantial portions of the Windows API into C++ classes. You can create Windows "objects" simply by creating instances of these classes. To create an application's window with a title and a default menu, for example, you simply declare an object of the ObjectWindows application class, and the window and supporting functionality are created (see Listing 21.1). You use this approach instead of making several calls to the Windows API via C function calls. ObjectWindows can cut down considerably on the amount of code a Windows program requires. It does, however, require a thorough understanding of C++ and object-oriented programming.

Listing 21.1. A "Hello World" program using the ObjectWindows application framework.

```
#include <owl.h>

class HelloApp :public TApplication
{
public:
  HelloApp(LPSTR AName, HINSTANCE hInstance, HINSTANCE hPrevInstance,
    LPSTR lpCmdLine, int nCmdShow)
    : TApplication(AName, hInstance, hPrevInstance, lpCmdLine, nCmdShow) {};
  virtual void InitMainWindow();
};
```

```
void HelloApp::InitMainWindow()
{
  MainWindow = new TWindow(NULL, "Hello World!");
}

int PASCAL WinMain(HINSTANCE hInstance, HINSTANCE hPrevInstance,
  LPSTR lpCmdLine, int nCmdShow)
{
  HelloApp HelloApp ("HelloApp", hInstance, hPrevInstance,
    lpCmdLine, nCmdShow);
  HelloApp.Run();
  return HelloApp.Status;
}
```

Resource Workshop

Windows programs contain many visual objects such as menus, dialog boxes, bitmaps, and icons. Collectively, these objects are called *resources*. Creating these resources is a large part of Windows programming. To aid you in creating resources, Borland includes a powerful tool in Turbo C++ for Windows called Resource Workshop. Resource Workshop contains a variety of graphical tools that enable you to create all the resources for your program by clicking and dragging. Resource Workshop also links the resources into your application. It even enables you to extract resources from one application and include them in another application.

Resource Workshop also comes with a special Borland .DLL called the Borland Windows Custom Controls (BWCC). BWCC is a set of icons, buttons, and dialogs that, in Borland's opinion, are more aesthetically pleasing than the Windows defaults. They are also designed so your user can more easily determine a button's function with a quick glance (see Figure 21.3). Instead of having a Windows Cancel button, which is an oval button with the word *Cancel* in it, BWCC adds a large red "X" to the word Cancel, giving the user a visual clue to the function of the button. Resource Workshop is a powerful tool that greatly simplifies one of the more confusing aspects of Windows programming.

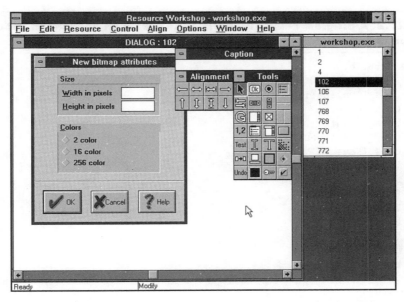

Figure 21.3. A dialog created with the Borland Resource Workshop. Notice the enhanced Borland Windows Custom Control buttons.

Borland C++ and Application Frameworks 3.1

Borland C++ is a mega-product that includes all the components of Turbo C++ and Turbo C++ for Windows plus additional enhancements. The box for Borland C++ weighs over 30 pounds. The software comes on 15 high-density, 3.5-inch disks—if the entire product is installed, it takes over 30M of hard drive space.

The DOS components of Borland C++ include the DOS Programmer's Platform. The compiler has been enhanced to support over a dozen code optimizations allowing the generation of smaller and/or faster code than Turbo C++. The 80386 instruction set is also supported. Borland C++ does not support the generation of 32-bit code or even protected-mode programming, but by using 80386 instructions in real-mode code, your program can be smaller and faster.

Also included is Turbo Vision, Borland's application framework for DOS (see Listing 21.2). Turbo Vision enables you to build event-driven, mouse-driven, windowed DOS programs. Although Turbo Vision and ObjectWindows share many of the same concepts, Turbo Vision source code is not portable to Windows and vice versa.

Listing 21.2. A program using Turbo Vision to create an application with a simple menu and dialog box.

```
#include <stdlib.h>

#define Uses_TApplication
#define Uses_TDeskTop
#define Uses_TEvent
#define Uses_TEventQueue
#define Uses_TKeys
#define Uses_TMenuBar
#define Uses_TMenuItem
#define Uses_TRect
#define Uses_TStatusDef
#define Uses_TStatusItem
#define Uses_TStatusLine
#define Uses_TSubMenu
#define Uses_TView
#define Uses_TWindow
#include <tv.h>

const int cmOpenFile   = 200;
const int cmNewWindow  = 201;


class THelloApp : public TApplication
{

public:
    THelloApp();
    static TStatusLine *initStatusLine( TRect r );
    static TMenuBar *initMenuBar( TRect r );
    virtual void handleEvent( TEvent& event);
    void HelloWindow();
};


static short wNumber = 0;

class THelloWindow : public TWindow
{

public:

    THelloWindow( const TRect& r, const char *aTitle, short aNumber );
```

```
};

class TInterior : public TView
{

public:

    TInterior( const TRect& bounds );
    virtual void draw();
};

TInterior::TInterior( const TRect& bounds ) : TView( bounds )
{
    growMode = gfGrowHiX | gfGrowHiY;
    options = options | ofFramed;
}

void TInterior::draw()
{
    char *hstr = "Hello World!";
    ushort color = getColor(0x0301);
    TView::draw();
    TDrawBuffer b;
    b.moveStr( 0, hstr, color );
    writeLine( 4, 2, 12, 1, b);
}

THelloApp::THelloApp() :
    TProgInit( &THelloApp::initStatusLine,
               &THelloApp::initMenuBar,
               &THelloApp::initDeskTop
         )
{
}

TStatusLine *THelloApp::initStatusLine(TRect r)
{
    r.a.y = r.b.y - 1;
    return new TStatusLine( r,
        *new TStatusDef( 0, 0xFFFF ) +

            *new TStatusItem( 0, kbF10, cmMenu ) +
            *new TStatusItem( "~Alt-X~ Exit", kbAltX, cmQuit ) +
            *new TStatusItem( "~Alt-F3~ Close", kbAltF3, cmClose )
        );
}
```

continues

Listing 21.2. Continued

```
TMenuBar *THelloApp::initMenuBar( TRect r )
{

    r.b.y = r.a.y + 1;
    return new TMenuBar( r,
        *new TSubMenu( "~F~ile", kbAltF )+
            *new TMenuItem( "~O~pen", cmOpenFile, kbF3,
                            hcNoContext, "F3" )+
            *new TMenuItem( "~N~ew",  cmNewWindow,   kbF4,
                            hcNoContext, "F4" )+
            newLine()+
            *new TMenuItem( "E~x~it", cmQuit, cmQuit, hcNoContext,
                            "Alt-X" )+
        *new TSubMenu( "~W~indow", kbAltW )+
            *new TMenuItem( "~N~ext", cmNext,     kbF6,
                            hcNoContext, "F6" )+
            *new TMenuItem( "~Z~oom", cmZoom,     kbF5,
                            hcNoContext, "F5" )
        );
}

void THelloApp::handleEvent(TEvent& event)
{
    TApplication::handleEvent(event);
    if( event.what == evCommand )
        {
        switch( event.message.command )
            {
            case cmNewWindow:
                HelloWindow();
                break;
            default:
                return;
            }
        clearEvent( event );
        }
}

void THelloApp::HelloWindow()
{
    TRect r( 0, 0, 26, 7 );
    r.move( random(53), random(16) );
    THelloWindow *window = new THelloWindow ( r, "Hello Window",
                                                ++wNumber);
```

```
     deskTop->insert(window);
}


THelloWindow::THelloWindow( const TRect& bounds, const char *aTitle,
               short aNumber) :
         TWindow( bounds, aTitle, aNumber),
         TWindowInit( &THelloWindow::initFrame )
{
    TRect r = getClipRect();
    r.grow(-1, -1);
    insert( new TInterior(r) );
}


int main()
{
    THelloApp HelloApp;
    HelloApp.run();
    return 0;
}
```

The Borland C++ Programmer's Platform includes the integrated debugger from Turbo C++, but also included is the stand-alone Turbo Debugger for DOS. Turbo Debugger is a more powerful debugger that permits debugging at the machine-code level and reverse execution of code (you can run your program backwards!). Like Turbo Debugger for Windows, it supports dual displays and remote debugging. If you have at least an 80386 processor in your computer, Turbo debugger also runs in "virtual DOS" mode. The debugger can therefore allocate a full 640K for your application to run in while the debugger is also running in other areas of memory.

You can use the DOS version of the compiler to create Windows programs. This way, you do not have to develop in the Windows environment to create Windows code. This also gives you the option of compiling Windows code using the command-line compiler, which many programmers prefer.

Borland C++ also includes the Windows IDE, compiler, and ObjectWindows from Turbo C++ for Windows. The compiler contains the additional optimizations discussed previously.

In addition to Turbo Debugger, Borland C++ includes *Turbo Profiler,* a tool that enables you to time the execution speed of every section of your code. This way, you can find out where your programs are spending most of their time and optimize those sections as desired. Both a DOS and Windows version of Turbo Profiler are included.

In addition to the built-in assembler, Borland C++ includes the stand-alone *Turbo Assembler*. Turbo Assembler is a Microsoft Macro Assembler (MASM) compatible assembler with object-oriented extensions. You can use it in conjunction with C/C++ code, or you can write stand-alone assembly language programs.

Another Borland C++ feature is the inclusion of the complete runtime library source code. If you ever wonder how a `printf()` function is written, just look at the source. You are also free to modify the source code for use in your own programs.

If you want all the functionality of Borland C++, but without all of the frills, you can buy Borland C++ without the application's frameworks and library source code. You'll save some money as well.

Borland C++ includes over 5,700 pages of printed documentation, including a three-volume Windows 3.0/3.1 API reference (available only online in Turbo C++ for Windows). Several documentation files on the program disks also can be printed out. All this is in addition to the 13M of online DOS and Windows hypertext documentation. Over 4M of example code and programs are also included.

Support

Borland offers extensive technical support for developers using its products. Borland sponsors a number of forums on CompuServe, including a Borland C++ for DOS forum and a Borland C++ for Windows forum. Questions posed on the forums are usually answered by a Borland representative within 24 hours. Other users often answer questions as well. Borland also maintains a free (except for the cost of the call) technical support hot line for general questions. You can also call Borland's Faxback line from your FAX machine and request to have technical documentation faxed to you. In addition, Borland publishes a free quarterly newsletter called "Borland Language Express." It contains product information, tips, and techniques regarding Borland's language products.

If you need more extensive and detailed support, Borland offers a fee-based support system. For an annual subscription fee, you get a toll-free technical support number, and you are always connected to a senior support engineer. You also get access to a special section of the Borland CompuServe forums reserved for support plan members. On these forums, a senior support engineer responds to your questions within two hours.

If you think a support subscription is overkill but you encounter a problem that requires detailed assistance, you can call a Borland 900 number and for a per-minute fee, a senior Borland support engineer will work through the problem with you, discussing your code line by line if necessary.

Vendor Information

Borland is currently the biggest player in the C and C++ market. As of this writing, Borland is developing a version of Borland C++ for IBM's OS/2 2.0 and Microsoft's forthcoming Windows NT. Both of these new products will include a version of ObjectWindows, which will allow for easier conversion of Windows 3.x code to these new environments.

The listing prices for Borland's C/C++ products at the time of publication were

Turbo C++, Version 3.0	$99.95
Turbo C++ for Windows, Version 3.1	$149.95
Borland C++ 3.1	$495.00
Borland C++ and Application Frameworks 3.1	$749.00

For more information on these C/C++ products, write or call Borland at:

Borland International
1800 Green Hills Road
P.O. Box 660001
Scotts Valley, CA 95067-0001
(800) 331-0877

Microsoft

Microsoft, developer of both DOS and Windows, is the world's largest PC software company. It has been producing PC C compilers since the early 1980s and has developed a well-deserved reputation for making compilers with some of the best optimizations available.

Another Microsoft hallmark is the capability of its various language products to work together. Indeed, all the C products discussed in this section have the capability to link their object code with object code created by most other Microsoft language products, resulting in executable programs.

Because Microsoft has been in the C market since long before the ANSI C standard was established, it took Microsoft some time to make its compilers ANSI-compliant. It could not totally embrace ANSI too quickly because code written for older versions of C would no longer compile. However, the latest version of Microsoft C/C++ fully supports the ANSI standard.

In terms of programming environments, Microsoft has done a bit of catching up lately. While Borland and others were producing slick, integrated development environments for their language products, most of Microsoft's offerings have been command-line based. Microsoft was also late to market a C++ compiler. Lately though, Microsoft has come roaring back with some modern and high-quality tools.

QuickC 2.5

QuickC is Microsoft's entry-level DOS C compiler, intended primarily for use as a learning tool. It features an easy-to-use, mouse-driven integrated development environment based on the "Quick" environment that made Microsoft QuickBASIC such a success. The Quick environment contains a single-file editor and the capability to compile, run, and debug a program all from simple menus.

The C-only language syntax is based on earlier releases of the Microsoft C compiler and is not 100 percent ANSI-compliant, but it should be close enough for most purposes. The compiler has very few optimizations and is geared more toward compiler speed than producing small, fast code.

The product features a tutorial text on C and an extensive hypertext help system covering most aspects of the C language and the use of the compiler.

One notable feature is that QuickC is the only C product mentioned in this chapter that can be realistically run on 8086/8088 hardware (XT class computers). If you still use that old XT, here's your chance to try C without having to buy a new computer.

QuickC includes a debugger that is a subset of Microsoft's famous CodeView debugger. You can set breakpoints and watch variables change as you step through your programs. In addition to the compiler and debugger, QuickC includes a linker, a librarian, and a sophisticated MAKE utility. The runtime libraries are complete and feature a very complete graphics library.

If you are new to C, or if you use C for small projects and for personal use, QuickC is a good, low-priced C tool.

QuickC for Windows 1.0

Like its DOS sibling, QuickC for Windows is intended for programmers who are new to C and new to the Microsoft Windows programming environment. It contains an easy-to-use Windows-based integrated development environment (IDE). In fact, QuickC for Windows is the only Microsoft C product with a Windows IDE. It features a multifile editor and the capability to edit, compile, debug, and run programs from the environment.

The C language implementation is based on Microsoft C 6.0, which is not 100 percent ANSI-compatible, but it is close enough for most purposes. C++ is not supported, however. You can use the compiler to generate Microsoft Windows programs only.

QuickC for Windows has two outstanding features. The first is the debugger. This is the only Windows-based product discussed in this chapter that enables the programmer to debug in a Microsoft Windows window. Other products have Windows debuggers, but they run in character mode.

The other major feature is a computer aided software engineering (CASE) tool called *QuickCase:W*. QuickCase:W enables you to draw your application's interface on-screen; then QuickCase:W generates commented C source code to create the interface as drawn. You then link the code created by QuickCase:W into your application. This approach is different from Borland's approach (using Resource Workshop to create screen elements that are then linked into your code), and from Microsoft's C/C++ compiler's approach (which uses special editors to create resources). QuickCase:W helps you cut down considerably on the code you must write. QuickCase:W performs the functions of many of the SDK tools, thus you can avoid buying the SDK.

Just like the DOS version, QuickC for Windows is intended as a low-cost learning tool for programmers who want to learn Windows programming without much investment. You must have the hardware to run Windows to use this product.

C/C++ 7.0

C/C++ 7.0 is Microsoft's first C++ product and its most ambitious language product to date. Microsoft has clearly been deemphasizing DOS and pushing Windows in the last few years—and this product is no exception. You can use C/C++ to create DOS applications, but the strong emphasis is on Windows programming.

C/C++ is actually two products in one. There is a C/C++ compiler and the complete Microsoft Windows 3.1 Software Development Kit (SDK). Until now, the Windows SDK has been a separate $500 product. As a result, this product is huge; the box weighs almost 50 pounds. The software comes on 21 3.5-inch, high-density disks. The product is optionally available on a CD-ROM, which is a more practical and convenient means of distribution. Fully installed, the compiler and SDK take over 30M of hard drive space.

The C language implementation is ANSI-compliant. The C++ implementation is based on the AT&T 2.1 standard, which is slightly different from the current 3.0 standard in the way it handles templates and exceptions. But this difference should not be considered a big stumbling block and, by the time you read this, it might have been corrected.

Microsoft's professional-level C compilers have long had a reputation for producing some of the smallest and fastest code, and C/C++ 7.0 is no exception. Dozens of optimizations are under the user's control.

One of the more interesting optimizations is the Microsoft *p-code system*. Rather than have your program compiled into machine code, you can have all, or part, of your code compiled into p-code or pseudocode. This code is then interpreted as it runs rather than running as native machine code. There is an execution speed penalty of up to 25 percent, but there is also a memory usage savings of up to 50 percent. On very large programs, using p-code might be the best way to get your program to fit in the available memory space.

Another state-of-the-art optimization is *auto-inlining*. If the compiler finds reasonably small and often-called functions in your code, it substitutes the body of the function for the function call in the object code. This makes your code bigger, but can also make it run much faster. Of course, it is up to you whether this optimization is used.

Programmer's WorkBench

Microsoft supplies an Integrated Development Environment (IDE) called the Programmer's WorkBench 2.0 (PWB) (see Figure 21.4). PWB contains an editor and has the capability of editing, compiling, running, and debugging programs all from the environment. PWB is an extendable environment that enables you to add your own features and link your own favorite utilities into it.

Figure 21.4. The Microsoft Programmer's WorkBench.

PWB is actually just a shell with added functionality. This functionality is due to the addition of extension files that add all the menus and options to support a given language. Naturally, C/C++ comes with all the necessary extension files to support both C and C++, but it also comes with extension files to support Microsoft's Macro Assembler, BASIC, Pascal, and FORTRAN. If you use any of these additional languages, you have only to include the appropriate file extension in the PWB directory, and all the appropriate menus and options are added to the PWB environment.

The PWB also includes an extensive hypertext help system that covers the entire C and C++ language, all library functions, the Windows API, and the use of all the included programming tools and utilities.

PWB is different from Borland's Programmer's Platform. Borland includes a version of the compiler and linker in its environment, whereas PWB works by running the command-line versions of these tools. When you combine source code files in a project in PWB and select the option to build a program, PWB creates a MAKE file on disk. PWB then runs Microsoft's MAKE utility (called NMAKE), which in turn calls the compiler and the linker. PWB is simply automating the running of the command-line utilities so you, as a developer, do not have to run through the steps.

PWB has been around for a few years, but earlier versions were marred by terrible performance and a clumsy interface. PWB 2.0 is a complete rewrite of the product, and it is much improved in both speed and usability.

Debugging

To debug programs, C/C++ includes a new version of Microsoft's CodeView debugger for both DOS and Windows. This powerful debugger supports sophisticated breakpoints and watches, and enables you to trace through applications. It supports debugging at the source-code or assembly-code level, and it also supports dual displays and remote debugging. You can control it with the mouse or keyboard. A command line modeled after the DOS DEBUG.COM utility is available.

To further aid in debugging and optimizing, Microsoft includes an object browser, which enables you to trace class hierarchies from derived classes to ancestors. Also included is Microsoft *Profiler*, a tool that analyzes the execution speed of sections of code to help you determine where the bottlenecks are.

PWB, the compiler, CodeView, and most of the other tools are character-based DOS programs despite the fact that Microsoft C/C++ is a product clearly aimed at Windows developers.

The Compiler

The compiler is strictly a DOS command-line tool made up of a series of .EXEs. Compile times tend to be slow. In fact, C/C++ has the longest compile and link times of all the products in this chapter. The compiler has a "quick compile" option that speeds the compilation considerably by eliminating most optimizations. You can use the "quick compile" option throughout the development cycle, and then turn the optimizations back on for the final version of the program.

To further speed compilation, C/C++ supports the use of precompiled headers. All the `#include` files are compiled to a separate file when the program is first compiled. On subsequent compiles of your source code, the header files need not be recompiled. This can save a lot of compile time, especially in Windows programs that have thousands of lines of header-file code per module.

The compiler runs only on an 80386-based (or later) computer. Even though the compiler is a DOS program, it usually must be run in a DOS session within Windows because the compiler uses the DOS Protected Mode Interface (DPMI) API as a DOS extender. The environment in which it is run, therefore, must provide DPMI services—which Windows does. The only way to run the compiler outside of Windows is to install a DOS memory manager that provides DPMI support, such as Qualitas' 386Max, on your computer. Microsoft provides a complimentary copy of 386Max with C/C++ for those who don't want to use Windows.

It should be noted that although previous releases of Microsoft's C compiler supported development of OS/2 1.x programs, C/C++ 7.0 does not. It is strictly a DOS and Windows development tool.

Windows Programming

As mentioned previously, C/C++ comes with the complete Windows SDK including documentation, utilities, libraries, example code, and help files. Everything you need to create Windows programs is included. In addition, C/C++ includes a Windows application framework called the Microsoft Foundation Classes (MFC). These C++ classes encapsulate much of the Windows API so you can use object-oriented programming techniques to build Windows applications. The MFC goes a long way toward simplifying Windows programming and cutting down the amount of code that must be written.

The MFC is well-organized; MFC classes and member functions follow the Windows naming conventions, making it easier to mix MFC code and straight Windows API calls without complicating the code too much. (See Listing 21.3.) Microsoft does not have an application framework for DOS applications.

Listing 21.3. A program using the Microsoft Foundation Classes application framework.

```
#include <afxwin.h>

class HelloWindow : public CFrameWnd
{
public:
    HelloWindow() { Create(NULL, "Hello World!",
    WS_OVERLAPPEDWINDOW, rectDefault); }
};

class HelloApp : public CWinApp
{
public:
    virtual BOOL InitInstance();
};

BOOL HelloApp::InitInstance()
{
    m_pMainWnd = new HelloWindow();
    m_pMainWnd->ShowWindow(m_nCmdShow);
    m_pMainWnd->UpdateWindow();
```

continues

Listing 21.3. Continued

```
    return TRUE;
}

// Declare an instance of the class HelloApp in order to run the program.
HelloApp helloApp;
```

DOS Programming

For DOS programmers, Microsoft includes an overlay manager called MOVE that permits DOS programs to swap parts of their code in and out of memory so large programs can fit in 640K. DOS programs also have access to non-Windows specific parts of the included class libraries.

To move DOS programs to Windows easily, Microsoft includes the QuickWin library. QuickWin allows standard DOS applications to run in a Windows window. The programs still run like DOS applications (they don't automatically get mouse support, for example), but they do use the Windows interface.

Documentation

The printed documentation consists of over 5,200 pages on the C/C++ compiler and tools, and almost 4,000 pages in the Windows SDK. In addition, all the reference material from the manuals is duplicated in 12M of hypertext help files for both DOS and Windows to allow easy access while you work on the computer. There are also over 5M of sample code and programs.

Support

Microsoft maintains an extensive support network for developers. It has several forums on CompuServe dealing with DOS, Windows, and programming tools. These forums are staffed by Microsoft technicians who answer all your questions. Also on CompuServe is the Microsoft Knowledge Base, a searchable database of common questions and answers, known bugs, and tips and techniques.

Microsoft has free (except for the cost of the phone call) support for questions regarding the setup and use of programming tools. Some limited assistance for programming problems is also available.

For developers who need help with the actual programming in C or C++, Microsoft offers a multi-tier, fee-based support system ranging from a 900 phone line for questions on DOS and Windows, to on-site consulting services for development problems. Microsoft also offers training courses through Microsoft University. It publishes the *Microsoft Systems Journal,* a bimonthly technical journal dealing with development issues, for a subscription fee. In addition, Microsoft Press publishes books and manuals dealing with Microsoft products.

Vendor Information

Microsoft is clearly pushing hard to regain its position as a language product leader. The competition in this market will mean even more and better products for developers.

The listing prices for Microsoft's C/C++ products at the time of publication were

Microsoft Quick C, Version 2.5	$99.00
Microsoft Quick C for Windows, Version 1.0	$199.00
Microsoft C/C++, Version 7.0	$495.00

For more information on these C/C++ products, call or write Microsoft at:

Microsoft Corporation
One Microsoft Way
Redmond, WA 98052-6399
(800) 426-9400

Zortech C++ 3.0

Symantec's Zortech C++ 3.0 is the current release of the most mature C++ compiler for DOS. Zortech's C++ has been around longer than both Borland's and Microsoft's implementations. It offers features that neither of its competitors has.

Zortech supports both ANSI C and C++ 2.1 (C++ 3.0 support is planned for the next release). The one package contains tools to build applications for standard DOS, 286 protected mode DOS, 386 protected mode DOS, Microsoft Windows 3.0, and OS/2 1.x. The package contains Windows software development tools and royalty-free DOS extenders. As of this writing, Windows 3.1 and OS/2 2.0 tools are still under development. Despite shipping on only eight 3.5-inch, high-density disks, a full installation of the product uses 20M of hard drive space.

Zortech comes with a DOS-based Integrated Development Environment (IDE) with a multifile editor that enables you to edit, compile, run, and debug programs within the same environment (see Figure 21.5). The integrated character-mode-only debugger supports dual displays and remote debugging. You can debug either on the source-code or assembly-language level and set breakpoints and watches. The debugger works in any of the supported programming environments.

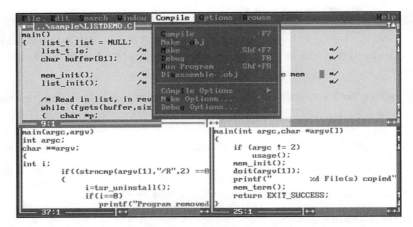

Figure 21.5. The Zortech C++ integrated development environment.

The compiler offers a wide array of optimizations, making it appropriate for professional development. It also can generate 32-bit code for use with the included 386 extender.

There are both real- and protected-mode versions of the compiler. However, only the most trivial DOS programs can be compiled using the real-mode tools. An 80286-based computer with at least 2M of memory should be considered a minimum system for any serious development.

Zortech C++ comes with a complete ANSI C library and C++ class library with full source code. It does not have an application framework for either DOS or Windows. Like both Borland and Microsoft, Zortech C++ comes with a library to enable you to run standard DOS applications in the Microsoft Windows environment.

This product is the only one in this chapter that can create non-Windows extended DOS programs (without third party software) or programs for the OS/2 1.x environment.

To aid in the development of Windows applications, Zortech includes a copy of Blue Sky Software's *Window Maker*. Window Maker is a prototyping utility and code generator. Windows resources can be drawn on-screen, and Window Maker generates C and C++ source code to create the interface objects, saving you considerable time.

Zortech C++ comes with over 3,200 pages of printed documentation. There is a reference manual for the Windows API, but no documentation on OS/2. You would have to acquire an OS/2 API reference from IBM—or a third-party—to program in that environment. There are a few sample programs for each of the supported runtime environments and almost 4M of hypertext help files.

Zortech support consists of a forum on CompuServe, a BBS, and telephone support (the BBS and phone support are free except for the cost of the phone call).

Vendor Information

With Borland and Microsoft so focused on the Windows market right now, Zortech is a good choice for programmers who have to satisfy customers in a variety of environments.

The listing price for Zortech's C++ at the time of publication was

    Zortech C++, Version 3.0 $699.00

For more information on Zortech's C++, write or call Symantec at:

    Symantec Corporation
    10201 Torre Avenue
    Cupertino, CA 95014-2132
    (800) 441-7234

Summary

Thanks in large part to the fine products produced by these vendors, C and C++ continue to be the primary languages used by software professionals in the PC arena. Each of these vendors has added features to its products to make them more powerful and more accessible to the new programmer.

The continuing adoption of graphical user interfaces by PC users and the explosion of object-oriented programming—both of which are well supported by C++—ensure that the demand for programmers with C++ skills will continue to rise.

address   A unique location of memory in a computer.

allocation   The creation of a block of memory for use by a program.

argument   A variable that is passed to a program, subroutine, or function.

array   A grouping of identical data types or structures. Individual elements of arrays are accessed by a unique indexing number called a subscript.

assignment statements   Used to assign values to a variable. An equal sign (=) is most often used to make an assignment.

batch file   An ASCII file containing a group of DOS commands that are executed one after the other.

beta test   Using other people to test your program after you're sure it is bug-free. (Your own test is the alpha test.)

binary file   A file that is accessed as individual bytes rather than structures (as with random-access files) or lines (as with sequential-access files).

BIOS (*B*asic *I*nput *O*utput *S*ystem)   The low-level instructions required to start the CPU and to provide support services (such as disk and printer interface) for the computer's operating system.

bit   A *b*inary dig*it*. The smallest unit of memory storage on a computer. A bit represents two states, off and on—also represented as 0 and 1, respectively.

Boolean expression   Any expression that evaluates to True or False. The expression 1 = 2 would evaluate to False, whereas 2 = 2 would evaluate to True.

Boolean operators   Values used in a Boolean expression that represent True or False. Languages such as C or C++ provide Boolean variables that can only represent True or False values.

branching   Changing the flow or order in which program statements are executed.

breakpoint   A marker in a program at which point execution stops for debugging purposes. Breakpoint support is available in most high-level languages.

bugs   Programming errors.

button   An on-screen graphical representation of a physical button.

bytes   The basic unit of memory in a computer. A byte—made up of 8 bits—can represent a number from 0 to 255.

case statement   Compares an expression with a series of evaluations.

CGA (*C*olor *G*raphics *A*dapter)   A standard 320 × 200 dot, color screen display. Also capable of displaying 640 × 200 black and white.

class   An object or programming entity comprised of a function or functions and the associated data structures.

client   On a network, a client is the computer or workstation that accesses the central computer or server. An application is usually contained on the main computer and serves the client computer. *See server.*

comment   An annotation or explanation of the purpose of a line or section of code. Comments are prefaced with a keyword or punctuation that varies by language.

compiler   A program that translates source code (QBasic, Turbo Pascal, C, and so forth) into a machine language executable file for later use. *See interpreter.*

conditional statement   Performs a test on an expression and causes your program to branch depending on the outcome of the test.

conditional test   Using a relational operator to test a number, expression, or event.

constant   A program data item that cannot be changed during the running of a program. Constants are usually set at compile time, and can be a number, character, or word that you put in a program. Also referred to as a *literal*.

construct   The organizational concepts of statements characteristic of a particular language. QBasic's FOR-NEXT construct is that it uses a discrete rather than an implied NEXT statement.

context-sensitive help   Help messages that are directed toward the current state the program is in rather than a generic help message. When in the file saving section of a program, for example, requesting help displays information on saving a file.

counter   A variable used to keep track of the number of times something happens. In a FOR-NEXT loop, the counter controls the number of times the loop is repeated.

CPU (*C*entral *P*rocessing *U*nit)   The CPU is the electronic device responsible for operations in a computer. These operations generally include interpretation of machine code instructions, memory control, system timing, and logical operations.

CUI (*C*haracter-Based *U*ser *I*nterface)   An on-screen environment based on text characters.

data   The values or information that a program processes or acts on during execution. Constants and variables are memory locations inside your computer that hold data.

deallocation   The releasing of a block of memory.

debug   The process of searching out and fixing errors (*bugs*) in a program.

declaration   A statement or statements—usually at the start of a program— that show the template of a subroutine, function, or object, or define the name and type of variables to be used. Also known as a *prototype*.

decrement   To decrease a value, normally by one.

dereference   Retrieving a value from a pointer or a variable.

device   A hardware input or output mechanism that is accessed by a programming language. High-level languages standardize output to the hardware through the use of device names such as filenames, COM*x*, LPT*x* and so forth. (The *x* refers to a number, such as COM1 or LPT2.)

dialog box   A small window that contains text, edit fields, or buttons for a user to select from. The user has a "dialog" with the program through the dialog box.

DOS (*D*isk *O*perating *S*ystem)   A software program that controls the input and output between the computer hardware and programs. DOS provides services for the programmer to access video monitors, printers, disk drives and com ports.

DPMI (*D*OS *P*rotected-*M*ode *I*nterface)   A standard in which programs and operating systems work together in a protected-mode environment. DPMI is used by DOS programs to access extended memory in Windows.

dynamic memory allocation   The process of allocating memory when needed and destroying or discarding it when finished. The opposite of *static memory allocation.*

EGA (*E*nhanced *G*raphics *A*dapter)   A standard 640 × 350 dot screen display.

element   Identifies an individual variable or location in an array.

encapsulation   The term for integration of data structures with functions or procedures, resulting in the creation of objects in OOP programming.

event-driven programming   Code that responds to an external event—such as a keypress or mouse click—and executes based on the event at that time. The opposite of procedural programming.

field   A variable or data location in a record or structure.

file   A collection of information stored as a discrete unit on a storage medium, such as a disk drive.

filter   A program that modifies data passed through it.

fixed disk drive   The permanent disk drive that most personal computers contain. The actual disk is not removable, unlike a *floppy disk.* Also called *hard drive.*

float   Short for floating-point number. Floating-point number can be in either single- or double-precision and represent numbers ranging from small fractional values to large values. Floating-point numbers can contain decimal points. Also known as *real numbers.*

floppy disk   A form of magnetic media that can store data or programs and that can be removed from the PC. A floppy disk refers to the physical characteristic that the disk-shaped medium is flexible.

flow   The order in which program statements are executed.

fourth-generation language (4GL)   High-level application programming languages associated with database products—xBase and PAL, for example.

function   A subroutine that returns a single value as the name of the function. Functions are called as variables in assignment statements.

global variable   A variable that is available for use by all functions or procedures in a program.

GUI (*G*raphic *U*ser *I*nterface)   A program interface based on a pixel-based graphic mode. A GUI interface characteristically contains pictures, icons, and graphical representations of real-world interfaces. An example of a GUI interface is a CD Player program with on-screen buttons that resemble an actual CD player.

handle   In standard programming: A unique integer that refers to an open file for access and manipulation of that file. In Windows: A unique integer assigned to an object, memory location, or device.

header file   Defines to the compiler certain built-in C routines your program uses later.

Hercules Graphics Adapter   A monochrome screen standard with a 720×348 dot display.

high-level language   A computer language with code resembling spoken or written English. High-level languages were designed to be more readily understood by humans. QuickBASIC is a high-level language.

increment   To increase a value, normally by one.

index   The element number in an array, or the record number in a random access file. Also used as a *counter* in a loop.

infinite loop   A loop that does not terminate once it begins.

inheritance   The property of an object-oriented language that allows a new class or object to be defined with the same properties of an existing class or object. An object that inherits properties is referred to as a *child* of the *parent* object.

input   Information that a program receives from data files, a keyboard, a serial port, or any other device.

integer   Any whole number. An integer cannot represent fractional or decimal values. A two-byte integer represents values between –32,768 and 32,767, whereas a long integer represents values between –2,147,483,648 and 2,147,483,647.

intelligent data structure   *See object or class.*

interface   The mechanism a computer uses to "talk to" or communicate with a user or hardware device.

interpreter   A program that reads source code and translates and executes a program, line by line.

ISAM (*I*ndexed *S*equential *A*ccess *M*ethod)   A system of indexing and file Input/Output commands for database support.

K (Kilobytes)   Approximately 1,000 bytes, but actually 1,024 bytes.

keyword   A command in a programming language. PRINT or INPUT are keywords in QBasic.

LAN (*L*ocal *A*rea *N*etwork)   A network that usually serves a single office or building.

library   A collection of precompiled code that is linked with a program to provide additional functionality.

local variable   A variable that is available for use only in the function or procedure in which it was defined.

logical drive   A software partition that is set up on hard drives and is referred to with a separate drive letter (such as D:, E:, or F:).

logical operator   An operator or statement that performs a logical function, such as AND, OR, and XOR.

loop   A statement or set of statements that are repeated until a specified condition is met.

low-level language   A programming language that directly represents machine code instructions and is designed to be "understood" by the computer rather than by humans. Assembly language is a low-level language.

macro language   A language used to create shortcuts and extend an application or system.

mainframe　A computer system consisting of a main computer and several satellite terminals.

meg　Short for mega (million). A million bytes of memory.

member function　A function or procedure contained in a class or object.

method　*See member function.*

modal　Software that operates in different modes. In the Windows environment, a modal dialog box Window is one that requires the user to answer before continuing with any other tasks.

multiple-dimensional array　An array that has more than one column of data. A spreadsheet would be represented by a two-dimensional array of rows and columns.

nesting　Placing loops in other loops.

network　A computer system in which two or more terminals are connected by hardware and software to share data, programs, and information.

null string　An empty string.

object　A program module that contains data structures bound to their functions or routines. Also called *classes* in C++.

operators　Symbols that cause a change in an expression. The equal sign (=) is an example of an operator.

optimization　The process of making code more efficient. It involves using knowledge of how instructions are executed by the computer.

output　Information returned by a program to the user through the screen, sound, files, printer, or other device.

PAL (*P*aradox *A*pplication *L*anguage)　Proprietary database language supported by Borland Paradox.

parameter　A variable or value that is transferred to and from a subroutine of the program.

polymorphism　The property of a class to take on many forms. An object member of a particular name can represent different functions. The object member's use is governed by the parameters with which it is called. An object can have a method called sum that can use single, double, or integer values. These values use different functions but share the same name.

portability   The capability of an application's program source code to be moved from one operating system or language to another. C programs are said to be portable because the source code can be understood by many different compilers.

private member   A C++ function that can only be accessed in its own class. The opposite of a public member.

procedural language   A language in which programs execute by calling procedures when needed. The opposite of an object-oriented language. QBasic is a procedural language—it uses a single thread of execution and calls procedures as needed.

procedure   A self-contained group or module of programming statements that performs a task and is called from a main program or other procedures. This block of code is given a name, and may or may not receive variables when called.

program   A set of programming statements or commands that direct a computer as to what to do.

prototype   A mock-up of a program used to simulate an application before actual programming is done. Also another name for a declaration of a function or subroutine.

pseudocode   A human-language representation of a program written as a narrative paragraph rather than actual code.

public member   A member function that can be accessed throughout the rest of a C++ program. The opposite of a private member.

pull-down menu   A horizontal menu bar that consists of a list of choices across the top of the screen, as well as vertical menus that "pull down" from these choices when selected.

Quick Libraries   A proprietary library used with Microsoft Quick Environments such as QuickC, QuickBASIC, or Visual Basic for DOS.

RAM (*R*andom-*A*ccess *M*emory)   The working memory that a computer uses to store programs, data, and output during the execution of a program. All data stored in the RAM is lost when power is off.

random-access file   A file containing identical data types, records, or structures that can be accessed by the program in a random order.

real number   *See float.*

record   A language construct that is referenced by a single name, yet contains several variables of the same or different types.

REM   Short for remark, it is one way to denote a comment in BASIC languages.

robust   A term describing the error-handling capabilities of a program. If a program can recover from errors easily, it is robust.

ROM (*Read-Only Memory*)   A computer's permanent memory, which contains programs that can only be executed—not changed or modified. The computer's BIOS is stored in ROM.

scientific notation   A shortcut method of representing numbers of extreme values. A large number is reduced to a single digit multiplied to a power of 10. The number 123,000 would be represented as 1.23e5.

self-modifying code   Code in which the program actually changes the executable statements while the program is running.

sequential-access files   Files that are accessed in a line-by-line format, such as text files.

server   A computer that contains a host database, operating system, or application and services client computers. A network is an example of a client/server system.

single-dimensional array   An array that has one list or column of data.

source code   The file (written in any language) containing the original, uncompiled set of instructions, written by the programmer.

spaghetti code   Quickly written, haphazard programs that have little or no structure.

SQL (*Structured Query Language*)   A language that enables the user to make inquiries to a database system. Traditionally used in miniframe and mainframe computer database products, but becoming more common on PCs.

static memory   Memory that is allocated at the beginning of program execution and is not discarded until the program terminates.

string   A variable that represents a collection of characters.

string terminator   The zero character placed as the last character of a C language string that identifies where the string ends.

structured programming   The style of programming whereby a program is broken into separate tasks or subroutines that are called when needed. Also called *modular programming,* because a large program is broken into small, easy-to-understand sections, or modules.

subroutine   A separate section of code that is accessed from the main execution through the use of a CALL, GOSUB, or GOTO statement. Also called a *procedure.*

syntax error   An error resulting from an incorrectly used keyword or typographical error.

tool bar   A set of buttons containing graphical representations or icons that are gathered in a line or box.

upward compatibility   The capability to run programs written on older versions of a compiler or interpreter on newer compilers or interpreters.

user interface   The portion of a program in which the user interacts with the computer, usually while entering and receiving data and information.

user-friendly   The ease at which a software application can be operated by a user.

user   The person or persons involved with operating or using a software package. The term usually means a person who, unlike the programmer, does not have insight into how the application was written, and therefore has only the program and the documentation with which to work.

utility   A program that does a specific task, such as displaying a sorted directory or formatting a disk.

validity checking   Using a procedure to verify that user input is in a specific range. A statement that checks that a date is a legal value, for example.

variable   A place holder for program values. Can refer to many types of values.

VGA (*Video Graphics Array*)   A standard 640 × 480 dot screen display.

WAN (*Wide Area Network*)   A network that services many offices or buildings, typically across city and state boundaries. An airline-reservation system would require a wide area network.

window   A rectangular area on the computer screen used to display data.

xBASE   A 4GL database language supported by dBASE IV, FoxPro, and Clipper, considered by many to be the "industry standard" database programming language for microcomputers.

Index

Symbols

E

J–K

L

N

P